The Unity of
Law and Morality

International Library of Philosophy

Editor: Ted Honderich

A catalogue of books already published in the
International Library of Philosophy
will be found at the end of this volume

The Unity of
Law and Morality
A Refutation of Legal Positivism

M. J. Detmold

ROUTLEDGE & KEGAN PAUL
London, Boston, Melbourne and Henley

K
332
.D47
1984

First published in 1984
by Routledge & Kegan Paul plc
39 Store Street, London WC1E 7DD, England
9 Park Street, Boston, Mass. 02108, USA
464 St Kilda Road, Melbourne,
Victoria 3004, Australia
Broadway House, Newtown Road,
Henley-on-Thames, Oxon RG9 1EN, England
Printed in Great Britain by
T J Press, Padstow

Library of Congress Cataloging in Publication Data
Detmold, M. J. (Michael J.), 1941–
The unity of law and morality.

(International library of philosophy)
Bibliography: p.
Includes index.
1. Legal positivism. 2. Law–Philosophy. 3. Juris-
prudence. I. Title II. Series.
K332.D47 1984   340'.1   83-21184

ISBN 0-7102-0030-7

To N.J.D.

CONTENTS

SYNOPSIS

ix

SOME TERMS

Rule   A method of deciding a case where a norm covering a class of cases is assumed to be binding and is applied.

Norm   A normative entity; an entity because it has come about, been decided or been promulgated (necessarily posited).

Reason Either a reason for action or a reason for belief. Reasons for action are what hard cases are decided by. All reasons for action are constituted by particular facts.

Principle A universalized reason for action. Principles are spurious norms. If, however, they are posited they are norms, and no longer the universalization of reasons for action.

Case   An individual practical question. Cases can be either single or strategic. The decision to adopt or reject a rule is the decision of a strategic case.

Hard case: non-rule case. The form of a hard case is ABC weighed against XYZ, where A, B, C, X, Y, and Z are all the relevant reasons for and against action. Action might be one action or any number of alternative actions; thus ABC might be the reasons for action p and XYZ either the reasons against p or the reasons for an alternative action q.

Weight The measure of passionate response by which hard cases are decided. Motivation determining the will.

The world: All the particular facts.

Adjudicate: Decide a single case.

Some Terms

Legislate: Decide a class of cases. Accordingly, lay down a norm covering a class of cases.

PREFACE

This book attempts an analysis of law. It is the product of one lawyer thinking about the nature of his thought in the law and wider as driven.

The title (and sub-title) are the consistent themes of what emerges rather than subjects in their own right.

The method is more the taking of problems as they come than the construction of a whole account and theory of the subject (or of the themes): as Socrates said to the Sophist, Protagoras:

'Cut up your answers into shorter
pieces, the better for me to follow you.'

(Protagoras, 334 D)

I

REASONS FOR ACTION

I.1

Practical thought is concerned with action. Reasons for action are sometimes thought to be either conditional (conditional upon some want or project) or unconditional. But if there were no unconditional reasons for action there would be no reasons for action. Conditional reasons (such as 'if I want to go to London I have a reason to be at the station at 8 o'clock') are theoretical not practical; not really reasons *for action* at all. On the conventional interpretation of Hume we would say that such reasons are the slaves of the passions; themselves inert practically.

Unconditional reasons for action are of two kinds: self-regarding and other-regarding.

Many self-regarding reasons are clearly conditional on my wanting something (for instance, if I want a Sung bowl I have a reason to buy one, or, if I want to go to London I have a reason to be at the station at 8 o'clock). It is tempting to think that all self-regarding reasons are conditional; and, for instance, say: if (when hungry) I want food I have a reason to acquire some. However, I think it is better to say of the basic human desires that they constitute unconditional not conditional reasons for action. This is a little tricky. Want and desire must be distinguished. Desire is a basic physiological state whose control on my action might simply be physiological; want is more an intellectual state and its control on my action is only rational (for this distinction see Benson (1968, 155). Hume made the distinction, too. Passions are secondary impressions; bodily sensations are original impressions (*Treatise*, vol. 2, part 1, section 1)). Now, in the case of the basic human desires (hunger, thirst, sex . . .) it seems that want can be omitted and the desire itself allowed to constitute an unconditional reason for action. Thus my desire for food (my hunger) is an unconditional reason to acquire food. I do not also have to want it. It seems silly to postulate a condition of wanting something which no sane man could fail to want (see Edgley, 1969, 161, and Nagel, 1970, 27–32). (Of course, I am not saying that no sane man would fail to feed himself – the reason to do so may be outweighed (by, say, religious reasons, or medical reasons) – only, that no sane man could fail to want to eat when hungry.)

I.2

The existence of other-regarding unconditional (or categorical) reasons for action is controversial amongst philosophers; not surprisingly, for if there are other-regarding unconditional reasons for actions the foundations of morality are laid.

William David Solomon argues (1975, 331) that, whilst one might accept something like:

(A)   If *P*'s doing *A* would cause suffering for other persons, *P* has a moral reason not to do *A*,

one could still ask whether:

(B)   If *P* has a moral reason for doing *A*, *P* has a reason for doing *A*.

The question is: is such a moral reason really a reason for action? This is a question of substance, for a moral reason need not even be a reason (it is not the case that if *P* has an imaginary child *P* has a child). Solomon contrasts the moral state of affairs with:

(C)   If *P*'s doing *A* is a means to something which *P* wants, *P* has a prudential reason to do *A*, and

(D)   If *P* has a prudential reason for doing *A* then *P* has a reason for doing *A*.

If someone denied D, for instance if he said he was thirsty but denied that his thirst constituted a reason for him to try to get a drink, one would conclude that either he didn't understand thirst or he didn't understand what it was to have a reason for action. He would have stated no rational position. But if he denied B, for instance if he denied that the fact that his act would harm another was a reason not to do it, we would not, Solomon argued, question his understanding.

Now, we have to be clear just what is involved in a denial that there are unconditional other-regarding reasons for action. Warnock (1971, 163–4) distinguishes between the existence of reasons and their weight. Moral reasons, he says, really are reasons for action and could not rationally be denied to be so, but it would not be irrational to hold that they were always outweighed by other (non-moral) reasons. Thus one could be rationally immoral.

This separation of the existence of reasons from their weight has bedevilled a lot of philosophy (as we shall see in chapter IV). A reason for action is a rational influence on action. If a fact has no influence on action then it is not a reason for action. Warnock's sceptic, therefore, if he admits that there are moral reasons, is required to admit that they have some influence on action, i.e. some weight. And if he were to go on to claim that they were *always* outweighed by other reasons, I think we would be inclined to doubt that he really admitted that there were moral reasons (unconditional other-regarding reasons) with weight. The only moral scepticism, therefore, which raises a question of philosophical interest is that which denies that there are any unconditional other-regarding reasons for action; and denies them completely, denies that others constitute any sort of consideration at all except as means to self-regarding ends.

A similar denial of self-regarding reasons, we have said, constitutes a failure of understanding. Can we not say the same thing of the moral sceptic?

If it is possible to establish that the set of others (the world) requires respect it is possible to establish the existence of other-regarding reasons for action. For if I respect others I have unconditional other-regarding reasons for action one way or another. If I respect you I have an unconditional other-regarding reason not to walk over you. If I forbear to walk over you for a self-regarding or conditional reason there is no respect for you involved. There may be respect for myself or for the project or want that provides the condition of my reason, but not respect for you. These are logical points. Respect for others entails the existence of other-regarding unconditional reasons for action. But what is there in the world that requires respect? The answer to this question since it will provide the foundation of unconditional other-regarding reasons for action will provide the foundation of morality and the answer to the moral sceptic.

Wittgenstein said: 'It is not how things are in the world that is mystical but that it exists' (*Tractatus*, 6.44). The pure existence of the world is mysterious. The importance of this for moral philosophy is that it identifies what in the world requires respect. Mystery requires respect.

There are two senses of the word 'mystery' involved here. In the weaker sense if the existence of the world were in principle explicable though not yet explained, there would be a mystery of a kind, requiring no doubt a modicum of self-regarding caution. But not respect. The stronger idea of mystery is needed for this, where the existence of the world is conceived as ultimately transcending explanation. The rationality of other-regarding un-conditional reasons for action depends upon what there is reason to believe about the ultimate nature of the world. If the existence of the world is beyond explanation it is mysterious, in the stronger sense of the word, and respect is required.

What explanation could be given of the existence of the world?

One explanation is the postulation of a necessary cause or reason, called God. Now, if God exists it is obvious that there is a foundation for morality: there is a simple basis for the requirement of respect for His creation, and every part of it.

But if we do not say that God exists, what explanation could there be of the existence of the world? Any non-theistic ex-planation must either enlarge the world, make it infinite, or in-finitesimal, or turn it in on itself to complete a circle. In each case the explanation postulates the existence of something about which the mystery of existence continues to obtain. This is the strong sense of mystery and there seems no way we can get away from it.

Of course, some things are beyond explanation for the simple reason that they are nonsense. I cannot explain the speed of a square, but this does not mean that any mystery attaches: the question is nonsensical, not mysterious. There are many philo-sophers who have questioned the logical propriety of the question why the world exists. But are there any who would dismiss it just as they would dismiss a question about the speed of a square? Take J. J. C. Smart for example:

> So the only rational thing to say if someone asks 'Why does this table exist?' is some such thing as that such and such a carpenter made it. We can go back and back in such a series, but we must not entertain the absurd idea of getting back to something logically necessary. However, now let us ask, 'Why should anything exist at all?' Logic seems to tell us that the only answer which is not absurd is to say, 'Why shouldn't it?' Nevertheless, though I know how any answer on the lines of the cosmological argument can be pulled to pieces by a correct logic, I still feel I want to go on asking the question. Indeed, though logic has taught me to look at such a question with the gravest suspicion, my mind often seems to reel under the immense significance it seems to have on me. That anything should exist at all does seem to me a matter for the deepest awe. But whether other people feel this sort of awe, and whether they or I ought to is another question. I think we ought to. If so, the question arises: If 'Why should anything exist at all?' cannot be interpreted after the manner of the cosmological argument, that is, as an absurd request for the nonsensical postulation of a logically necessary being, what sort of question is it? What sort of question is this question 'Why should anything exist at all?' All I can say is, that I do not yet know. (1955, 46)

The inability to answer a question in a logically proper way may be because the question is nonsense, it may be because the question poses a mystery in the weak sense (that is, the answer is, for any one of a thousand reasons, not yet known), or it may be because the question is mysterious in the strong sense. No one experiences awe as to the outcome of a whodunnit. Smart's awe is clearly a recognition of strong mystery.

Perhaps some moral sceptics would be happy to admit all this. But it would be a fatal concession on their part, for the mystery of the existence of the world obtains for every particular in the world. Any particular might itself be the whole world and the mystery would be the same: it is not the size of the world that is mysterious, but the fact that any part of it exists. Thus the mystery of existence cannot be dismissed as remote metaphysical speculation. It obtains for every particular encountered. There is only one possible answer to this point. There would be no distribution of mystery to all the particulars of the world if there were a unique entity such as a necessary being that attracted to itself the whole mystery of existence. But we have already put aside for our present purposes the moral consequences that might attach to the existence of God.

Perhaps some moral decisions are made without encountering particulars; these would be moral judgments about (universal) properties and relations. But such judgments would be purely theoretical: a practical decision is necessarily a decision in relation to at least one particular. Thus no practical decision can avoid the mystery of the world.

We may approach this point from a different direction. In his analysis of the sublime Kant says: 'The feeling of our incapacity to attain to an idea *which is a law for us* is respect' (*Critique of the Aesthetical Judgment*, 27). Developing this idea in Kant, Iris Murdoch wrote:

> What stuns us into a realisation of our supersensible destiny is not, as Kant imagined, the formlessness of nature, but rather its unutterable particularity; and the most particular and individual of all natural things is the mind of man. That is incidentally why tragedy is the highest art, because it is most intensely concerned with the most individual thing. Here is the true sense of that exhilaration of freedom which attends art and which has its more rarely achieved counterpart in morals. It is the apprehension of something else, something particular, as existing outside us. . . . Kant was marvellously near the mark. But he thought of freedom as the aspiration to a universal order consisting of a pre-fabricated harmony. It was not a tragic freedom. The tragic freedom implied by love is this: that we all have an indefinitely extended capacity to imagine the being of others. Tragic, because there is no prefabricated harmony, and others are, to an extent we never cease discovering, different from ourselves. Nor is there any social totality within which we can come to comprehend differences as placed and reconciled. We have only a segment of the circle. Freedom is exercised in the confronta- tion by each other, in the context of an infinitely extensible work of imaginative understanding, of two irreducibly dissimilar individuals. Love is the imaginative recognition of, that is respect for, this otherness. (1959,51–2)

6

'The sublime' is an enjoyment and renewal of spiritual power arising from an apprehension of the vast formless strength of the natural world. How close this is to being a theory of tragedy, if we think of the spectator as gazing not at the Alps, but at the spectacle of human life. (1959–60, 268)

It is particularity which escapes law (explanation). Particulars when stripped of their attached (universal) properties and relations are pure existence. Thus the correspondence between the rather remote metaphysics of Wittgenstein and Iris Murdoch's practical moral philosophy is clear.

Perhaps the moral sceptic will admit the mystery of the world but deny that it requires respect. This would be sufficient to deny the basis for the claim that there are unconditional other-regarding reasons for action. But such a position is not logically in order. How could one who affirmed mystery but denied respect be thought to have made his meaning clear? We are talking of the stronger sense of mystery here, where the world is conceived of as ultimately transcending explanation. What could we make of one who affirmed that such was indeed the ultimate nature of the world but also held that it was not to be respected? Would we not have to conclude that he, like the prudential sceptic who said he was thirsty but denied that it was a reason to get a drink, did not understand his terms? The two words 'mystery' and 'respect' seem intimately connected in meaning (as Kant's definition shows).

Another way of making this point is in terms of beauty and love.

The common idea that beauty is in the eye of the beholder is actually the opposite of the truth. For it is particulars (indubitably out in the world) which are beautiful: it is self-evident that a class (which may well be in the eye of the beholder) cannot be beautiful. Beauty is experienced in the confrontation of an 'irreducibly dissimilar individual' (Murdoch), something or someone free of me (outside of me) in the sense of my being unable to subsume it into an explanation. The world, of course, is full of men whose business it is to deny this - the manufacturers of Hollywood sex symbols, the pedlars of package tours (the Alps), and the thousand and one other pornographers whose money comes from the false eros embodied in the class images that they put in the place of beauty. And full of men who purchase the pornographers' wares and retreat from particulars into the dreary solipsism of

7

images. Now, the correlative of beauty is love. It is not possible to affirm the beauty of a particular but deny love. But is that not what the moral sceptic is doing when he denies respect? The affirmation of the mysterious particularity of the world is an affirmation of beauty. The denial of respect for that world is simply a denial of love.

I.3

There are reasons for belief and reasons for action; and also reasons for private judgement in the sense established by Iris Murdoch (1970, chapter 1), though perhaps this might best be regarded as a category of reasons for belief. An analysis of law must be concerned principally with public judgment (what a judge does when he settles a law case), and this clearly is a case of action. Thus reasons for action are fundamental to an analysis of law.

There are also in law reasons for ordinary actions. That I promise to pay you money is a (legal) reason for me to pay it. It is also a reason for a judge to give judgment against me. These are different reasons, and this creates problems. In IX.12 we introduce a principle of correspondence which solves some of them.

I.4

Only facts (including future facts) are reasons for action (see Raz, 1975, 16–20). Sometimes it is thought that my belief that something ought to be done can be a justifying reason for my action. But this is fallacious. My belief can be an explanatory reason: you can explain that the reason why I acted was my belief that such-and-such. But my belief cannot be a justifying reason for the action it contemplates, for it does not justify that action. If you are not a criminal but I believe you are and I arrest you, my action is not justified by my belief. I do not have a reason to arrest you; I only believe I do. As Raz put it: 'to decide what we should do we must find what the world is like, and not what our thoughts are like' (1975, 18). Of course, beliefs are themselves facts in the world and, as facts, are reasons for certain actions: for example, if I believe there are pink elephants in the sky I have a reason to consult a doctor.

But what sorts of facts are to be taken to constitute reasons for action? Suppose in law there is a precedent case giving support to the principle that I ought to exercise care towards my neighbours. Now, we shall want to say here that there is a legal reason to exercise care. But what is the reason? Is it that so and so is my neighbour? Is it that there is a source of law for the principle that one should exercise care towards one's neighbours? Or is it that one should exercise care towards one's neighbours (i.e. can such a principle itself exist as a fact and be a reason)? In short is the reason the existence of my neighbour, the existence of the source of law, or the existence of the principle?

Raz's definition of fact is wide enough to allow the third possibility if our principle is reformulated as a value: 'facts are not contrasted with values but include them' (1975, 18), and Raz gives as an example of this: 'it is a fact that human life is the supreme value'. This 'fact' would constitute, for instance, a reason not to kill. No doubt there are reasons not to kill, but is this the reason? And is it a fact? Raz significantly clarifies the analysis of moral and legal thought by insisting that only facts are reasons. But to allow principles or values into the definition of fact nullifies the clarification.

Obviously if a principle has been laid down, say in a statute, there is a fact. The fact then is that the principle has been laid down; the fact is not the principle itself. Where could the principle itself, as opposed to its promulgation, exist or occur? Or 'that human life is the supreme value'; where could that exist or occur? You might say it exists or, by-passing that problem, that it is a fact, but why should I believe you? Is it to be taken as a moral truth whose existence is not contingent but in some sense necessary? We shall later reject that possibility(IV.3 and IV.4); but even if you could demonstrate such existence how could a non-contingent fact be a reason for action? (one reason for this question is: how could I weigh it against a reason constituted by a contingent fact?).

There is another way to make this point. We shall later see (IV.2) that such a principle as we have been discussing, 'I ought to exercise care towards my neighbour (*prima facie*)', is equivalent to 'There is a reason to exercise care towards my neighbour.' Now, if I am asked what is my reason to exercise care I cannot reply that the stated reason is my reason ('my reason is that there is a reason . . .' is no answer at all). Since the principle and the reason are equivalent I cannot reply with the principle either. Thus the principle cannot be a reason. And nor can 'that human life is a fundamental value', for that, too, has an equivalent reason.

Of course, as we have said, that the principle or value has been laid down or decided would be a fact which could constitute a reason. But this is not to say that the principle or value could itself be a fact.

I.5

Facts and possible facts present a seemingly endless array of different and overlapping reasons for action of all degrees of generality (compare Hampshire's thesis of the Inexhaustibility of Description, which holds that for any moral case the relevant facts can never be exhaustively stated: see I.10): thus 'that Harold is in front of my car is a reason for me to take care' might rather be 'that I am driving down a busy street is a reason to take care' (or the fact might be that Harold may be injured, or killed, or impinged upon, or prevented from keeping an appointment . . .); or, sometimes alternatively, 'that Harold is in front of my car is a reason to apply the brakes' (or decelerate, or call out, or turn the steering wheel . . .).

I.6

Probability raises many philosophical difficulties. In the analysis of reasons for action one problem is that the degree of probability of a fact ought to affect its weight as a reason. Reasons for belief and reasons for action are here interrelated (see Raz, 1975, 21). Thus, 'The probability that it will rain is a reason for taking an umbrella' must often be analysed as 'There is a reason to believe that it will rain, and that it will rain is a reason for taking an umbrella'. But not always; for the degree of probability will often affect the weight of the reason for action: for example the location of an umbrella might present a degree of inconvenience only to be outweighed by a virtual certainty of rain. Here we would have to say that the probability that it will rain (in whatever degree) is the reason for taking an umbrella.

Likewise, in a law case the probability of a fact can affect the weight of the reason it constitutes. This is not often seen, for the simple reason that, at least in the cases of present and past facts, the case of proof is usually detached. Thus a fact X which, let us say, is a reason for judgment for the plaintiff might have a certain degree of probability; but whether this fact is proved will be settled by various rules and reasons of evidence and proof, and if it is proved its probability becomes irrelevant. Assume X is proved under a rule specifying the degree of proof required. Such a case would have to be analysed as at least two cases; the first case is a case of proof, and the second, which follows the decision of the first and therefore assumes that X is proved (the separation of cases requires this assumption), is a case in which X, without any complicating factor of probability, is weighed. The separation of reason for belief and reason for action is best seen in those cases where the case of proof is detached.

However, even when detached, the case of proof itself is often complex. The reasons (principles) of the law of evidence are reasons for action – the action is the action of deciding the case of belief – and these are related in a complex way to the reasons for belief in the case.

Future or wide facts tend not to be subject to decisions of proof: for example in a hard punishment case the probability of, say, repentance is given weight proportionate to its degree; or the probability of deterrence; or in a constitutional case if the issue is between on the one hand a strict and therefore more certain construction of the Constitution and on the other a liberal and therefore vaguer one, the weight to be attributed to certainty in public arrangements would vary with the degree of probability of the wide range of facts about social behaviour which constitute this certainty.

I.7

There are brute facts and there are evidential facts. A brute fact is a fact which goes to make up a less-brute fact (see Anscombe, 1958a, 69): for example, the facts that I said 'I promise p' and that you relied on me are brute relative to the fact that I promised p, and this latter fact is in turn brute relative to the fact that I owe you what I promised.

In practical decisions when it is necessary to weigh reasons the degree of bruteness of the facts which constitute the reasons must be settled; I suggest, however, that the weight of the fact that I promised as a reason for action is exactly equal to the sum of the weights of its brute facts.

Evidential facts, by contrast with brute facts, have no weight as reasons for action. For example the fact that Harold confessed to a murder or the fact that he had a blood-stained knife in his possession have no weight as reasons to convict him. They do have weight, however, as reasons for belief, and enter into the proof of the fact that Harold committed the murder. They are not brute to this fact, and it is only this fact which has weight as a reason for action (the action of convicting him).

Though the sum of the weights of a set of brute facts equals the weight of the fact they constitute, it is not without practical importance which I address myself to in a hard decision. Perhaps it is true to say: the greater the bruteness of my reasons the more discriminating and therefore more likely to be accurate is my hard decision. Institutions have a very significant action here: by my institutions I have become used to, for instance, the concept, promise, and I therefore tend to think of the fact of a promise rather than of its brute facts.

I.8

It is well-known that Searle (1969) thought he had derived an ought from an is.

The derivation is:

(1) Jones uttered the words 'I hereby promise to pay you, Smith, five dollars.'
(2) Jones promised to pay Smith five dollars.
(3) Jones placed himself under (undertook) an obligation to pay Smith five dollars.
(4) Jones is under an obligation to pay Smith five dollars.
(5) Jones ought to pay Smith five dollars.

In practical cases facts constitute whatever the reasons are for the action in question and I have to weigh them against whatever the facts (reasons) are against the action. It doesn't matter whether I take the brute fact (I said . . .), the institutional fact (I promised . . .), or its extension (I am under an obligation . . .) as the basis of my decision whether or not to keep my word, for it is obvious that one cannot change the weight of a set of facts by analysis.

There is perhaps some plausibility on the face of Searle's claim to have produced an ought from nowhere. A claim to have produced the weight of a reason for action, however, would immediately be rendered implausible by the question: what degree of weight? And if there is no weight there is no reason; for what sort of reason for action could it be that has no weight, that is, no influence on action? Actually the 'ought' in Step 5 of Searle's analysis is highly confusing.

Step 5 might itself be taken to state a fact. This becomes plausible as soon as we see that Step 3 is a metaphorical statement of fact which gets progressively odder as it is worked out logically. 'Jones placed himself under an obligation . . .' is a metaphor which leads to 'Jones is under an obligation . . .' in the way that the non-metaphorical 'Jones placed the chair under the tree' leads to 'The chair is (at some time) under the tree.' The metaphor might well be distrusted at this point. But when it leads to Step 5, Jones ought (metaphorically) . . ., which we might render as 'What Jones is under has a normative quality' (by analogy with 'What the chair is under has a vegetal quality'), the metaphor has clearly become confusing. Still, Step 5 metaphorically states a fact which might be sorted out and weighed. The weighing, that is, the decision of the practical case, at whichever of the five levels of fact it proceeds, is not assisted by the derivation.

Searle's derivation is not a normative one at all. It is nothing but the analysis of facts, confused somewhat by metaphor. The normative element in his case is given independently of his derivation by the weight that is attached to the fact that Jones promised . . . at whatever level of analysis that fact is taken.

I.9

Only facts can be reasons for action; and, it seems, only contingent facts.

Contingent facts mark a change in the world to which a

passionate response is possible. Necessary facts don't do this. I could no more act in passionate response to $2 + 2 = 4$ than I could to $2 + 2$ by itself or 4 by itself. We have to be careful here. The discovery of a necessary fact (perhaps with a cry of *Eureka*) may well be a reason for action (telling the world, applying for a Nobel prize . . .), but the fact that is the reason here is the discovery. And secondly, there is a loose sense in which the fact that $2 + 2 = 4$ might be taken to be a reason for action. Suppose I have to solve the stated sum. Does not the fact that $2 + 2 = 4$ give me a reason to write 4 as the answer? No. The fact that the sum is required for something or that I will fail an exam unless I write 4 are the operative facts.

Of course, not all contingent facts give reasons for action. The height of Mount Everest is a contingent fact, but, given ordinary human life-spans, hardly a change in the world.

For more general purposes, D. M. Armstrong makes a similar argument when he rejects as existing in the world: 'transcendent universals, a realm of numbers, transcendent standards of value, timeless propositions, non-existent objects such as the golden mountain, possibilia and/or possible worlds, "abstract" classes which are something more than the aggregate of their members, including unit-classes and the null-class' (Armstrong, 1978, 128). The idea behind this is similar to the idea of a change in the world, for these things are rejected by Armstrong on the ground that they possess no causal power.

No doubt philosophers will continue to postulate funny entities; what is quite clear, however, for an analysis of law is that golden mountains and null classes will never occasion law-suits. Nor, even, will transcendent standards of value (IV.3).

I.10

The facts of a practical case give me the reasons for deciding it one way or another. But 'fact' is a word that covers a lot of problems.

The facts will state a series of acts, events and states. A fundamental ambiguity here is whether the acts, events and states are to be taken as particulars or universals. No doubt the facts of any case are very complex; Hampshire's thesis of the inexhaustibility of description is helpful here:

14

Any situation which confronts me, and which is not a situation in a game, has an inexhaustible set of discriminable features over and above those which I explicitly notice at the time because they are of immediate interest to me. . . . When it comes to giving an account of the reasons for an action, or course of conduct, one picks out a few salient desires and beliefs from the foreground of consciousness . . . (Hampshire 1978, 30–1. Incidentally, Hampshire is wrong in thinking that legal judgments are different in this regard)

But still there is an important question of whether a practical decision is to be based upon this inexhaustible set of particulars or that at least equally inexhaustible set of properties and relations (universals) of which the particulars are the instantiation. For any described particular, no matter how complex, there stands in correspondence a highly limited universal; and it is a point of some importance to know which of these, the particular or the universal, is at the basis of practical decisions. For example, Harold is the manufacturer of a bottle of ginger beer into which he negligently introduces a dead snail, thereby causing injury to a purchaser of the bottle from a café at Paisley. He is also a Protestant, plays chess and loves his wife, etc., etc. Is my practical decision (my legal decision if I am a judge) to be based upon the seemingly inexhaustible particulars of which we have but commenced description, or on the corresponding highly limited universal, wife-loving, Protestant, chess-playing, manufacturer of ginger beer, etc., etc.: that man who . . . (which could only be Harold) or a man who . . . (which could be anyone)?

Perhaps the thesis of the inexhaustibility of description misses this point. For the world might be much simpler than it is, and description not inexhaustible. But still, in this simple world, the question would arise whether a case is to be decided on the basis of its particulars or on the basis of the corresponding set of (now exhaustively defined) universals. Hampshire's argument is aimed against what he calls a computational style of morality. And what this argument really needs is particulars. For what is ultimately beyond the grasp of a computer is not complexity, but particulars. For this reason, in a simple world one would still want to argue against the computational style of morality.

The view that a practical decision is not based upon the

particulars of a case but rather on the corresponding set of highly limited universals is implicit in much moral philosophy. But there are two objections to it: the first suggestive, and the second conclusive. The suggestive objection depends upon the nature of the determination of the will of the acting subject. There can be subjective and objective determinations of the will. The simplest example of a subjective determination of the will is a habit: if I have a habit of doing something, then when the appropriate circumstances come along my will is determined more or less automatically, as though programmed to respond to the circumstances whenever they arise.

Now, in practical cases if judgment were on the basis of the universal properties and relations that obtained rather than particulars it would tend to be judgment where the will was determined subjectively. Perhaps if universals are real (as Armstrong (1978) has argued) we would want to say that the first time I encountered and responded to a particular universal or a particular arrangement of universals my will was determined objectively. But once encountered, then, given a degree of memory, there would be no further question when another particular instantiation of the universal came along – my will would be determined as if programmed. If, on the other hand, it was always determined by particulars this would necessarily be objective: programme and response to particulars are logically incompatible.

The conclusive objection depends upon the practicality of practical judgments. In practical cases judgment is in the end applied to particulars. In law cases, for example (though the point applies to all practical cases), if Harold is the defendant judgment is against Harold, the particular, not against that highly limited set of properties and relations (universals) of which Harold is an instantiation (and in ordinary practical cases action is against the particulars involved). This I take as obvious, without the necessity of reflecting on the problem of a sheriff wondering whether he ought not to execute judgment against this instantiation of Harold's properties and relations in case another happens to turn up. Now, accepting this, the question is what is sufficient to connect the judgment of the case to the particular Harold. If the judgment were a judgment about a set of highly limited universals there would seem to be no reason to apply it to any particular instantiation of those universals rather than another; and we would have no explanation for the fact that a judgment actually is applied to one particular rather than another. Judgment is against Harold, not any Harold II who might turn up with the relevant (universal) properties and relations. The problem is to account for this connection of the judgment to Harold, the particular. Of course, I *would* apply it to Harold if my will were subjectively determined to do so (if that were the way I were programmed). But there would seem to be no reason to do so. Any 'reason' presented for the application of the judgment to the Harold is itself subject to these difficulties. For instance, you might say: the reason for applying the judgment to this particular Harold is that it was this particular Harold who did the particular act. But this 'reason' itself might be stated in terms of correspondingly limited universals: apply judgments to persons with (Harold's properties and relations) who do acts of (whatever the sort). Thus we are left with precisely the same problem: is there reason to connect *it* to the particular Harold? If there is no reason, as seems to be the case, then a conception of practical judgment as based upon universals would be incorrigibly theoretical.

If, on the other hand, practical judgment is determined by particular facts (that is, it is particular facts which are reasons for action) there is no difficulty in accounting for the application of such judgments to the relevant particulars (Harold, rather than Harold II). It would seem that we have to say that practical judgment, because it is practical, that is, concerned with action, must necessarily be judgment on the basis of particulars. Reasons for action, therefore, are founded on particulars. (The Common Law has always known this: it will not decide hypothetical cases.)

An important consequence of this conception of practical judgment is that it opens the analysis to love and its correlative, beauty. Only particulars can be loved and only particulars can be beautiful. And, furthermore, it establishes the connection of practical thought to the mystery of the world. A particular is pure existence, and that is what is mysterious. As Wittgenstein said, the mystery of the world is not how the world is but that it is (*Tractatus*, 6.44). The mystery of the world is distributed to the particulars of the world, for any one of them might alone constitute the world, and the mystery would remain.

If practical judgments are based upon particulars not universals, what is the status of universalization in moral thought?

R. M. Hare is prominent among the many philosophers who have thought that moral judgments have to be universalizable. Hare's main argument is that moral judgments have a descriptive element (1963, chapter 2), and it is this which makes them logically universalizable. To say that this thing is red is to say that it is a thing of a certain kind, and that commits me logically to saying that anything like it in the relevant respect is also red (1963, 11). So, to say that something is good commits me logically to saying that anything like it in the (describable) respects is also good:

> [P and Q are pictures.] Suppose that either P is a replica of Q or Q of P, and we do not know which, but we do know that both were painted by the same artist at about the same time. Now there is one thing that we cannot say; we cannot say 'P is exactly like Q in all respects save this one, that P is a good picture and Q not'. If we were to say this, we should invite the comment, 'But how can one be good and the other not, if they are exactly alike? There must be some *further* difference between them to make one good and the other not.' Unless we at least admit the relevance of the question 'What makes one good and the other not?' we are bound to puzzle our hearers; they will think that something has gone wrong with our use of the word 'good'. (1952, 80–1)

Perhaps Hare is right in this argument. For judgments of goodness may properly be taken as intrinsically theoretical, judgments not necessarily resulting in action at all, and therefore not raising the problem of connection to a particular, or not in anything like as pressing a form as practical judgments. Judgments of what ought to be done, on the other hand, are practical ('this is a wrong act' may have a theoretical sense and Hare's argument may apply to it; but in that event it is not equivalent to the practical 'this ought not to be done'). The examples that Hare uses (this is red, this is good . . .) are examples where a (universal) property is attributed to a particular; and of course this commits one to other applications of the universal. It is part of the meaning of universal that this should be so. But practical judgments do not attribute universals. They determine the will in relation to action against particulars. And if they are conceived of as judgments about universals, then, as we saw in the last section, they lose their practical sense.

Something like this has been perceived by the many philosophers who have remarked against Hare that the requirement of universalizability is a formal shell, devoid of substance. At most it is perhaps a rather vague guard against hypocrisy: if I make a judgment about you I should be prepared to be judged myself. But given a thick skin and an heroic disposition there is not much that cannot be universalized. Thus too much is authorized: there is no question of (objective) truth in issue, no connection to the substance of the world. What is superior in a moral philosophy based upon particulars is first, its intrinsic practicality and second, that there is an immediate connection to that which is at the heart of all substance, the mystery of the world. It is particulars not universals which are mysterious.

I.12

To admit other-regarding, unconditional reasons for action is of interest in the Prisoners' Dilemma.

The dilemma is this (it is now to be found in a very wide range of philosophical literature):

Suppose two prisoners are interrogated separately. Each knows that if neither confesses they will each get a short sentence. If one confesses but the other doesn't the one will be released and the other will get a large sentence. And if both confess they each get a middling sentence.

The standard matrix to present this dilemma is as follows (where C = co-operate with the other prisoner, i.e. not confess; and D = defect, i.e. confess; and the numbers 1 to 4 represent the increasing order of desirability of outcome, e.g. heaviest sentence = 1 and release = 4):

	C	D
C	3 3	1 4
D	4 1	2 2

It is thought that this demonstrates a paradox. The rational *joint* action is to co-operate (i.e. not confess) for then each gets 3, whereas if both defect each gets 2. But for each individual the rational course is to defect whatever the other does. For if the other co-operates defection gives 4 instead of 3 and if the other defects it gives 2 instead of 1. Thus if each individual makes the individually rational decision a result is produced (2 instead of 3) that would be jointly irrational.

But it is irrational to overlook other-regarding reasons for action. The dilemma is based upon self-regarding reasons only.

Let the orders 1–4 in the matrix represent quantitative judgments as to the weight of self-regarding and other-regarding reasons for action. Thus *for each individual* co-operation is superior to defection. For each the following reasoning obtains:

If the other co-operates my co-operation gives $3 + 3 = 6$ whereas my defection gives $4 + 1 = 5$. If the other does not co-operate my co-operation gives $1 + 4 = 5$ whereas my defection gives $2 + 2 = 4$. Therefore, whatever the other does, it is rational to co-operate.

There is no paradox on these quantities. The rational joint action corresponds to the rational individual action.

(There are two problems here. First, how reasons for action have quantities rather than orders. This is taken up in chapter XI. And second, how they have the stated quantities. Some quantities (where, for instance, a self-regarding reason is given more than twice the weight of an other-regarding reason) preserve the dilemma.)

II

RULES

II.1

The world is a mystery. This is the basis of moral thought. But we appropriate the mystery (reduce it to our grasp and ownership) with no less audacity than Prometheus, who stole fire from the gods. One of the forms into which we put our acquisitions is rule. The use which we make of rules (like our use of fire) is to enable us to carry on. Now, wanting to carry on is a pervasive human inclination, but wanting is no final mark of moral authenticity. Putting aside more dubious special revelations, our present and evident token of the mystery of the world, and of its moral quality, is beauty and its correlative, love. But beauty, indifferent to passing events, fails to authenticate our wish to survive.

The form of all rules evidences, invariably, an act of formidable audacity: no part of moral thought which might otherwise influence judgment in the matters covered by the rule is left to stand. Law, that vast array of rules, is precisely this, the clearest example of it; it is a settlement, an end to questions, a substitution of certainty for truth; it is a reduction to the grasp of men of the mystery of things.

Legal positivism, a philosophy of law that has been dominant for over a century and a half, disguises the audacity of rules by holding that the logical character of judgment under rules is such that one can make it without being committed to that judgment in any ultimate moral sense. On this view nothing conclusive is done by our taking a rule: no moral question is importantly prejudiced. But

21

the view is a false one. Rule judgment is not just legal judgment or chess judgment, but ultimate moral judgment; and nothing less than this is the responsibility of those who make it. The normal expression by legal positivists of this false doctrine is to say that rules, including legal rules, are provisional or *prima facie*, and that for any decision under a rule the full moral question awaits separate answer. This is the most significant part of their thesis of the separation of law and morality.

II.2

What could we make of a judge who at the conclusion of a capital case declared that he sentenced the prisoner *prima facie* to be hanged? What would the prisoner make of it? Initial confusion, caused only partly by the linguistic oddity of the pronouncement, would perhaps give way to hope (for the sake of simplicity we exclude appeals, prerogatives of mercy, hangmen's strikes, and such like). What would lawyers make of it? Let us assume that the status of the sentence comes up for formal decision (perhaps the judge dies between sentence and execution). The problem would be to know whether the prisoner had actually been sentenced, for the form used suggests in its odd way that finality has been deferred. Perhaps it could be treated as a whimsical equivalent of the ordinary form of sentence (I sentence you to be hanged). Unless so, if it meant something less than that, we would have to say that no legal sentence had yet been given. A legal sentence, it seems, has to be in substance conclusive not *prima facie*. So, either the sentence means 'I sentence you to be hanged' or it is no sentence at all. But the thesis of the separation of law and morals has it that legal judgment is in some sense *prima facie* judgment. Why is a *prima facie* sentence, then, not in order as it stands? This is puzzling, and indicates a need to look more closely at the nature of legal judgment.

Suppose, that one way or another a proper legal sentence is obtained from our judge. What sort of decision has he made, what sort of act has he performed?

The thesis of the separation of law and morals takes many forms. But when Raz says (1975, 147) 'that the primary organs [courts] follow and apply the rules of recognition does not entail that they hold them to be morally justified' he is applying the thesis in a widely accepted way. How does this form of the thesis fit our case? Let us suppose that our judge in making his sentence is following and applying a rule of recognition which identifies a certain statute prescribing the death penalty (rule of recognition is here to be understood in the sense of H. L. A. Hart's analysis in *The Concept of Law*). Now, could the thesis hold in this case? Could it be that our judge's following and applying the rule of recognition does not entail that he holds it to be morally justified? This could only be true if the following were non-contradictory:

(A) The prisoner ought to hang, but it is not the case (morally) that the prisoner ought to hang.

Before examining (A) a couple of comments are necessary. The first part of (A) states the legal norm which is constituted by the combined operation of the rule of recognition and the capital statute. The function of this legal norm is to justify the capital sentence; if it does not do this it is irrelevant to the legal situation of the sentencing judge, and to our purposes, too (our analysis is of law and therefore of *legal* judgment).

'The prisoner ought to hang' and 'it is not the case that the prisoner ought to hang' are formulated generally. The question for a judge, however, is the more specific: whether he ought to sentence the prisoner to be hanged. There are some important differences between these forms. I have chosen the more general form for the purposes of this chapter because it is the more conventional and convenient form of legal norms. The arguments of this chapter apply just as well, however, to the more specific:

(AA) I ought to sentence the prisoner to hang, but it is not the case (morally) that I ought to sentence the prisoner to hang.

To get back to (A), if (A) is a contradiction (and I think it is) then the entailment which the thesis of the separation of law and morals rejects obtains.

Proponents of the thesis, defending the sense of (A) or something like it, have maintained that the first part of (A) is a legal not a moral norm, and that legal norms have only a *prima facie* force. The following is not contradictory, they correctly point out:

(B) *Prima facie* the prisoner ought to hang, but it is not the case (morally) that the prisoner ought to hang.

But (B) has to be rejected as a justification of our judge's sentence since the only sentence (B) is capable of justifying is a *prima facie* sentence, which is no sentence at all.

That a *prima facie* norm such as the first part of (B) cannot justify a conclusive (non *prima facie*) sentence is perhaps not self-evident. The question must be taken strictly. If some extra norm or fact is injected into the argument then a justification can be produced: for instance, if we can say there is no further relevant norm, then a *prima facie* norm becomes conclusive. But this is not a case of a *prima facie* norm itself justifying the sentence. An argument for that sort of justification is either irrational or illogical. It is irrational if it says we ought to do what we *prima facie* ought to do (we ought to sentence the prisoner if we *prima facie* ought to sentence the prisoner); and it is illogical if it equates what we *prima facie* ought to do to what we ought to do. (It is also, of course, immoral: i.e. immoral to do other than what one ought to do; but that is beside the point.) We conclude that a *prima facie* norm cannot justify a conclusive (proper) sentence. Thus (B) must be rejected as a justification of a conclusive (proper) sentence.

How else might (A) be defended? Consider:

(C) According to the law the prisoner ought to hang, but it is not the case (morally) that the prisoner ought to hang.

There are three possible ways of interpreting the first part of (C). According to the first it is not a norm at all, but rather a description of the content of a given legal system:

(C1) The fact is that according to the law of (a given community) the prisoner ought to hang, but it is not the case (morally) that the prisoner ought to hang.

Obviously there is no contradiction in (C1), but it will not do as a justification of the judge's sentence because the mere external existence of a norm can by itself justify no practical decision. The second way of interpreting (C) is to regard its first part as normative in the ordinary way ((C2), formulated identically to (A) with the addition of the words 'according to the law'). What could we now make of the words 'according to the law'? Either these

24

qualify the norm in a normative way or they are redundant and can be ignored. I can see no other way that they could qualify the norm normatively than by making its force *prima facie*. This would reduce (C) to (B), and we have already rejected (B) as a justification of the sentence. If the words are redundant contradiction is plain.

There is a third way of interpreting (C) if we accept Joseph Raz's analysis of normative statements. According to Raz there is a type of normative statement which is neither an ordinary normative statement nor a statement of fact about someone's normative beliefs (neither (C2) nor (C1)), but which states what ought to be done from a certain point of view without endorsing that point of view.

> The use of this type of normative statement is more frequent than might be thought . . . If I go with a vegetarian friend to a dinner party I may say to him, 'You should not eat this dish. It contains meat.' Not being a vegetarian I do not believe that the fact that the dish contains meat is a reason against eating it. I do not, therefore, believe that my friend has a reason to refrain from eating it, nor am I stating that he has. I am merely informing him what ought to be done from the point of view of a vegetarian. Of course, the very same sentence can be used by a fellow vegetarian to state what ought to be done. But this is not what I am saying, as my friend who understands the situation will know. (Raz, 1975, 175)

Let us now formulate (C3):

> (C3) From the legal point of view the prisoner ought to hang, but it is not the case morally that the prisoner ought to hang.

Now, if this is contradictory the entailment under consideration obtains. Perhaps it is not (though this is a difficult question); in which case (C3) confirms a certain form of thesis of the separation of law and morals. But it will only be a significant one if the first part of (C3) is able to justify a sentence, for only then will it concern legal judgment and decision. But (C3) cannot justify a sentence, because these statements from 'points of view' do not justify practical decisions. This can be seen if we look further at Raz at dinner.

Suppose after stating what ought to be done from the vegetarian point of view, Raz returned his own meat to his host:

Raz: I will not eat this meat.

Host: Why is that? I didn't know you were a vegetarian. I thought a moment ago you were merely speaking from the vegetarian's point of view.

We can understand the puzzlement here. It is simply that no such decision as Raz has made is justified by this 'statement from the vegetarian point of view'. Nor can we say it is justified in the case of the vegetarian either; for the vegetarian himself does not make or act on that sort of statement. In fact no decision at all is justified by a statement from the vegetarian point of view. The same is true for the legal point of view too. No legal decision is justified by a statement from the legal point of view. Thus (C3) cannot justify a sentence.

Raz supports the thesis of the separation of law and morals by consideration of the case of an anarchist posing as a judge (1975, 148). It is not easy to see how an analysis of legal thought can be concerned with impostor judges. Perhaps, however, whether a man is an impostor is extrinsic to the problem of meaning and entailment which concerns us now; so we shall consider a defence of (A) that relies upon this case of an anarchist posing as a judge. Raz says: 'An anarchist . . . may become a judge on the ground that if he follows the law most of the time he will be able to disobey it on the few but important occasions when to do so will do most to tend to undermine it.'

Now, (A) might be made to read:

(D) The prisoner ought to hang (in order to increase the potential for undermining the system), but it is not the case (morally) that the prisoner ought to hang.

The 'ought' in the first part of (D) is a technical one – it is a statement of what ought to be done to produce a certain end. This technical ought could not save (A) for it is not capable of supporting a sentence: the only sentence it could justify would be one conditional on the pursuit of the impostor judge's end, and a conditional sentence of that sort would be as objectionable and as null as a *prima facie* sentence, and for similar reasons (of course, the impostor might conceal the condition and deliberately misstate the sentence in order to achieve this end, and actually succeed in his deceit, but that says nothing about our questions of meaning and entailment). The first part of (D) can certainly be made categorical, when the (argued) moral desirability of the end is put into the norm. And then it will justify a sentence. But (D) then becomes (D1), and is an obvious contradiction:

(D1) The prisoner ought (morally) to hang [the reasons to undermine the system can be set out] but it is not the case (morally) that the prisoner ought to hang.

Not every use of the term 'morally ought' necessarily marks a conclusive ought. I can say 'morally, I ought not to do X, but since it is legally required I ought to do it'. This is a confusing use of the word 'moral' which, for our own part, we later reject (II.9). However, the sense here is clear enough: the first ought is *prima facie* or in some other way non-conclusive. If the first ought in (D1) were of this sort then contradiction would be avoided, but in this event (D1) would not justify the sentence, even for an impostor judge, since it would be equivalent to (B). This, of course, will always be the case when the norm to justify the sentence is non-conclusive.

We may say the following about (A). Either its first norm is non-conclusive or it is conclusive. If it is non-conclusive it cannot justify a sentence. If it is conclusive A is contradictory and the entailment under consideration holds, that is, our judge's following and applying the rule of recognition does entail that he holds it to be morally justified. Since only the conclusive form is able to justify the sentence, this entailment always holds for this sort of legal decision.

II.3

What is a sentence? This question, and its equivalents for other sorts of judicial actions, is obviously at the heart of the problems discussed so far. A *prima facie* sentence is not a sentence. Well, why not?

Two possibilities for the analysis of a sentence seem open. First, we might regard a sentence by a judge as an act of will; a decision *to* act; like an ordinary decision to act, except that it is taken on behalf of the community. Second, we might be able to regard it as an authoritative certificate as to what the law requires to be done to the prisoner in question. As an authorized act of will the sentence would constitute a lawful direction to officials to act accordingly; as an authoritative certificate it would be picked up by a supervening legal rule which would thereby arrange the legal state of affairs, including the obligations of officials. How would these lines of analysis apply to a *prima facie* sentence?

Could such a sentence be taken by a hangman as a lawful direction? Hangmen, no doubt, are not given to taking fine points, but it is no fine point to maintain that a *prima facie* capital sentence is not a direction to hang; for if it is anything at all it is a direction whose operation is deferred. Thus if the first line of analysis is taken we have to say that a *prima facie* sentence fails to perform the legal act required of it. What about the second line? Could the *prima facie* sentence operate as an authoritative certificate?

So far as the rule which is to pick it up is concerned, there is no reason why it should not. What the signal is which activates a rule is largely a contingent matter, and so it could be the case that the rule arranging the relevant obligations was by its terms to be activated by the signal, *prima facie* sentence. In this case obligations would be arranged accordingly, including that of the hangman. The thesis of the separation of law and morals would hold in this form of sentencing decision, for the decision would not entail moral justification. The judge would simply certify, uncommitted in any conclusive way to the death of the prisoner, what sentence the law required, and the supervening rule would pick up his certificate as a signal for the required arrangement of obligations (just as it might pick up the declaration of a computer). But this line of analysis fails. A judge's sentence is not just a certificate, and not just a signal.

If we take the case of the hangman himself, we can see clearly that at least he must make a willing decision which is more than certificate or signal. Obviously his decision to apply the rules and directions requiring execution can be regarded neither as certificate nor signal activating a rule, for there is no one in the legal system left to be certified to or signalled to or to apply that further so-activated rule. Let us say that the hangman follows and applies the rule of recognition identifying the capital statute and the judge's sentence as law. Obviously in the hangman's case this entails a claim to moral justification. His case is much clearer than the judge's; for if the first part of (A) ('the prisoner ought to hang') is qualified, there is no semblance of justification for his pulling the lever. No actual pulling of the lever could possibly be justified by:

(B) *Prima facie* the prisoner ought to hang, but it is not the case (morally) that the prisoner ought to hang.

The *prima facie* qualification must be removed from (B) leaving an obvious contradiction. Thus we can say that at least the hangman must make a full willing moral decision such that his following and applying the rule of recognition of statutes and sentences does entail that he holds it to be morally justified (weakness of the will excluded: see II.4).

The question now is whether an analysis of law is possible which has hangmen acting with moral responsibility in this way but judges acting without moral responsibility.

What precisely is our hangman's responsibility for a decision to hang? Generally, responsibility is diminished when one's act is directed by someone in authority. Is there to be any diminution in this way of the hangman's responsibility for the execution which he performs? Obviously yes; for his case is not at all like that of a lynch mob which takes the law into its own hands. If the execution is morally wrong he is certainly responsible for his part in the wrong; but not to the extent that a lynch mob is responsible.

No doubt some of the total responsibility can be passed to Parliament, which made the capital law. But there is one part of it which cannot. An important part of the moral question whether the prisoner ought to hang is whether Parliament ought to be obeyed (for it is Parliament's statute which requires the hanging). And Parliament itself can take no responsibility for the answer to that question: it is not logically possible for Parliament to say anything significant on whether it ought to be obeyed (any attempt to do so would lead to infinite regression). We therefore have to consider what is the hangman's responsibility for the moral decision to obey Parliament in this case of Parliament's requiring that the prisoner be hanged. Can he pass any of it to the judge?

If our judge's sentence were simply a signal or a certificate that the law applied to the prisoner, then he would say nothing at all on the moral question of whether Parliament ought to be obeyed; and

29

the full responsibility for this decision must be the hangman's alone. Can hangmen be expected to be versed in the problematics of legal obligation and its relationship to moral obligation? Yet the certificate and signal analysis of a judge's sentence places the responsibility for a decision in these matters on the shoulders of the hangman. Only the most doctrinaire adherence to the thesis of the separation of law and morals could insist that such matters are for hangmen rather than for those wise and learned men that we set up on high in robes of scarlet; and even then it would only be a thesis of the separation of law and morals for judges – there can be no such separation for those who have to perform the executions. Any analysis which concludes that hangmen are to take the whole of the responsibility for such decisions on legal obligation and judges none is false; not only false in the moral way, in that it unfairly places a burden on people ill-equipped to bear it, but false also in its understanding of the conceptual structures that underlie the establishment of courts.

We conclude that a judge's sentence must be regarded as a responsible direction to officials to carry out its terms; and that a *prima facie* sentence fails as a sentence, first, because it cannot constitute that direction, and second, because it shirks proper judicial responsibility.

II.4

A full-blooded (fully-willed) direction by a judge to hang is what is required. Can a judge not make up for the inconclusiveness of '*prima facie* the prisoner ought to hang' by an act of will; thus allowing (B) (*prima facie* the prisoner ought to hang, but it is not the case (morally) that the prisoner ought to hang) to stand as a sufficient justification of the sentence? But, obviously, since the first part of (B) is *prima facie* it does not justify that act of will. This is perhaps not a conclusive argument because the point of introducing will to the analysis was to do something over and above the justification. The real difficulty in introducing will is with the second part of the normative statement which makes such a will conclusively (morally) unjustified. Might not a judge nevertheless will the hanging? This turns into the difficult and widely fascinating philosophical problem of akrasia or weakness of the will: is moral backsliding possible?; is it possible for me to do what I know I morally ought not to do? More particularly for present purposes, we might ask whether the thesis of the separation of law and morals can be saved by taking law as moral weakness. (A) would become:

(E) The prisoner is to hang (weak moral but legal will), but it is not the case (morally) that the prisoner ought to hang.

This is not a very comfortable position for a theorist of law to take. It is one thing for him to argue for a separation of law and morals; but quite another to insist upon an analysis which requires judges to be seen paradigmatically as moral backsliders; and moreover, backsliders acting with no sufficient legal justification, either, for the first part of (E) is a mere act of will stating no justification, legal or of any sort (once a justification is put into it we are forced back to one or another of the earlier variations of (A) already examined).

However, the most conclusive way to deal with (E) is to reject the possibility of weakness of the will; this is done in V.13.

II.5

The preceding argument is not restricted to the case of criminal sentences, but applies to all legal decisions. A *prima facie* judgment for a plaintiff is as objectionable as a *prima facie* sentence, and so on. Thus it is a general truth about any decision under legal rules that the legal norm justifying the decision entails the corresponding conclusive moral judgment.

 Prima facie sentence is an odd notion. Perhaps it is meaningless; an improper construction; a thing not to be accommodated in language at all. So be it. But *it ought to have been* able to have been accommodated if the thesis of the separation of law and morals had held, and if judges when they sentenced criminals were doing no more than certifying what the law required. Anyway, the notion can now be abandoned and our conclusions stand without reference to it:

(a) legal decisions entail a claim to their moral justification.
(b) legal decisions are made with moral responsibility for what they require.

31

II.6

When Kelsen held that it was not possible to maintain at the same time a legal norm and an inconsistent moral norm he had seen the truth that legal norms were logically conclusive. The way Kelsen assured this logical feature was by requiring that the validity of the historically first constitution be presupposed (this was his *grund-norm*). This systemic ground of validity carries right through the hierarchy of legal norms and has the effect of excluding external (non-systemic) questions. If such questions are excluded legal norms are conclusive. It is ironical that the moral vacuity of the *grund-norm* has been thought to indicate that Kelsen's is an extreme form of the thesis of the separation of law and morals. Kelsen is a much subtler thinker than that, and in truth this moral vacuity has the opposite effect. It breaks down the separation of law and morals, for it ensures that a real answer to a legal question entails the same answer to the corresponding moral question.

II.7

Hart on a number of occasions argued against Kelsen on this point, adopting amongst other things the *prima facie* idea, or a variation of it. According to the way he presented the matter in his report of his visit to Kelsen ('Kelsen Visited', 10 U.C.L.A., L.R., 722–8) (B) would become:

(B1) There are good reasons for requiring the prisoner to hang, but it is not the case (morally) that the prisoner ought to hang.

But (B1) is not significantly different from (B). The only sentence it is capable of producing is 'There are good reasons for hanging you', which is unsatisfactory as a sentence in the same way as our *prima facie* sentence.

But Hart should not be arguing against Kelsen on this point. For in Hart's own concept of law there is the basis for Kelsen's conclusion. The internal attitude to rules (a crucial part of Hart's analysis) excludes considerations beyond a certain point (that point being the boundary of whatever rule the attitude is internal to). Like Kelsen's *grund-norm* it guarantees that the legal norms which justify judgment will be conclusive, not *prima facie*; so that it is not possible for people displaying the internal attitude to talk of the law as merely good reasons. The judge of our example when he sentences the accused displays an internal attitude to the rule of recognition, and that entails the exclusion of questions beyond the rule of recognition. If further questions are excluded then the legal reasons are not merely good ones, they are conclusive. So, as in Kelsen, the corresponding moral norm is entailed by an internal legal decision.

It is strange that the similarity between the two ideas, internal attitude and *grund-norm* has usually been overlooked, not least by Hart himself. Hart's insistence on a distinction between himself and Kelsen on this point is substantially misconceived. Hart says:

> That it is logically impossible to regard a particular rule of law as valid and at the same time to accept, as morally binding, a moral rule forbidding the behaviour required by the legal rule . . .
> [does not] follow from the account of legal validity given in this book. (1961, 246)

But precisely that does follow whenever the regarding of a particular law as valid is internal. And it will be internal in most cases that are of interest to legal philosophy. The internal attitude to rules is analysed in the next chapter.

II.8

For the thesis of the separation of law (and rules in general) from morals two senses of the moral justification of a rule must be distinguished. In the first sense a rule is morally justified if morally it ought to be followed. This is the practical sense of moral justification – that which relates to practical decision – and is the sense considered by the argument of this chapter. The second sense is a largely non-practical sense, usually more suited to idle reflection. It is that if the making of the rule were at issue it would be morally justified to make the same rule. Of course, for legislators this is also a practical sense, but for most practical decisions the making or unmaking of a rule is not at issue.

It is not clear when Raz argues (in the passage quoted earlier as an example of the separation thesis) that the application of a rule of recognition does not entail that it is held to be morally justified which sense of moral justification he intends. If he intends the second sense then he is clearly right, for the application of a rule does not entail that the rule is morally to be chosen were its making in issue. But this second sense is not one which is philosophically interesting (the issue in Nazi Germany was whether to obey the rules not whether to repeal them). Nor does it support any thesis of the separation of law and morals. It is merely one example of the more general thesis, which no one at all would want to deny, that rules are sometimes binding even when they ought to be otherwise. This thesis exposes one of the logical features of a rule. It is not a thesis of the separation of law and morals, for it applies to *legal* criticism of a legal rule as well as to moral criticism: for instance, when a court follows the rule of a precedent case even when it would be minded on *legal* grounds to decide its case otherwise were there no binding precedent; and it applies to moral criticism of a moral rule, too. In fact it applies to either legal or moral criticism of either a legal or a moral rule. It would only constitute a thesis of the separation of law and morals if law were all the rules and only rules, which it is not. The argument of this chapter has been concerned to refute the thesis in the first, stronger, practical and interesting sense.

II.9

Rules, we have said, are appropriations of the mystery of the world, occupations of the whole field of moral thought. It may be morally wrong to make these appropriations, or at least to make them as frequently and immodestly as we do. And we may, of course, and often do, make the wrong appropriations; that is, we make rules that ought to be otherwise in the second sense of II.8. But we have to say, despite these qualifications, that judgment under rules is moral judgment (of course, as on any definition of moral, a particular judgment may be mistaken moral judgment). This follows from a simple idea of moral judgment: a conclusive judgment about life, liberty, property and the like (matters of importance, certainly including all the matters of law) is a moral judgment.

Now, much may be thought to turn on this definition of 'moral'.

We are arguing against the separation of law and morals; but the argument will be no more useful or interesting than its definitions. The definition we have proposed may be thought to have begged the whole question.

One of the most muddling things in moral philosophy is the idea that the word 'moral' refers to a limited area of practical thought; for instance, when it is said that there are moral reasons for action and other sorts of reasons as well. There are (so we have argued: I.2) unconditional other-regarding reasons for action; but to call these or some other limited class of reasons for action moral reasons makes confusion. This can be demonstrated by an example.

Suppose, Robert, Harold and I are drifting in an open boat and I am in control of just enough food to save one of us (if it is shared we all die). I have an other-regarding, unconditional reason to give the food to Robert, a similar reason to give it to Harold, and a self-regarding, unconditional reason to give it to myself; and I must decide on the balance of reasons what to do. There is a moral decision to be made here. It seems clear that my whole decision is the moral decision, and not just the decision between Robert and Harold (if it were just the decision between Robert and Harold, then when judging my own claim I would be deciding between morality and self-interest). To refer to my whole decision is the way the word 'moral' is conventionally used: the extent to which self-interest should be allowed weight against the interests of others is taken to be almost paradigmatically a moral question. If such a decision is the moral decision then I cannot contrast moral reasons (in favour of Robert and Harold) with self-regarding reasons. Either all the reasons are moral reasons, because they all go into the moral decision, or none are. There is a well-known puzzle which plays upon this really very simple issue.

If (it is said) I ought morally to do p and I ought on some other ground, let us say self-interest, to do some incompatible thing, q, then if the question of what conclusively I ought to do is a question of what I ought morally to do, there is no contest between p and q; for, *ex hypothesi*, I ought morally to do p. So, since the possibility of contest must be admitted, it is suggested that the final 'ought' is not a moral ought, implying that final or conclusive judgment is not moral judgment (see Williams, 1978, 91–109).

The puzzle depends upon the construction of a special compartment for morality; it is to be set up in this way:

1 I ought *prima facie* to do [what I ought conclusively morally to do].
2 I ought conclusively morally to do *p*.
3 Therefore I ought *prima facie* to do *p*.
4 I ought self-interestedly to do *q*.
5 (Requiring a judgment between 3 and 4.)

Setting up the problem in such a way does not allow the final decision to be a decision as to what I ought conclusively morally to do, for if it were, there would be no reason to go past 2. But, of course, everything depends upon the compartment made by the square brackets in 1, for which no justification is available. And as we ordinarily consider these matters we do not have this compartment, for we do not ordinarily keep 4 out of 2 (quite ordinary usage has it that judgment between my own interests and another's raises a moral issue).

The ordinary usage by which the statement in 2 is conclusive not merely morally but absolutely, might, of course, need amendment. It is sometimes possible for philosophers to show that ordinary usage needs amendment. But not in this case. The compartmental view of moral judgment really reduces to absurdity. For it requires us to say that selflessness is no virtue; not merely no moral virtue, but no virtue at all! Consider our earlier example of the open boat. If I give the food to Harold or Robert rather than to myself this is no moral virtue on the compartment view (only my decision between Harold and Robert could display that virtue). But the absurdity is greater than this, for we are forced on the compartment view to say it is no virtue at all. What sort of virtue could it be? Certainly no prudential virtue – indeed precisely the lack of it. The absurdity of the compartment view is simply that selflessness can be nothing but a lack of prudence.

If it were possible for some version of the compartment view to survive this analysis it might be said that the argument of this chapter establishes that legal judgment is final or conclusive judgment, but not that it is moral judgment. Some version of the thesis of the separation of law and morals might then be saved. But it would have no point.

The point of Hart's insistence on the separation of law and morals was precisely that it was a separation of law from what is conclusively required:

What surely is needed in order to make men clear-sighted in confronting the official abuse of power is that they should preserve the sense that the certification of something as legally valid is not conclusive of the question of obedience. (1961, 206)

Hart is right in his conception of the problem. What could be the point of maintaining the thesis in any other form? To say that the certification of something as legally required is not to certify that it is morally required is, if 'moral' is to refer to a compartment, no more interesting than to say that such a certification is not necessarily politically sound, or prudent, or necessarily in accordance with the principles of the Oddfellows, or with some other compartment of thought. What is really at stake in this issue is a certain notorious conception of law; that which activated the positivist attitude to Nazi Germany; that which allows a Roman Catholic judge to issue decrees for divorce. On the arguments of this chapter such Roman Catholic judges make a very grave mistake about their role. Nothing is exclusively Caesar's. Anyway, that is the issue of interest and importance; and only the wide definition of 'moral' raises it.

II.10

A favourite case in legal philosophy is Nazi Germany: were the laws, so-called, of that regime law but immoral, or not law at all? Hart has stated the positivist view as follows:

What then was the concern of the great battle-cries of legal positivism: 'The existence of law is one thing; its merit or demerit another'; 'The law of a State is not an ideal but something which actually exists . . . it is not that which ought to be, but that which is'; 'Legal norms may have any kind of content'?

What these thinkers were, in the main, concerned to promote was clarity and honesty in the formulation of the theoretical and moral issues raised by the existence of particular laws which were morally iniquitous but were enacted in proper form, clear in meaning, and satisfied all the acknowledged criteria of validity of a system. Their view was that, in thinking about such laws, both the theorist and the unfortunate official or private citizen who was called on to apply or obey them, could only be confused by an invitation to refuse the title of 'law' or 'valid' to them. They thought that, to confront these problems, simpler, more candid resources were available, which would bring into focus far better, every relevant intellectual and moral consideration: we should say, 'This is law; but it is too iniquitous to be applied or obeyed.' (1961, 203)

Now, the arguments of this chapter show that the positivist position is logically impossible for lawyer, citizen or judge. 'That X ought to be done is the law' is, when said by lawyer, citizen or judge, equivalent to 'X ought legally to be done'. Thus, 'that X ought to be done is the law' and 'X ought not (morally) to be done' is a contradiction; and judge, lawyer or citizen is required to remove one side of it – to say either 'that X ought to be done is the law, and it is not the case that X ought not (morally) to be done' or 'it is not the case that that X ought to be done is the law and X ought not (morally) to be done'.

In the passage quoted, Hart is clearly addressing himself to the problem of judge, lawyer and citizen as well as to 'theorists'. But what of a sociologist?, one concerned to observe and examine legal systems in a scientific way. Is a sociologist going to want to take Hart's positivistic view? In one sense yes; in that a sociologist need not too much allow his own judgment of the moral quality of the laws he observed to influence his classification of them as laws. But the moral judgments of lawyers, judges and citizens have a primary significance for the sociologist: their statements are the raw material of the sociologist's investigations, and if they say, and adhere to it, that certain norms of their community are not morally to be obeyed, then, no matter what other contradictory things they say under the influence of bad philosophy (e.g. that the norms, though they ought not to be obeyed, *are* the law), they are really saying (assuming that they adhere to their stated moral judgment) that they are not law, and a sociologist must classify accordingly.

II.11

Suppose you and I invent a version of Christians and Lions which lays down a complex set of rules for determining which Christians are to be thrown to which lions. And suppose we play the game and that I am the judge and you the executioner. It would be absurd for me subsequently to claim that I merely certified the application of a rule and took no moral responsibility for the taking of life. But is that claim any less absurd in the case of the judges of a legal system?

It might be said that killing for the sake of community is justifiable in a way that killing for fun is not. (How? Well, we don't have to play *that* game; we could play chess, instead. But we don't have to have *that* community, either (it is surely not claimed that no community is possible without hanging). Community is a more important value than fun? But each is indispensable to our carrying on: life without fun would be as impossible as life without community.) Even if this claim could be supported it is beside the point, for what is in issue is only where moral responsibility lies.

II.12

(A) No woman shall procure her abortion.
(B) No vehicle shall be driven on the right hand side of the road.
(C) A valid contract shall be made in the following way . . .

These are three very different norms and commonly they or something like them are legal rules. It is easy to see the sense in which the settlement of a morally controversial matter such as rule (A) can be said to appropriate the mystery of the world; but what of (B) and (C)?

(B) in one sense is morally uncontroversial: it does not seem to matter which side of the road a community drives on so long as one is clearly chosen. Nevertheless, single cases of the application of a rule raise moral issues. And no matter what the moral strength of my reason in a single case for driving on the right (perhaps avoiding a pile-up of cars in order to take someone to hospital) the whole moral discourse about it is precluded (appropriated), for the rule is absolute and that is an end of the matter (if the rule has exceptions then the rule with its exceptions is absolute and the same character obtains: the exceptions will not exhaust the moral possibilities in single cases).

(C) gives a facility or a power. I don't have to make contracts; what, then, is appropriated? Well, powers entail duties of recognition. Unless there is a duty in someone to recognise an exercise of power there is no power. Thus (C) entails a duty in someone (usually a court) to recognize a contract made pursuant to its terms. And this, notwithstanding an indefinite number of possible single case moral objections, is absolute.

II.13

The *Agamemnon* of Aeschylus is a metaphor of the appropriation of mystery by law.

The mystery of the world is the domain of the Furies (amongst other fantastical personifications of the things that really disturb us), who in my opinion are to be respected. Athene, when she established law in Athens, claimed the power to set the Furies to rest. The context of this claim was the tragedy that was abroad in Greece on the return of the heroes from Troy. Agamemnon is slain by his wife and her lover; and Orestes, therefore, is bound to avenge his father's murder. The particular tragedy of this is that it requires him to kill his own mother. He does, and the Furies, naturally, seek him out:

Orestes [seeing the Furies approach]:   Ah, ah!
Look, women, see them, there! Like Gorgons, with grey cloaks,
And snakes coiled swarming round their bodies! Let me go!

Chorus: Most loyal of sons, what fancied sights torment you so?
Stay! You have won your victory; what have you to fear?

Orestes: To me these living horrors are not imaginary;
I know them – avenging hounds incensed by a mother's blood.

Chorus: That blood is still a fresh pollution on your hands,
Therefore your mind's distracted. What more natural?

Orestes: O Lord Apollo! More and more of them! Look there!
And see – their dreadful eyes dripping with bloody pus!

Rules

Chorus: Go quickly then where cleansing awaits for you; stretch out
Your hand to Apollo, and he will free you from this torment.

Orestes: I know you do not see these beings: but I see them. I
am lashed and driven! I can't bear it! I must escape!

Aeschylus, *The Choephori*,
1049–1062 (trans: Vellacott)

What shall Orestes do, for in tragedy there is no solution?

When shall be solved this long feud's argument?
When shall the ancestral curse relent,
And sink to rest, its fury spent?

(*Choephori* 1074–6)

Athene's solution is to establish a court of standing jurisdiction:

Citizens of Athens! As you now try this first case
Of bloodshed, hear the constitution of your court.
From this day forward this judicial council shall
For Aegeus' race hear every trial of homicide.
Here shall be their perpetual seat, on Ares' Hill.
Here, when the Amazon army came to take revenge
On Theseus, they set up their camp, and fortified
This place with walls and towers as a new fortress-town
To attack the old, and sacrificed to Ares; whence
This rock is named Areopagus. Here, day and night,
Shall Awe, and Fear, Awe's brother, check my citizens
From all misdoing, while they keep my laws unchanged.
If you befoul a shining spring with an impure
And muddy dribble, you will come in vain to drink.
So, do not taint pure laws with new expediency.
Guard well and reverence that form of government
Which will eschew alike licence and slavery;
And from your polity do not wholly banish fear.
For what man living, freed from fear, will still be just?
Hold fast such upright fear of the law's sanctity,
And you will have a bulwark of your city's strength,
A rampart round your soil, such as no other race
Possesses between Scythia and the Peloponnese.
I here establish you a court inviolable,

41

Holy, and quick to anger, keeping faithful watch
That men may sleep in peace.

(*Eumenides*, 678–706)

So law is established, and the power and mystery (the jurisdiction, so to speak) of the Furies is appropriated. Orestes is tried and acquitted. To the Furies, Athene says:

Let me entreat you soften your indignant grief.
Fair trial, fair judgment, ended in an even vote,
Which brings to you neither dishonour nor defeat.
Evidence which issued clear as day from Zeus himself,
Brought by the god who bade Orestes strike the blow,
Could not but save him from all harmful consequence.
Then quench your anger; let not indignation rain
Pestilence on our soil, corroding every seed
Till the whole land is sterile desert. In return
I promise you, here in this upright land, a home,
And bright thrones in a holy cavern, where you shall
Receive for ever homage from our citizens.

(*Eumenides*, 792–803)

A short bargaining session follows, and then the poet has the Furies submit. This is the submission of mystery to law. But what is the *real* disposition of the Furies in this matter? We know what the poet had them do, but are we to believe it? It is the answer to this most difficult question (a variation on our earlier one about the status of our wanting to survive) which sets the balance in moral thought between law and the deeper moral questions which we have referred to as mystery.

Christopher Robin knew the comfort and safety of rules, and, his young eyes not yet being closed to the terrible beauty of the world outside them, he saw the necessity of a move similar to Athene's:

Whenever I walk in a London street,
I'm ever so careful to watch my feet,
And I keep in the squares,
And the masses of bears,
Who wait at the corner all ready to eat
The sillies who tread on the lines of the street,
Go back to their lairs,

Rules

> And I say to them 'Bears,
> Just look how I'm walking in all of the squares.'
> (A. A. Milne, *When We Were Very Young*)

Kindly bears.

III

THE ANALYSIS OF RULES

III.1

Rules have puzzled moral philosophers in the following way: let us say that on the whole balance of reasons I ought not to kill whales. How could there as well be a rule that I ought not to kill whales for what could rule add to the original judgment that I ought not to kill whales? If there is the rule that I ought not to kill whales then I ought not to kill whales; but that is already given by the balance of reasons without the requirement of a rule. Rule, therefore, seems otiose. On the other hand if it is not the case on the balance of reasons that I ought not to kill whales then certainly a rule that I ought not to kill whales would add something significant. But how could there be that rule (particularly a moral rule) if it is not the case that I ought not to kill whales? (see for a statement of these problems Warnock, 1971, ch. 5). In short: if I have reasons for action or against action how could I be said to have a rule, for either the rule is against the reasons or it adds nothing to them?

Legal philosophy provides the beginnings of an answer to this puzzle when it shows how in law I can be bound to obey a law (rule) which is wrong at least in the sense that it ought to be repealed. But the problem is wider than this, for there are many other sorts of rules, including ordinary moral rules, to which the standard arguments of legal philosophy do not apply. The analytical problem is to establish a separation of what, under a rule, I ought to do or judge from what in truth (meaning on the whole balance of reasons) I ought to do or judge (see Warnock,

1971, ch. 5 and Raz, 1975, chs 1 and 2), a separation of rule from reasons.

III.2

All rules are found in language, so we shall have to look to the way they stand and move in our speech:

(A) Harold: Don't eat with your fingers.
   Johnny: Why not?
   Harold: Because to do so is bad manners.
   Johnny: So what?
   Harold: Just do as I tell you.

(B) Judge: I am inclined to think, Mr Featherstone, that your argument overlooks the Corporate Mergers (Share Structure) Act.
   Featherstone Q.C.: Indeed, your honour. I submit that the Corporate Mergers (Share Structure) Act is nothing more than a desperate attempt by the snivelling lackeys of Capitalism to resist the movement of History.
   Judge: Kindly keep to the point, Mr Featherstone.

(C) Brother John: It is time for prayer, Brother Laurence.
   Brother Laurence: We are going to talk to ourselves again are we, Brother John?
   Brother John: Come on, Brother Laurence. Pray for grace.

(D) Harold: You may not move your rook diagonally.
   Johnny: Why not?
   Harold: That is the rule.
   Johnny: So what?
   Harold: Look, do you want to play chess or not?

In each of these conversations there is evident a boundary, an attempt by one of the parties to break through that boundary, and a resistance by the other. In each of our cases the boundary is constituted by a rule: 'one ought not to eat with one's fingers', 'statutes ought to be obeyed', 'pray at such and such a time', 'rooks may not be moved diagonally', are all rules, and the attempt to break through the boundary which each constitutes is an attempt to put at issue the bindingness of the norm which the rule establishes, that is, to reduce the question to reasons. In a sense it is an attempt to speak outside the rules.

The sense of boundary in these conversations is critical in the analysis of rules. When we say things which use a rule or apply a rule we are not seeking a position outside the rule. We are addressing what is normally assumed to be the point. The rule defines an area of discourse within which there is much to be said. What is said is normative and therefore committed talk; but the commitment is displayed rather than put in issue. Were the commitment to be put in issue then the talk would concern the rule itself and would have gone beyond the boundary that the rule constitutes.

Featherstone's statement in conversation (B) implies a value judgment that such statutes are not to be obeyed. It puts the bindingness of the rule that statutes ought to be obeyed in issue. It speaks beyond the confines of that rule. The judge says it is beside the point. But how could that be? The judge is proposing to apply the statute, and Featherstone says the statute ought not to be applied – how could that be beside the point? It is beside the point because it is not within the appropriate area of discourse; it is outside the boundary that the rule constitutes.

Most lawyers would see immediately that Featherstone's statement was beside the point. Some, however, might offer the explanation that it was beside the point because it was a political rather than a legal argument. But this common idea is confused. It is, in fact, a variation of the confused thesis of the separation of law and morality attacked in the last chapter. Law, it would be said, is separate from politics, and both from morality. But we have shown there is no such separation, there are no such categories, at least not for the serious purposes of legal or moral decision, to which both the judge and the lawyers address themselves. The great Australian judge, Owen Dixon, put the matter as follows:

> it has often been said [of a certain doctrine of Australian
> Constitutional law] that political rather than legal considerations
> provide the ground [of the doctrine] . . . The Constitution is a
> political instrument. It deals with government and governmental

powers. The statement is, therefore, easy to make though it has a specious plausibility. But it is really meaningless. It is not a question whether the considerations are political, for nearly every consideration arising from the Constitution can be so described, but whether they are compelling. (*Melbourne Corporation* v. *The Commonwealth* [1947] 74 C.L.R. 31, 82)

There is but one question, that of compellingness; just as there was in the example of the last chapter but one question, that of whether the accused ought to hang.

Featherstone's speech addressed the issue of compellingness; it could not be dismissed as beside the point by virtue of category. Rather, it is beside the point because it operates outside the rule which lawyers and judges in ordinary circumstances regard as enclosing the point. It is in that sense an external statement; a statement beyond the boundary of the rule. By contrast, ordinary rule discourse, the hundred and one things that can be said about the Corporate Mergers (Share Structure) Act without putting its bindingness in issue, is internal discourse.

To distinguish these modes of talking by the terms external and internal raises a slightly tricky problem of terminology, for H. L. A. Hart in *The Concept of Law* has used these terms to signify what are not necessarily the same things. There are, however, no terms half so appropriate.

Let us say I am playing chess with you and you move the piece of ivory which stands as your rook diagonally and I say to you:

(A) You ought not to move this piece diagonally.

This statement is about a certain thing in the world. It is not a statement about rooks. It is intended as a practical statement connecting to action in respect of a certain thing in the world (you may say a certain rook if you like). It is not intended as a theoretical statement of the sort I would make were I teaching you the rules of chess; though it may take that form (where for example I say 'rooks ought not to be moved diagonally' and mean by it (A), strictly conceived).

Now, so far as the truth of (A) is concerned, unless there is a rule on the matter, which is binding, to the effect that rooks ought not to be moved diagonally it will ordinarily not be the case that you ought not to move this piece of ivory diagonally (assume you own the chess set and, special rules aside, can do what you like with any part of it). Thus the existence and bindingness of a rule on the matter seems to be necessary for the truth of my statement. It is not sufficient that there simply *exists* a rule, for such a rule might be in some other game which we are not playing; the rule must be a relevant rule if my statement is to be true, i.e. a rule binding upon us in our immediate context.

Now, how is this bindingness accounted for? I am not asserting it – it is most likely that you have simply made a careless mistake about the piece, confusing it with a bishop, perhaps. Thus there is no reason in ordinary contexts for me to think you are disputing the bindingness of the rule and thus no reason for me to assert it. Indeed, were I to assert it my statement would be as odd, as inappropriately heavy, as Featherstone's about the capitalists. A second way to see this is to see that if after my stating (A) you gave me the answer 'I'm not playing chess' I should be entitled to be annoyed. But what could be the justification for my annoyance? My claim is an outrageous one: it is that you are not entitled to move a thing which you own from one place to another. Your answer, 'I'm not playing chess' is a perfectly proper answer in terms of truth to the assertion of such a claim. I would be a fool to think it was not. Yet still I am annoyed. I am annoyed because you continued to sit there seeming to contemplate moves. I have no entry to your mind. Was I not entitled to assume you were playing chess? You have made me look a fool. If I had known you were not playing chess I should not have bothered to say anything about your piece of ivory. I am annoyed because I was not asserting anything so outrageous as your answer suggests I was: your being bound not to move in some way something which you own.

Bindingness is not asserted, yet it is essential to the truth of my statement. It follows, I think, that it is assumed.

This assumption defines internality: if I make the assumption my statement (A) is internal; if I don't, it is external (and then 'I'm not playing chess any more.' is an appropriate answer). It is not the mere fact of my making an assumption which defines internality, for there may be assumptions in (external) statements of fact about a rule, too: for example, when I say:

(B) The rule against moving rooks diagonally was scrutinized by the International Chess Conference, 1949,

48

I assume rather than state that the rule exists. It is the type of assumption on which the definition of internality turns.

The assumption of bindingness is an assumption of the ultimate bindingness of the norm of the rule. It must be of the ultimate bindingness of the norm. Anything less would preclude the possibility of a rule decision to act, for it would necessitate some further deliberation before action. The totality of this assumption corresponds with our earlier argument that rules appropriate the whole field of moral thought. Statement (A) is a chess statement. Chess is not exempt from the arguments of the previous chapter. If you think that games like chess have nothing to do with what is ultimately required (morality) consider this example: you can make a dying parent happy by the acclaim that will come to you from appearing to win a game. Will you do so by secretly breaking a rule? This is a moral problem requiring an ultimate decision about which the rule of the game gives an unequivocal answer, which you can only reject by rejecting the game (preferring to play your own secret game in order to achieve what you conceive to be a moral purpose). Conversely, you might maintain a strict thesis of the separation of chess and morals, maintaining that you have no responsibility for the happiness of your dying parent by virtue of the judgments that you make in the chess game. The whole of the previous chapter could have been written around this example. Its mistake is exactly the same as the mistake of the legal positivists.

Assumption of bindingness in the case of public rules has two elements. When I make (A) as an internal rule statement I assume two things:

(1) that it is the case ultimately or morally that rooks ought not to be moved diagonally; and
(2) that you (and usually, but not necessarily, a wider audience or community of other players, referees, etc.) accept that it is the case ultimately or morally that rooks ought not be moved diagonally.

(The norm in this rule is: rooks ought not to be moved diagonally. For simplicity and as a general formula we may say that in an internal rule statement I assume:

(1) the bindingness of the norm; and
(2) that you accept the bindingness of the norm.)

If the second of these assumptions is false, my statement (A) breaks down in a conversational sense. It does not become false or meaningless, for it might still be the case, even though you don't accept the rule, that you ought not to move your rook diagonally (for example, you may have made a special promise). It breaks down in the sense that if I am to try to convince you in the matter the rule-statement will not do. I shall have to start again; go into the whole question and adduce reasons rather than make assumptions. This point is better made by another example, for there is not much sense to external talk about rooks.

In *Madzimbamuto* v. *Lardner-Burke*, decided soon after the unilateral declaration of independence in Rhodesia, the issue was whether the foundation of law in Rhodesia was the old order or the new. Let us say that the question was the application of a statute of the old order, the same question in form as arose in our conversation (B) where Featherstone Q.C. made an external argument about the application of a statute. Now, in such a case the rule of recognition itself is the issue, and therefore external assertions about its bindingness are in point. Featherstone's speech in such a case might be able to be rejected; but only on the ground that it is a bad argument, not on the ground that it is beside the point.

The equivalent of (A) in this context is:

(A1) Statute X ought to be obeyed.

In normal contexts this is stated internally with the two assumptions mentioned (the bindingness of the norm 'statutes ought to be obeyed' and the fact that you accept the bindingness of the norm), and there would be resistance to their being put into issue. But in a revolution if (A1) is stated internally it is liable to break down: in particular the second assumption is liable to be false, i.e. it is liable not to be the case that you accept that statutes ought to be obeyed (not that you reject it, just that you don't now acccept it), and if I continue to assume that you do accept it we shall get nowhere. Our argument will proceed only if I recognize that what I took to be a rule case has ceased to be so, and thus that the matter is entirely open to the full range of reasons.

III.3

(A1) ('statute X ought to be obeyed') would usually be asserted internally. But it might be asserted externally, where I am not relying on any rule. Which it is depends upon conversational context and my intention.

III.4

The puzzle about rules (III.1) generates a problem of establishing a separation of what under a rule I ought to do or judge from what on an ultimate judgment of the balance of reasons, that is morally, I ought to do or judge. Assumption satisfies this analytical requirement, for when I decide on the basis of an assumption I exclude the present consideration of that question of moral truth.

On the other hand, it is still the case that although I don't presently consider moral truth any decision that I make under the rule entails a claim to its ultimate (moral) justification in the sense established by the last chapter. In making a rule decision I assume the bindingness of the norm of the rule, that is, I assume that it gives the ultimately true (moral) answer to the class of cases which it defines, of which my single case (my actual practical problem) is one; and the claim to that truth in my single case is entailed by my decision.

III.5

Internal statements and attitudes were an important part of H. L. A. Hart's *Concept of Law*. It is clear that these, for Hart, were attitudes and statements which made certain assumptions. It was important for Hart's positivism that these assumptions be paradigmatically assumptions of fact, not of bindingness. Thus in a note at the end of his book he says:

> normally, when a lawyer operating within the system asserts that some particular rule is valid he does not *explicitly state* but *tacitly presupposes* the fact that the rule of recognition (by reference to which he has tested the validity of the particular rule) exists as

the accepted rule of recognition of the system. (1961, 245;
Hart's emphasis)

Here Hart's lawyer makes the legal equivalent of the assumption
in our chess statement (B) (III.2), the assumption of the *fact* that
there is a rule, but not the assumption of statement (A), the
assumption of bindingness. This, however, is inadequate as an
analysis of law. For one thing, since the mere fact of the existence
of a rule is, without normative addition, incapable of justifying a
practical decision, the assumed fact is at least as incapable. And a
conception of internal attitude and statement which does not
justify in any way a practical decision (hang the prisoner, take the
defendant's chattels, deliver the goods under the contract, etc.) is
obviously inadequate as an explanation and elucidation of the
thought which does lead to such decisions. This might not be
obvious to an extreme positivist (which Hart is not), who would be
content to insert the required normative element separately after
all the (purely descriptive) legal statements are in. But this
extreme positivism drains legal language of all normative character
and is therefore obviously analytically inadequate. A second
reason why Hart's formulation is unacceptable is that if the
assumption is only of fact we are not able to distinguish internal
statements from external. We can refer again to:

(B) The rule against moving rooks diagonally was scrutinized
     by the International Chess Conference 1949.

And perhaps, to make the point about law, we might say:

(B1) the rule of recognition in the Afghan legal system was
      scrutinized by a visiting sociologist in 1949.

As we saw in III.2, these statements assume rather than assert the
fact of the existence of the relevant rule, and they are external not
internal.

Since this formulation by Hart in the notes of his book is
inadequate, it is no surprise that the text puts the matter
differently:

Statements of legal validity made about particular rules in the
day-to-day life of a legal system, whether by judges, lawyers, or
ordinary citizens, do indeed carry with them certain presupposi-
tions. They are internal statements of law expressing the point

of view of those who accept the rule of recognition of the system and, as such, leave unstated much that could be stated in external statements of fact about the system. What is thus left unstated forms the normal background or context of statements of legal validity and is thus said to be 'presupposed' by them. But it is important to see precisely what these presupposed matters are, and not to obscure their character. They consist of two things. First, a person who seriously asserts the validity of some given rule of law, say a particular statute, himself makes use of a rule of recognition which he accepts as appropriate for identifying the law. Secondly, it is the case that this rule of recognition, in terms of which he assesses the validity of a particular statute, is not only accepted by him but is the rule of recognition actually accepted and employed in the general operation of the system. (Hart, 1961, 105)

Thus, for Hart, it seems that apart from the assumption of fact there is also an assumption of appropriateness. It is not easy to be sure what Hart has in mind here. 'Appropriate' cannot mean 'legally appropriate'; for on any version of Hart's concept of law it is this appropriateness which establishes legality, thus 'legally appropriate' would be circular. 'Appropriate' must therefore be something independent of the law. Does it mean normatively appropriate, that is, binding? What could it mean short of that? If it did mean something short of that it would not be able to justify the legal decision in question without normative addition. How would it then be 'appropriate'?

Joseph Raz identified a type of normative statement which is neither a descriptive statement about a normative opinion nor an ordinary normative statement, but a third type which states normatively what ought to be done from a certain point of view without committing the speaker to that point of view (see II.2). Could this be the explanation of Hart's 'assumption of appropriateness'? Could it be that a person making a legal judgment assumes the appropriateness of the rule of recognition in the sense of its being appropriate 'from the legal point of view'?

The objection to this is that as we saw in II.2 statements or propositions from points of view do not justify practical decisions. Thus this explanation of 'appropriateness' will not suffice as an analysis of the legal thought which manifestly does lead, without addition, to decision. We may conclude that in the analysis of the internal point of view 'appropriate' must mean 'binding' in the sense we have defined as the first assumption of the internal point of view, i.e. the assumption that the norm of the rule is binding. Thus Hart's judge or other internal person who applies the legal system's rule of recognition assumes that it provides the 'appropriate' binding solution to the class of cases which it defines, of which his single case is one.

It follows that Hart was wrong to draw a distinction between his theory and Kelsen's in the matter of conflict between law and morals. Hart said:

> Kelsen's view . . . is that it is logically impossible to regard a particular rule of law as valid and at the same time to accept, as morally binding, a moral rule forbidding the behaviour required by the legal rule. No such consequences follow from the account of legal validity given in this book. (1961, 246)

Kelsen's view was logically sound. If an assumption of bindingness (in Kelsen's terms the postulation of the *grund-norm*) is a requisite of a legal statement an assertion of non-bindingness, moral or of any sort, which must destroy the assumption, will vitiate that statement. The same is true of Hart's concept of law. If the earlier argument is right an assumption of 'appropriateness', meaning bindingness, is a requisite of an internal legal statement, and so the statement will be vitiated by an assertion of non-bindingness ('non-appropriateness').

Hart's mistake, I think, was to try to run two incompatible analyses together: the analysis of sociological statements, where existence can be separated from bindingness and thus from moral statements; and the analysis of internal normative statements, where it cannot. *The Concept of Law* suffers throughout from a failure to separate these things.

III.6

Kant distinguished ethical and juridical legislation on the basis of internal and external incentives. The internal incentive was the idea of duty itself (the purely moral way of acting), the external incentive was 'derived from the pathological grounds determining choice, i.e. from inclinations and disinclinations . . .' (Kant, *Metaphysics of Morals*, 219). Thus legal duties (duties in accordance with juridical legislation) are only external because juridical legislation does not require that the internal idea of duty be the ground of the agent's choice (simple obedience to a statute, whatever the motives, is enough for Parliament, and coercion is its method of achieving it).

Though the law (*recht*) requires no more than external obedience, internal obedience is possible and, indeed, by definition morally proper. Such an internal judgment excludes inclinations and disinclinations, but it would not do justice to Kant to say that it displayed an assumption of bindingness. On his conception of moral judgment, the judgment is as full as it could be: nothing moral is merely assumed. If, however, a wider conception of moral judgment is taken (as, for instance, it is by Hume) in which the inclinations and disinclinations have their part, a Kantian (internal) moral judgment is a rule judgment, for it makes a conclusive judgment without judging the matter in full; thus we can say it assumes the answer to the *full* moral question, and is internal in our sense as well as Kant's own.

The essence of law for Kant is external obedience (though internal obedience is possible); thus there is no close relationship between Kant and modern theorists such as Kelsen and Hart for whom the essence of law is internal obedience. For Kelsen, the presupposition of the *grund-norm* (which constitutes the internal point of view) has no real moral component: it is not an expression of respect for duty for duty's sake (and thus not internal in Kant's sense). And Hart's conception of the internal point of view comprises a motley of things besides Kant's pure moral obedience (Hart, 1961, 198).

III.7

It is well-known that political or treason trials tend to break down as rational exercises. One of the reasons for this is that judge and prisoner tend not to talk to one another in roughly the way in which the judge and Featherstone were not talking to each other in conversation (B) in III.2, and this failure is compounded in the various other relationships that spring up with other participants and officials. The way in which people talk or don't talk to one another is critical in an analysis of rules.

Let us say that a judge makes the internal statement to the prisoner 'statute X ought to be obeyed' (A1). Of course, he won't often actually say this, but it or something like it will be implicit in the trial and in many other things that the judge will actually say. In stating (A1) the judge makes the two assumptions of rule statements, and in particular he assumes that the prisoner accepts the bindingness of the legal system's rule of recognition. But this is precisely what the prisoner, being a political prisoner, does not do. And if assumptions are not common any conversation breaks down. Yet the judge is likely to persist with this assumption, even to the point of having the prisoner bound and gagged.

There are only two possible characterizations of such behaviour. Either the trial is a show trial or the judge is being particularly obtuse.

It is a show trial if the judge is content with the breakdown of his conversation with the prisoner. He might well be content, for there will usually not be lacking other participants and officials who do accept the assumptions of (A1), and the trial may therefore constitute a successful conversation with them. But because he is not speaking to the prisoner but about him it is a show trial.

Alternatively, the trial is a mess. The judge may genuinely try to accord the prisoner proper respect: try to talk to him and to get him, as he would conceive it, to understand (A1). But this is obtuse. Even if it is the case that the rule of recognition ought to be obeyed (i.e. that the judge is ultimately (morally) right, not the prisoner) it is obtuse of the judge to assume that the prisoner accepts the rule when he knows that he doesn't. Only logical confusion could give an air of respectability to such a proceeding.

There is no realistic third alternative. It is usually not possible in a legal trial for a judge to address himself externally and seriously to the question of the bindingness of the rule of recognition. For one thing, a political prisoner is likely to be more adept than the judge at that sort of (external) argument.

The only thing to be done with political prisoners, therefore, if show trials and public displays of judicial obtuseness are to be avoided, is to have them treated as prisoners of war. This accords with the logical proprieties: war is the proper characterization of the relationship involved in such cases. When men no longer share assumptions there is left just man against man in the world. 'Hereby it is manifest, that during the time men live without a common power to keep them all in awe, they are in that condition which is called war; and such a war as is of every man, against every man' (Hobbes, *Leviathan*, part 1, ch. 13). When the common power is a rule of recognition and it collapses because the assumptions constituting it collapse there is war: 'the nature of war, consisteth not in actual fighting; but in the known disposition thereto, during all the time there is no assurance to the contrary' (*loc. cit.*). When judge and prisoner are no longer bound together by common assumptions there is war between them.

Of course, there may remain another sort of common power to keep all in awe including the prisoner, viz. the brute force that the judge has at his command; but that will usually accord with the prisoner's interpretation of the trial, not the judge's.

Kelsen's interpretation of such a situation is with the prisoner's: without *grund-norm*, that is, without the assumption of the bindingness of the rule of recognition, there is mere force, not law:

> From the point of view of normative jurisprudence, the order to pay taxes differs from the gangster's threat . . . by the fact that only the tax order is issued by an individual who is authorised by a legal order assumed to be valid. (Kelsen, 1945, 176)

Kelsen's whole theory of the *grund-norm*, his most important single idea, was a response to the problem of distinguishing the demand of a tax collector from the demand of a gangster. It is sometimes misunderstood. The *grund-norm* is not the ultimate norm in a legal system, whose bindingness is presupposed or assumed. Rather, it is the (normative) assumption of bindingness itself. The ultimate real norm of a legal system is the rule of recognition, in Kelsen's terms the historically first constitution. This is, in the pre-supposition of the *grund-norm*, assumed to be binding, upon which event (i.e. the making of the assumption) the whole set of subjective meanings operated on by the *grund-norm* become objectively binding, including the demand of the tax collector. In outward manifestations there might be no distinction at all between a tax collector and a robber; the words used in each demand might be identical, and all other facts might be, too; hierarchical support, a system of enforcement, and so on. But our (lawyer's) internal way of regarding the tax collector is what makes the difference. We assume the bindingness of the system of which he is part, and the whole structure of legality follows. Without that legality there is mere force, that is to say, war. War is the proper characterization of the relationship between judge and prisoner when they no longer share the assumptions that constitute a common rule of recognition.

As I wrote this, Irishmen were starving themselves to death and were allowed to do so because of a conversational breakdown similar to that in a political trial. The Irish claimed to be prisoners of war; the English that they were convicted criminals. But in this conversation the sense of the category, convicted criminal, depended upon the subsistence of the common assumptions which constituted a rule of recognition, and the mere use of the term 'prisoner of war' was sufficient to show that these assumptions were not common to both parties. The English were wicked if they persisted knowing the conversation had broken down in this way; and obtuse if they did not know it.

III.8

Hart said that one speaking from an internal point of view presupposed or assumed the general acceptance of the rule of recognition (1961, 105 and 245). This is insufficient for a rule of recognition, for unless this general acceptance includes the acceptance of the person addressed by the statement the conversation will break down.

But what if you and I are eccentric? Let us say that you and I and no one else assume the bindingness of a validifying rule. Is it a rule of recognition? Well, what else could it be? It performs the logical function of recognition, of making valid; and it is a rule that you and I have. Our acceptance would have to be manifest: we would have to enforce our rule of recognition, at least substantially, and recognize no other. What of importance could be added by a more general acceptance? Kelsen made the effectiveness of an historically first constitution (rule of recognition) a condition of the presupposition of the *grund-norm* and thus a condition of legal objectivity. But effectiveness here means substantial enforcement and an absence of competitors (see 1967, 47–8); it says nothing about the size of the effective community. If you and I thought about our minuscule community we might well agree that it would be better to reserve the word 'law' for larger communities; but nothing much can turn on this. Of course, legal conversations tend to be wider than simply between you and me. It is not just that I can expect others to have similar conversations with similar assumptions (that sort of general acceptance), but that our actual conversation is wider than just between you and me. If I am a judge I am likely to be speaking via court records and orders, law reports, newspapers and other media to a very wide range of other judges, lawyers, officials and citizens, all of whom are 'you' in my second assumption ('that you accept the bindingness of the rule of recognition'). If any of you speak or act inconsistently with that assumption (particularly those in power; if for instance you are a sheriff and refuse to enforce my order) then it tends to be difficult for the assumption to survive. This is the same thing as saying that it tends to be difficult for the legal system to survive. A legal system is an ongoing conversation constituted by the two assumptions of the rule of recognition.

III.9

A legal system is an ongoing conversation constituted by certain assumptions. It derives its unity from the interlockment of these assumptions and in particular from the interlockment of the set of second assumptions, 'that you accept the bindingness of the rule of recognition'. All citizens in a legal system make this assumption (one who does not make it is an outsider at war with the community), and there is therefore a wholesale interlocking which constitutes the unity of the legal system. A legal statement is a statement which makes this assumption and the first one.

If these assumptions are not made, any ensuing statement is external, and we have lost the thing, law. The rule of recognition is then no longer a present rule. As Kelsen put it, the officials of the system would no longer be taken as legal authorities but just so many robbers (or a chess piece no longer a rook, just a piece of ivory). This is true even with a normatively *supporting* external statement: for instance, that the legal system ought to be obeyed. That it ought to be obeyed does not distinguish a legal system from the system of commands of a gang of robbers, for there are many situations where a gang of robbers ought to be obeyed (e.g. to save a hostage's life). Consider:

(C) The rule of recognition ought to be obeyed.

This is, in usual contexts, an external statement and it supports normatively the legal system in question. It is external because it asserts rather than assumes the bindingness of the rule. It is not a legal statement, and does not catch the primary sense of 'law'. Suppose a judge is required by law to enforce the rules of an association, say the Oddfellows. The law supports normatively the rules of the Oddfellows, but this does not make our judge's statements statements of Oddfellowship. They are external to the institution of Oddfellowship and remain statements of law. This analysis can be applied to (C). It is, though normative, external, and therefore not legal. (In the second chapter of *Taking Rights Seriously*, Ronald Dworkin regarded (C) as internal. This mistake vitiates most of the argument of the chapter.)

Depending on the assumptions behind (C), it might be a religious statement (I might be assuming that God has commanded the obedience) or a moral statement (I might be assuming the bindingness of a moral rule such as that democracies are good) or a statement in a game invented by the board of directors of a multi-national corporation for their amusement, or a statement of promise-keeping (it might be the consequence of a judicial oath – if I obey or apply the law strictly because of my oath I am a promise-keeper, not a lawyer or a judge). The same analysis holds for other sorts of external statements. For example:

(D) The rule of recognition is a manifestation of social consciousness.

(E) The rule of recognition is a function of the material interests of the ruling class.

These are not legal statements.

What is it that distinguishes legal statements from other sorts? The answer seems to be an internality, or a certain assumption of bindingness, as Kelsen clearly saw, and Hart not so clearly. The rejection of (C) (the *assertion* of bindingness) as legal makes law necessarily a matter of assumption, and legal system correspondingly a complex of interlocking assumptions.

Do rules create institutions? What are institutional facts? And tied up with these questions is the difficulty of distinguishing substantive rules from the rules of the language necessary to talk about them and use them.

Hare remarks:

> Unless a sufficient number of people were prepared to assent to the moral principles which are the constitutive rules of the institution of promising, the word 'promise' could not have a use. To take the extreme case: suppose that nobody thought that one ought to keep promises. It would then be impossible to make a promise; the word 'promise' would become a mere noise. (Hare, 1964, 124)

Now this extreme case is ambiguous. It could be that nobody has thought about the question of keeping one's word; or it could be that everybody has thought about it and thinks that one ought not or that it matters neither way. In the latter case Hare is surely right: there could be no expectation in any putative promisee, no sense of commitment to him and thus no promise. But in the former there could be.

Suppose I am the first man in this society to make a statement of my intention to another intending that he should rely upon it for his purposes. The word 'promise', of course, would not yet exist; but I might immediately invent it and explain its meaning, for the practical problem to which I would wish to apply it is quite intelligible – is the fact that I said to another I would do something, on which statement I intended that he should rely, and on which he did rely, a reason for me to do it? This is a simple moral problem to which there (as yet) attaches no institution. It is also obvious that it is not a rule case – it is the first case ever to arise, thus there could be no rule. We shall call all non-rule cases hard cases. This is a hard case where I weigh the reasons to keep my word – but I am being unnecessarily scrupulous in saying 'keep my word'; there are no questions begged if I now use the word available to me, 'promise' – a hard case where I weigh the reasons to keep my promise against the reasons not to do so.

Now, rules might develop: my own personal rule, for I might have other cases; or a community rule, for the idea that it is important to keep one's word might catch on. What the terms of the rule are will depend upon the language available: it is of no importance (except as a matter of economy) whether it be in terms of 'promise' or some alternative set of constituting, brute words. Let us say the norm is: promises ought to be kept. Is there now an institution? Perhaps; but is it in any more interesting a sense than that in which any key word in any norm might be said to create an institution? Are we to say that intentional killing is an institution if there is a norm: intentional killing is prohibited? Perhaps we would say no. But if the norm is: murder (meaning: intentional killing) is prohibited, we might now wish to say yes: murder is an institution. So a key idea is bruteness. Intention and killing are brute to murder. Intention and saying 'I promise . . .' are brute to promising, and so on. Institutions, therefore, seem to be simply matters of the linguistic economy involved in having concepts for sets of brute facts (less brute facts Anscombe calls them – see 1958a). We do not need the word 'murder' for we could construct the same norms with intention and killing. Nor 'promise'. Nor 'out' in cricket, for the rule of that game would lose nothing in point of meaning if whenever the word 'out' occurred we had its brute constituents (innings terminated, must leave the pitch).

Thus Hare has not put it quite right when he says:

> It may seem as if the 'brute fact' that a person has uttered a certain phonetic sequence entails the 'institutional fact' that he has promised, and that this in turn entails that he ought to do a certain thing. But this conclusion can be drawn only by one who accepts, in addition, the non-tautologous principle that one ought to keep one's promises. For unless one accepts this principle, one is not a subscribing member of the institution which it constitutes, and therefore cannot be compelled logically to accept the institutional facts which it generates in such a sense that they entail the conclusion . . . (1964, 126)

The brute facts do entail the 'institutional fact' in a language which contains the appropriate definition. One is committed to this linguistic fact (one is in a sense committed to every linguistic fact of this sort in every language in the world) but not necessarily to the bindingness of any set of rules which uses it (or to any use of it at all – Hudson's advice is apposite: if one doesn't like the entailments one had better stop using the language – see Hudson, 1965, 193).

The Analysis of Rules

What is misleading about Hare's remark is that a commitment to the institution, which is really just a commitment to a definition is identified with a commitment to substantive (non-linguistic) rules using the institution.

Hare's discussion of institutions is a response to Searle's well-known derivation of 'ought' from 'is', which has fascinated philosophers for some time. This derivation is:

(1) Jones uttered the words 'I hereby promise to pay you, Smith, five dollars.'

(2) Jones promised to pay Smith five dollars.

(3) Jones placed himself under (undertook) an obligation to pay Smith five dollars.

(4) Jones is under an obligation to pay Smith five dollars.

(5) Jones ought to pay Smith five dollars.

Now, in rule cases I don't derive the norm 'promises ought to be kept' from anything. I start with it, add a factual premise, and derive a conclusion from them. The normative force of the whole activity comes from the assumption of the bindingness of the norm, not from any derivation of an 'ought' from an 'is'. Thus the derivation has no practical significance in rule cases (it has no significance in non-rule cases (hard cases) either: I.8).

Searle clearly thinks, however, that the derivation is of practical significance; and one of the examples by which he demonstrates this is of a rule case:

> We are in our half of the seventh inning and I have a big lead off second base. The pitcher whirls, fires to the shortstop covering, and I am tagged out a good ten feet down the line. The umpire shouts 'Out!' I, however, being a positivist, hold my ground. The umpire tells me to return to the dugout. I point out to him that you can't derive an 'ought' from an 'is'. No set of descriptive statements describing matters of fact, I say, will entail any evaluative statements to the effect that I should or ought to leave the field. 'You just can't get orders or recommendations from facts alone. What is needed is an evaluative major premise.' I therefore return to and stay on second base (until I am carried off the field). I think everyone feels my claims here to be preposterous, and preposterous in the sense of logically absurd. Of course you can derive an 'ought' from an 'is', and though to actually set out the derivation in this

63

case would be vastly more complicated than in the case of promising, it is in principle no different. By undertaking to play baseball I have committed myself to the observation of certain constitutive rules. (Searle, 1969, 185)

But if the rules are applied in this situation (as they are) there *is* evident an evaluative major premise: it is whatever the rule is which prescribes the consequences of batsmen being tagged out. The reasoning is:

1 Anyone tagged out must leave the play.
2 Searle was tagged out.
3 Searle must leave the play.

That is, of course, a simple matter which should occasion no fuss. But, as Searle knows, there is a fuss, for his objection between bases is preposterous. Why is this? It is preposterous for Searle to require the premises to be spelt out because all participants are internal to the rules and therefore assume the bindingness of the norm (the evaluative major premise), 'anyone tagged out must leave the play'. It is always preposterous for another to question one's assumption *if one continues to make it.* Searle's situation is no different from that of a revolutionary questioning Parliament's sovereignty in a court which continues to assume it.

The preposterousness of requiring the evaluative major premise has misled Searle into thinking that in his baseball case a real normative conclusion is derived from a fact. It is true that the major premise is in a sense not present in the situation. Searle wants to say that since it is not present the reasoning proceeds in its absence from fact to conclusion (from 'is' to 'ought'). But this does not follow. Searle's argument is based upon an inadequate analysis of rules. It overlooks the way in which the assumption of bindingness in rules, like any assumption, is both present and not present. The rule, the evaluative major premise, controls the situation despite being in this way not present.

III.11

Established decisions have a logical character similar to rules (see Raz, 1975, 65–72). If I have a rule, then when the time comes to implement the rule I do not go into its merits unless I cancel it or suspend it; similarly, if I have made a decision on a practical question then when the time comes to implement that decision I do not again go into the merits of the issue it decided unless I cancel the decision. While it subsists I assume its bindingness upon my action. If I do not assume its bindingness it follows that I have cancelled or suspended it – and the matter is again one for rules and reasons. Decisions are usually personal and private, and like private rules they do not usually have the second assumption of public rules, the assumption of your acceptance (III.2). Court decisions where they are precedents are in a sense public decisions but their operation is principally as rules (how they operate in this way is the problem of *ratio decidendi*: IX.3).

> To decide to take the bun is *not* to commit oneself to the imperative 'take the bun'. . . . Deciding involves deliberating which, being a verbal process, issues most naturally in a verbal formula. But the formula for decision is not 'take the bun' . . . it is 'I shall take the bun'. (Nowell-Smith, 1958)

But suppose, having decided to take the bun, I ask myself again whether I ought to take it. What answer do I have to this question? I think there are three sorts of answers. The first two are in their different ways unrestricted answers (external, we might say, by analogy with rules). First, I could make an answer based upon the balance of reasons for and against the action (go into the decision again in a full and unrestricted way). Second, I could go in full into the reasons for and against reconsidering the decision. If I decided that on the balance of reasons I ought not to reconsider my decision my answer would be to reject my second thoughts. But the third sort of answer is radically different – it is restricted or internal.

An example of this third sort of answer would be something like: 'Oh yes, I've already decided. I ought to take the bun.' This does not go into the reasons for and against taking the bun – indeed they might be beyond recall (another example would be more plausible here) – and it does not go into the reasons for and against reconsidering the decision. Indeed, it does not say anything *about* the decision at all, whether it is justified (first answer), or ought not to be reconsidered (second answer). It

65

points to it or manifests it – as we put it a moment ago it applies it internally.

But what exactly is it that is applied internally? If the form of my decision were, as Nowell-Smith suggests, 'I shall take the bun' it could not be applied to answer my question, 'ought I to take the bun?', for 'I shall' is no answer at all to 'ought I?'. Some normative addition and further decision would be required. To be able to apply the decision internally (without any normative addition) its form needs to be normative.

The non-normative form 'I shall take the bun' would do in the case of the second answer where I decide against reconsideration; but only because this is not a true answer to the question, but a rejection of it. I shall take it that it is possible strictly to answer the question 'ought I to take the bun', and to do so without reconsidering the merits of my decision to take the bun. This requires that there be a norm whose bindingness on my action I assume. And its form in this case must be: I ought to take the bun.

Both rules and decisions have an internal aspect. The main difference between them seems to lie in the type of norm that each contains; a norm in a rule covers a class of cases, but the norm in a decision covers a single case (rules, one could say, though loosely, are decisions of classes of cases).

Suppose I agree to pay you some money for goods which you deliver and the time comes for my payment. If I have a rule on the matter, say, that contracts ought to be performed, then I assume the bindingness of that norm. But suppose I have no rule and must make a decision on the balance of reasons (a hard case). Suppose my decision is that I ought to perform this contract. The contrast between the norm of the rule and the norm of the decision can easily be seen: the norm of the rule is 'I ought to perform contracts' and the norm of the decision 'I ought to perform this contract'.

Conversely, *commitment* belongs more to choosing than to deciding. I can commit myself or become committed in two main ways. (a) I may have taken such steps as to make a certain course of action inevitable or more nearly inevitable than it was before. Thus, if I have bought a train ticket and have no more money, I am now committed to going by train and not by bus (if I go at all). (b) I commit (engage) myself when I promise to do something, even, perhaps, when I announce my decision to do it. But a private unannounced decision does not commit me to anything. If this account of commitment is correct, it seems clear that when I choose (embark on a course of action) I do, very often, commit myself. I am to some extent committed when I book a room at an hotel, to a less extent when I announce to my family that I have chosen the Metropole, but not committed *at all* when I have merely decided which hotel to go to. (Nowell-Smith, 1958, 64–5)

But I am committed when I make a practical decision.

The commitment involved in decisions (and in rules, too) is primarily of the first of Nowell-Smith's types.

To take a practical decision is to become internal to it. This internality constitutes my decision: it is a subsisting decision in so far as I have an internal attitude to the norm of the decision; if I look at it externally (in either of the two ways mentioned) it is obvious that the decision is not a subsisting decision. The equivalent is true of rules. And to become internal to a rule or decision is to 'take steps' which make a certain course of action (that action directed by the norm of the rule or decision) 'more nearly inevitable than it was before'. This relative inevitability is the product of the psychological hold that an assumption has on one: it is often very difficult to abandon assumptions.

The second type of commitment is involved too; mainly in public rules (of which legal rules are, of course prime examples) but also, to a lesser extent, in publicly manifested private rules and private decisions by which I hold myself out as intending to do something.

III.12

The concept of a practical decision is needed in the analysis of conditional reasons.

Conditional reasons can only be weighed with and against reasons with the same condition. If A is a reason to p, conditional upon project j, and X a reason not to p, conditional upon project k, I cannot without more make a judgment in the matter. I must proceed to weigh the reasons to want j against those to want k, and if these are diversely conditioned I must repeat the process until I reach reasons which are identically conditioned or unconditional. Then I can make a judgment. If this judgment is of unconditional reasons my decision is in itself a practical one, an immediate determinant of the will. But if the judgment is not of unconditional reasons but of (identically) conditioned reasons it is not yet practical. If I wish to make a practical judgment, I must go further until I reach unconditional reasons or else I must base my decision on a previous decision in favour of the project which the common condition states. In this latter case the decision is practical by virtue of the assumption of bindingness of the norm of the previous decisions (an assumption gives practical content to decisions as well as to rules: see III.11). An example of this would be where a judge decides a hard case on reasons conditional on his wanting the survival of society, without attending to the practical question which this project raises. He may have previously decided to seek the survival of his society; in which case the norm of this decision, and the assumption of its bindingness, gives the practical content of his current decision. However, he probably hasn't attended to questions about survival for years. Perhaps never: one can be gradually inducted, without conscious decision, into a society's projects, just like its rules. One way or another he is likely to assume that the project of the survival of his society is to be pursued; and being in this way internal to it he is likely to give as short shrift to one putting the project in issue as the judge gave in our earlier example (III.2) to Featherstone putting his legal system's ultimate rule of recognition in issue.

Conditional reasons of the sort we have been discussing are sometimes called reasons for action. But this is really misleading. Suppose a judge sentences a criminal to gaol in order to deter future offences. For many purposes we can say that he has a reason for action (the action of sentencing the criminal) which is conditional upon the project of deterring future offences. But all he has really is a reason for belief in a certain means–end efficacy: a belief that gaol will have the effect of deterring. This is devoid of practical content. Such reasons are in themselves only theoretical (more like reasons for belief). In our example the only way a practical content can be injected into the conditional case is by a decision in favour of, or some other adoption of, the project of deterrence, and this means that the practical content of the sentencing case (its connection to action) is given by the assumption of bindingness which that decision or other adoption constitutes.

Suppose Harold is in front of my car and that this gives me reason to apply my brakes. Is this an unconditional reason? It might be. But it might also be a reason conditional upon a project of mine: save lives. In which case my reason is not a reason for action but a reason for belief in the efficacy of braking for the project of saving lives; and it is the project which supplies the practical force, the determinant of the will.

Sometimes it is difficult to distinguish a case where my action is controlled, say, by my project to save lives from where it is controlled by a rule to save lives, for both go by assumption. The difference is that in the latter case there is a norm covering a class of actions, so that my question in respect of a particular life-saving action would be whether it is a life-saving action within the terms of the norm. In the project case, on the other hand, my question would be of the efficacy of the action for the project of saving lives, and if necessary it would have to be weighed against other possibly efficacious actions for which there are similar (conditional) reasons. In reality I would tend to have both a rule and a project and move easily between the two in a complex of rule cases and project cases.

Sometimes conditional reasons look like unconditional reasons. Perhaps I am a judge with a project of preventing offences. That my putting a certain criminal in gaol will prevent offences is therefore a conditional reason for me to hand down the gaol sentence. But in the absence of this project it might be an unconditional reason for the same action. The difference between the two is, however, considerable. In the first place, as we have seen, the conditional reason is not a reason for action at all. And secondly, I can only weigh an (opposing) unconditional reason (say, that the criminal's family will suffer) against another unconditional reason. To decide my case, therefore, if I wish to press the reason of family suffering, I would have to cancel my project of preventing offences. What would be left then would be the unconditional reasons, on the balance of which I would decide. Perhaps my decision is to restore the project; this would then bring back into relevance the means of accomplishing the project.

Of course, I may have more than one project, and they may be incompatible. Let us say that as well as the project of prevention I have the project of reforming criminals, and that gaoling the criminal in question will diminish his chances of reform. This is like the clash of incompatible rules. One project must collapse; but the likelihood is that both will; in which case I will have the following case of now unconditional reasons: 'that gaoling the criminal will [certainly, probably possibly . . .] prevent future offences is a reason to send him to gaol' against 'that gaoling the prisoner will [certainly, probably, possibly . . .] lead to his corruption is a reason not to send him to gaol'.

Weighing a conditional reason against an opposing reason with the same condition is, we have seen, a theoretical exercise. An example would be: if I want the survival of society there is a reason to impose a sentence that will deter criminals, weighed against if I want the survival of society there is a reason to impose a sentence that will not alienate criminals. This is in itself theoretical, and the weighing is radically different from the weighing in a practical judgment. It is more a matter of measuring probabilities and quantifications of achievement, whereas in a practical judgment weighing is a response to opposing passionate commitments.

1 If I want the survival of society there is a reason to impose a sentence that will deter criminals.
2 I want the survival of society.
3 Therefore, there is a reason to impose a sentence that will deter criminals.

This is a practical syllogism, but practical according to the argument of this section only by virtue of the second premise. The first premise is theoretical and, though as we have seen it could be weighed with and against other reasons which have the same condition (for instance, 'if I want the survival of society there is a reason to impose a sentence that will not alienate criminals'), the balance so produced would remain theoretical and would justify no practical judgment.

The practical premise would normally be implicit. Thus, Anscombe says:

The role of 'wanting' in the practical syllogism is quite different from that of a premise. It is that whatever is described in the proposition must be wanted in order for the reasoning to lead to

70

The Analysis of Rules

any action. Then the form 'I want a Jersey cow, they have good ones in the Hereford market, so I'll go there' was formally misconceived: the practical reasoning should just be given in the form 'They have Jersey cows in the Hereford market, so I'll go there.' (Anscombe, 1957, 66)

Here the want is displayed, implicit rather than in issue as a premise would be in issue. As in rules, assumption is suitable for the analysis. We say simply the want, the practical base, is assumed. Thus people display these sorts of internal attitudes, too:

> Let us now consider an actual case where a desirability characterisation gives a final answer to the series of 'What for?' questions that arise about an action. In the present state of philosophy, it seems necessary to choose an example which is not obscured by the fact that moral approbation on the part of the writer or reader is called into play; for such approbation is in fact irrelevant to the logical features of practical reasoning; but if it is evoked, it may seem to play a significant part. The Nazis, being pretty well universally execrated, seem to provide us with suitable material. Let us suppose some Nazis caught in a trap in which they are sure to be killed. They have a compound full of Jewish children near them. One of them selects a site and starts setting up a mortar. Why this site? – Any site with such-and-such characteristics will do, and this has them. Why set up the mortar? – It is the best way of killing off the Jewish children. Why kill off the Jewish children? – It befits a Nazi, if he must die, to spend his last hour exterminating Jews. (I am a Nazi, this is my last hour, here are some Jews.) Here we have arrived at a desirability characterisation which makes an end of the questions 'What for?' (Anscombe, 1957, 72)

The idea of an end to a certain series of questions is very important: as in rules the internal attitude is defined by (confined by) a boundary. And as with rules one *may* go beyond it, become external: the Nazi may consider whether he wants to be a Nazi at all. But as Anscombe says that is not a continuation of the series; it is outside the game, a different game.

These wants, externally judged or internally displayed, we have been calling projects, and shall continue to do so. And the internality may be internality to what was a conscious decision.

71

But more likely, particularly in examples like Anscombe's, it will be internality to a want or project of one of my communities into which I have grown: I grow into my communities' decisions as well as their rules.

III.13

Any internal practical decision, whether it be under a rule or under an established decision, is a case of subjective determination of the will. The norm of the rule or established decision is assumed to be binding, and this assumption makes a programme. There is no question of the will being determined by a passionate response to the (objective) world, as there is when an external decision is made (V.11). The only objective reference when an internal decision is made is the existence of the facts upon which the norm operates. The *practical* determination of the will is subjective.

IV

THE WEIGHT OF REASONS

IV.1

The weight of a reason for action means the degree of passionate response to the fact which constitutes it. Traditionally opposed to a conception of the passions in moral thought is Kant's conception of moral principles that can be known *a priori*. We shall take it that the concept '*a priori*' means in moral thought the quality of something's being known independently of (contingent) passions.

Dworkin (1977) argues that an analysis of law (and wider moral thought) must distinguish rules and principles: rules are applied all-or-nothing, whereas principles apply by weight. Rule cases are to be distinguished from what we are calling hard cases by their quality of absoluteness. If there is a rule it applies absolutely; that is to say, either it applies or it does not. Whereas in what we are calling a hard case, where there is no rule (or previous decision), the field of moral thought, instead of being occupied by an absolute, is open to the whole flux of moral reasoning; and it is plausible to hold (as Dworkin does) that the moral things which determine hard cases are relative not absolute (though many problems lurk, particularly the problem of moral freedom which so concerned Kant).

We shall call principles such as Dworkin postulates *prima facie* principles. Many philosophers use the concept '*prima facie*' to mark the relativity of moral thought; some say 'other things being equal'; Dworkin has principles with weight. There may be some differences between these things. But they cannot be important

73

ones; for clearly something like weight is necessary to determine whether the application of a *prima facie* principle has been rebutted or whether other things are not equal. We shall embrace all in the term '*prima facie* principle'.

IV.2

Consider the following inferences:

(A)(1) One ought to exercise care towards anyone in front of his car (*prima facie*).
    (2) Harold is in front of my car.
    (3) Therefore, I ought to exercise care towards Harold (*prima facie*).
(B)(1) Harold is in front of my car.
    (2) That Harold is in front of my car is a reason for me to exercise care towards him.

(A1) is a *prima facie* principle, and it is the universalization of (B2), a reason. It is the logical character of each to be weighed against other principles and reasons; (B), because it is *a* reason amongst others, and (A), because its application is merely *prima facie*.

If (A1) were laid down, decided, or came about as by custom, it would be a norm and could be applied either externally or internally. If applied externally its having been laid down would be taken as a fact constituting a reason for action (the common lawyer's notion of *stare decisis*, perhaps, or some other idea of respect for established norms):

(C)(1) It has been laid down that one ought to exercise care towards anyone in front of his car.
    (2) That it has been laid down . . . is a reason for me to exercise care towards anyone in front of my car.

If, on the other hand, it were applied internally it would be as a rule:

(D)(1) One ought to exercise care towards anyone in front of his car.
    (2) Harold is in front of my car.
    (3) Therefore, I ought to exercise care towards Harold.

Inference (D) is the form of rule judgments; inferences (B) and (C), the form of hard judgments. That 'ought' appears in (D), the form of rule judgments, and not in (B) and (C), corresponds with the view taken by Anscombe (1958b) that 'ought' is a relic of an earlier law-based conception of morals. That (B) and (C) give the form appropriate to a hard case is confirmed by the fact that only they purport to state a justification (a reason for action). (D) says nothing of the justification of its norm: it is a mere logical truth, appropriate, therefore, in the case of rule application where justification is assumed.

Inference (A), however, as a type is spurious, because *prima facie* principles, which constitute its major premise, are spurious. This can be seen from the following case:

Suppose I make promises to two different people and it turns out that either one of the promises but not both can be kept. How do I decide? If the fact that I have promised is in each case a reason to keep the promise the problem can be clearly stated: I weigh the reason that there is to keep one promise against the reason to keep the other, and decide on the balance. There is no logical difficulty with this: the idea of conflict is perfectly in order. However, if in that case I were to try to decide by weighing *prima facie* principles of the (A1) form I could not do it for I would have to weigh the promise-keeping principle against itself, which is absurd. No matter how much the promise-keeping principle is refined to cope with this difficulty (e.g. keep promises of this sort in preference to that) it fails, for the case can always be raised of two inconsistent promises of 'this' sort. Even a principle of temporal priority fails here for no one would maintain that a trivial promise must be kept in preference to an important one merely because it is prior in point of time. Only the facts which attach to each promise and to the consequences of its breach can solve the conflict. Now, facts constitute reasons; and so long as you have different facts it is possible to say you have different reasons (the relationship between fact and reason was analysed in chapter I). Thus there is no difficulty in postulating a conflict between reasons to keep promises no matter how refined the facts are. Thus you never reach the point, which we have seen you must do with principles, where you are forced to say that you are weighing something against itself.

There is a more fundamental way to show that *prima facie*

principles are spurious. They purport to be things to be weighed (*prima facie* rather than absolute). However, the weight that such a principle has in any particular conflict can only be determined by the facts, which can vary indefinitely (think of our promise example: the seriousness of either promise can vary indefinitely according to its facts). But facts are reasons, not principles. Hence the primacy of reasons for action, as in inference (B), over *prima facie* principles, as in inference (A).

Of course, inference (A) looks in order logically speaking; and *looks* superior for it. But the question is of the simple status of the *prima facie* principle (A1), not the validity of any inference. If (A2) is, by itself, insufficient justification for (A3) (if I believe it is insufficient justification) how could (A1) help the situation? You might say that (A1) added to (A2) makes (A3) logically required. But I mean: if I don't see (A2) as *itself* sufficient justification for (A3) (and to see this I would have to see (B) as the governing inference), what reason could I have for accepting (A1)? Where could I suppose it came from?; where in the world could it exist? If it had been laid down, decided, or come about as by custom, it would exist as a norm exists; but then the form of the reasoning would be (C) or (D). Someone might say, following Kant, that (A1) is an *a priori* moral truth, or something like that, but, as we shall see, the *prima facie* character which introduces the element of weight excludes that possibility, and anyway, how could I believe it, given that I don't regard (A2) as sufficient in itself?

Many philosophers say that moral requirements have to be universalizable; that this is a prerequisite to their being called moral. In the case of rules this is not more important or interesting a requirement than that a rule must speak in classes; certainly there is no need to say there is anything distinctively moral about a rule's requiring classes. In the case of principles like (A1) what could *it* be that has been universalized? If inference (B) is insufficient by itself to produce a practical decision it is nothing. Universalizing it, meaning universalizing reasons into *prima facie* principles, would universalize nothing. Of course, it might enable us to get over the is/ought gap. However, if that gap can be passed just by saying something (A1) for which there is no *other* justification, it should not have worried us in the first place.

We have described each of (A), (B), (C) and (D) as inferences. But clearly they are different types of inference. Inference (A) is valid by entailment: the conjunction of (A1) and (A2) entails (A3). But clearly, on the other hand, (B1) does not entail (B2); for if I were to affirm (B1) but deny (B2) I would be guilty of no logical mistake. I would certainly not contradict myself, as I would do were I to affirm (A1) and (A2) but deny (A3). So what is the nature of the inference (B)?

I think we have to say that since, unlike (A) and (D), it is not a purely logical inference it is an inference of moral substance; it expresses a substantive moral judgment. There are, however, many philosophers who say that it cannot stand by itself; that it requires, under pain of being defective, a universalized major premise, (A1). But I don't see this. The only thing that could be missing from (B), since we have decided that it is a substantive not a logical inference, is the justification of its substantive moral judgment. But precisely that is missing from (A); there is no justification in (A) of (A1), its substantive moral judgment. Thus if anything is lacking from (B) it is at least equally lacking from (A). Actually, I don't think (B) lacks anything; the justification of its substantive moral judgment is (B1), Harold is in front of my car. But philosophers have thought that moral judgments to be such must be universalizable: not universalizable and they are not moral judgments.

Two senses of universalization must be distinguished. 'That Harold is in front of my car is a reason for me to exercise care towards him' could be universalized to either:

(a) that Harold is in front of one's car is a reason for anyone to exercise care towards him or,
(b) that anyone is in front of my car is a reason for me to exercise care towards him.

Universalization of the first sort raises the problem of the objectivity of reasons. This we discuss in chapter V. Universalization of the second sort raises the issue we have been discussing between inferences (A) and (B).

We have argued that reasons (as in inference (B)) have primacy over *prima facie* principles (as in inference (A)) because of their immediate connection to facts. The objection that inference (B) needs to be universalized into inference (A) need not in its modern form trouble us at this stage, for all it amounts to is the claim that the universalization is a kind of side entailment (see, for example,

Hare, 1963, ch. 2). It is not claimed that the form of (B) is improper, but simply that if I maintain (B2) I am forced logically to admit also its universalization, (A1). Kant's conception of universalization was more profound than this and related intimately to his conception of the *a priori* character of moral principles (modern moral philosophers who discard the *a priori* but keep the universal form corrupt Kant). It will be argued in the next section that *prima facie* principles cannot be *a priori*.

Notwithstanding their spuriousness *prima facie* principles can be harmless enough. They can stand as the entailed universalization of reasons for those who think that is important; and for those who think it is not important or indeed those who think it is logically improper (we argued in I.10 that hard decisions are made by reference to particulars not universals) they are harmless enough as loose references to certain classes of reasons. In much of this chapter we talk of *prima facie* principles rather than reasons because that is the currency of a relevant contemporary work. The argument will not by this misfire so long as the weak and harmless meaning of 'principle' is understood.

IV.3

Suppose you make a promise to someone and on your way to perform it you come across a person who has been injured in a road accident and requires your help. You cannot both keep your promise and help the injured person. What are you to do? Of course, you might decide by rule, but let us assume you don't, i.e. that the case is a hard case.

This conflict between the promise-keeping principle and the Samaritan principle is about as simple a moral hard case as you could get. It might be thought because it is a conflict case to be not typical. This is not true. Most (perhaps all) moral hard cases are cases of conflict, for there is usually (perhaps always) something to be said on the other side of a moral question. Shall I go into the street and kill a stranger? No. But there are reasons to do so. Prevent whatever harm the man is certain to do at some time in the rest of his life. This is outweighed, of course, but so too might the injury or promise be trivial, and therefore easily be outweighed by the other.

There is one fact about the conflict (or to be precise, two) which makes it very complex, and this fact has far-reaching implications in moral philosophy, for it renders implausible the idea that there can be significant *a priori* principles of moral thought. The fact is: the problem is solved by judgment as to the respective seriousness of the breach of promise and the injury, *and the seriousness of each of these varies indefinitely.* Obviously if the promise is trivial and the injury serious the Samaritan principle determines the case. And vice versa. And if both are serious or both trivial the case is difficult. There is an indefinitely graduated scale of seriousness for both principles (I can go on forever changing the facts of my examples, making promises slightly more important and injuries slightly more serious). There is therefore an indefinitely extending scale in which the principles alternate in overtaking each other (now decide for the promise, now the injury, now the promise, now the injury . . .).

This scale can be represented as follows:

Suppose the facts of the case are *A a B b C c D d . . . N n. A* is the bare fact of a promise, and *a* the bare fact of an injury. The simple principle 'keep promise where *A*' will work where *A* is the only fact. Likewise, the simple principle 'help where injury' will work where *a* is the only fact. Where, however, the facts are *A a* neither works. More complex principles are required, which take a more discriminating view of the facts (perhaps picking aspects of the seriousness of the injury and the importance of the promise). Let us suppose these principles follow this scheme: keep promises where *A* or *A a B* or *A a B b C* or *A a B b C c D* or *A a B b C c D d E . . . N*, but help an injured person where *A a* or *A a B b* or *A a B b C c* or *A a B b C c D d* or *A a B b C c D d E e . . . N n.* Even though we have made it easy for the analysis by assuming that *A a* gives a result rather than an even balance, it is apparent that an indefinite number of distinct *a priori* principles is needed (or if you like one indefinitely complex principle).

It is implausible to suppose that there might be an indefinite number of distinct *a priori* principles responding to the indefinite number of facts in the world (or one indefinitely complex principle). If this is recognized the moral philosopher finds himself in a dilemma. He seems forced to admit to his analysis something which, like Hume's passions, is capable of accounting for the complexity of moral problems because it is capable of varying indefinitely in intensity according to the variation of facts. But if he does this, is not morality just a matter of psychological contingency, and hopelessly subjective? The solution is to find what is objective and non-contingent in the operation of the passions (then and only then, we may remark by the way, would the use of the word 'reason' in the title of this chapter be justified).

Thomas Nagel in *The Possibility of Altruism* seeks to resolve the dilemma by arguing *a priori* for altruistic (other-regarding) reasons for action. In our example there would be an other-regarding reason to keep the promise and an other-regarding reason to help the injured person. These reasons are not subjective or psychologically contingent, Nagel argues, because they are *a priori*. But the difficulty with Nagel's analysis is that there is lacking a satisfactory *a priori* account of the varying weight of these reasons. If his *a priori* analysis succeeds all he does is to establish the existence of the reasons for action. But what is it to establish the (objective) existence of a reason? Does that guarantee any weight at all? If so how much? What could be the minimum quantity? How could the weight vary in accordance with the facts, as it must do if reasons are to solve problems of the sort we have discussed? Nagel shows at the end of his argument that he thinks that principles can be developed to decide between conflicting reasons. The purpose of his whole enterprise is the Kantian one of establishing an *a priori* and therefore rational basis for moral thought. If these conflict-resolving principles which Nagel thinks can be developed are not themselves *a priori* the enterprise obviously fails. But they cannot be *a priori* given the possibility of indefinite alternation just established. If Nagel's proof of the existence of reasons does not guarantee any weight at all (as I think must be conceded) what is it that is established, for what could be the significance of a reason without weight? It could have no function in moral thought; so what, morally speaking, could it be? It does not seem to make any sense at all to separate the existence of reasons from their weight: the ontology of reasons for action must at the same time be an ontology of their weight.

IV.4

Kant recognized the possibility of conflicts of *a priori* moral principles, and the *Metaphysics of Morals* has many appendices adumbrating casuistical questions in which judgment is required in order to resolve such conflicts. The nature of casuistry is not at all clear in Kant. By what does one decide casuistical questions? Sometimes there will be a third *a priori* principle by which to decide; but this is an unsatisfactory answer to the problem because it is always possible to change the facts and postulate the conflict with that third principle. Kant would then need a fourth, and so on. As IV.3 shows there is no definite limit to this and the plausibility of supposing an *a priori* character soon runs out. It seems that the will must in the end be determined in such cases by something other than *a priori* principles.

Modern moral philosophers are inclined to say that it is determined by the agent weighing the conflicting principles (see e.g. Dworkin, 1977, ch. 2). Variations of this notion are that such principles are merely *prima facie*, or such as to apply only when other things are equal. These, we have said, are not important variations, for clearly weighing or something like it is necessary to determine when a *prima facie* principle is rebutted or whether all things are not equal.

The introduction of weight as a means of determining the will between competing *a priori* principles does not save Kant's conception for, as we have seen in IV.3, it makes no sense to suppose that weight with its indefinite graduation can be *a priori*; and it makes no more sense to postulate a separation of existence from weight. As with reasons (IV.3), we have to say that once weight is introduced as the determinant of the will it is weight that carries the whole practical significance. Thus principles if they are to be practical must be a function of their weight, in no practical sense separate from it. Since the weight of principles is not *a priori* their existence is not, either.

Weight is a cardinal concept. Perhaps an *a priori ordering* of principles is a more plausible basis for Kant's conception. However, this too must be abandoned as soon as the indefinite alternation of principles shown in IV.3 is contemplated. For any pair of competing principles by alternating critical changes to the facts (our example alternated changes in the seriousness of an injury, attracting the Samaritan principle, and in the seriousness of a promise, attracting the promise principle), we can postulate an indefinite number of changes in the order of the competing principles, thus rendering any *a priori* sense in the order implausible.

Kant's conception of *a priori* principles of practical reason is not saved by their modern interpretation as *prima facie* principles of the (A1) sort. The corollary of this is that the spuriousness of *prima facie* principles (merely the universalization of reasons, which have primacy) is not avoided by any Kantian connection.

IV.5

> Then Socrates sat down and – 'How fine it would be, Agathon,' he said, 'if wisdom were a sort of thing that could flow out of the one of us who is fuller into him who is emptier, by our mere contact with each other, as water will flow through wool from the fuller cup into the emptier. If such is indeed the case with wisdom I set great value on my sitting next to you . . .' (Plato, *Symposium*, 175 D. Loeb translation)

How are reasons transferred from one person to another? More specifically, how do we learn from others to judge and act for reasons? In legal philosophy a central part of these questions is whether the reasons which determine legal hard cases could exist dependently upon precedent and statute, that is upon some contingent enunciation in one form or another in the institutions of a community. If they could that would be a way of the authors of these institutions transferring reasons to others.

The depth and difficulty of this problem is not to be mistaken. A precedent decision, for instance, might lay down a norm 'people ought to exercise care towards their neighbours'; and it would not be difficult to see how this norm existed simply by virtue of having been laid down, nor to see how it could be used in a subsequent case either as a rule or by virtue of the reason of *stare decisis* (respect precedents). But in this latter case the operative reason, the one which has weight in the subsequent decision is *stare decisis*, not 'people ought to exercise care towards their neighbours' (its form is inference (C): see IV.2). This neighbour principle is, because it has been promulgated, a norm; and its promulgation is a fact constituting the reason of *stare decisis*. The deeper, more important problem relates to the neighbour principle itself, as a principle or reason with weight, not as a norm supported by *stare decisis*. Can this principle or reason itself exist and have weight dependently upon precedent or statute? (Of course, there is an equivalent problem with *stare decisis* itself: can *stare decisis* exist and have weight dependently upon precedent or statute?)

Suppose that a precedent or statute stated that such-and-such was a principle or reason, and that courts were required to weigh it. What could a court make of this?

In answering this question we shall make much reference to the work of Dworkin. For ease of terminology, we shall talk of principles not reasons. The harmless sense of the term is intended. Reasons still have primacy. The whole of the following discussion (and the whole of Dworkin's work) could be put in terms of reasons.

Suppose that a precedent or statute stated that such and such was a principle and that courts were required to weigh it. What could a court make of this? So long as 'such and such' was clear, the court's problem would be with the weight of this *prima facie* principle. Principles are not rules, and therefore nothing is to be assumed about their operation and nothing is to be excluded. A principle must therefore operate in competition with other relevant principles. For a court to press its case to a conclusion it must face the fact that no principle is absolute (rules are absolute because they are made absolute: they are precisely an exclusion of all those things which would compete). So the problem of the weight of principles, which is simply the problem of their competing with counter-principles, will have to be faced. Is it possible for the institutions of society to inform a judge about the weight of a principle?

Dworkin, though he has done much to clarify the logical character of *prima facie* principles, has not attended clearly to this problem of weight (in this he is like Nagel: IV.3). The problem arises acutely and clearly only in the case of a judge who knows there is a principle he is required to weigh but does not know what weight to attach to it. In most cases judges do know this and our problem is avoided, or at least they know it sufficiently well to be able to come to a decision in a case in hand. In *Riggs v. Palmer*, one of Dworkin's paradigm cases (1977, ch. 2), an important principle was the wrongness of a man's profiting from his own wrong. Happily for legal systems, judges do know, no doubt roughly and in some cases controversially, how to weigh that principle. It simply is not like a principle, say, of the wrongness of any man who happens to be called Harold profiting in life. If a judge were given the information in a statute or precedent case that this latter was a principle which he was required to weigh, what could he do with it? How could he assign it any weight at all?

He might be told by the statute or precedent to assign it total or absolute weight, that is, take it to outweigh all other principles. But then it would be a rule, not a principle at all. Similarly, if he were told that it was in certain cases to outweigh a certain other principle or set of principles, it would in those certain cases operate as a rule. The reason is that the judge in these cases is required not to go into the real question of weight but to assume the bindingness of the dictated answer to the question. The extremes, no weight or total weight, do not create a problem. The only course open to our judge in the case of the principle against people called Harold is, it seems, to assign the principle an arbitrary weight. But that is not to weigh it; it is simply to decide a case arbitrarily. Our question is: can a legal system by its institutions, which we know can pass or establish rules, pass or establish anything which will give a judge the information he needs to weigh an extraordinary principle like the one against people called Harold? The question in this extraordinary case raises our issue clearly. In a more ordinary case of a principle to which I attribute some weight where the question is of an increase or decrease of that weight, the issue is the same, though somewhat disguised.

Dworkin presents a (somewhat) extraordinary case thus: Hercules J. is deciding the constitutionality of certain abortion laws, and in particular he is considering the weight of the principle of respect for human dignity.

> Hercules might think dignity an unimportant concept; if he were to attend a new constitutional convention he might vote to repeal the due process clause, or at least to amend it so as to remove any idea of dignity from its scope. He is nevertheless able to decide whether that concept, properly understood, embraces the case of abortion. . . . It is, of course, necessary that Hercules have some understanding of the concept of dignity, even if he denigrates that concept; and he will gain that

understanding by noticing how the concept is used by those to whom it is important. If the concept figures in the justification of a series of constitutional decisions, then it must be a concept that is prominent in the political rhetoric and debates of the time. Hercules will collect his sense of the concept from its life in these contexts. He will do the best he can to understand the appeal of the idea to those to whom it does appeal. He will devise, so far as he can, a conception that explains that appeal to them. (1977, 127)

There is a lack of clarity here. What is it to 'have some understanding of the concept of dignity'? Does someone who thinks dignity 'an unimportant concept' understand it? What could it be, we might ask, to understand the principle against people being called Harold? I understand the meaning of all the words I have used in formulating this extraordinary principle. But I have not the faintest understanding of the principle at all. The reason for this, it would seem, is that I can see absolutely no value in it, and thus could give it no weight. More specifically, when confronted by a Harold I would have no reason by virtue of his name to act differently towards him from the way I would act towards a Michael. On the other hand, I can see the value of respect for human dignity. Thus when I see that you are human I have all sorts of reasons for action and judgment.

For me to see this value it must in some way be independent of any statement of it; otherwise I would see nothing in the statement. To see the value of a principle is to be committed to it, that is, to be committed to assigning it a certain, though over cases infinitely variable, weight. This is a logical truth. To see the value of something is to be committed to its having weight in moral thought. Thus it seems that a judge can only understand and weigh a principle if he is himself committed to it; and he must be committed independently of any enactment or establishment of that principle by the institutions of society – if he were not he could make nothing of the enactment. Thus statute or precedent can only effectively lay down a principle if the principle is one already. And that, of course, is to say that statute and precedent cannot effectively lay down principles.

There is one exception to this. A statute (or precedent) may impose a rule that a certain principle (or reason of course: we are talking for the moment of *prima facie* principles) is *not* to be weighed, i.e. is to be of no weight (just as it may impose a rule that it is to be absolute). Such laws may be repealed, and a statute (or precedent) requiring a principle to be weighed may not be a nullity if it is such a repeal. But, of course, the weight, now, as it were, freed by the repeal, is still independent of statute.

Principles, therefore, as a matter of logic cannot be dependent for their existence, as rules can, on some contingent enunciation in the institutions of society.

Perhaps this will be thought a too hasty conclusion. We may have proved that the weight of a principle cannot be determined by a statute or precedent, but the weight of a principle, it might be said, is different from its existence, and we have not shown that its existence cannot be determined by statute or precedent. This objection, however, does not make sense, for it implies that a particular principle might exist independently of its weight. And how could this be? If a principle had no weight it would have no function in moral or legal thought; and what then would be the point of according it existence? (this was the mistake Nagel made in relation to reasons: IV.3).

Dworkin thought that Hercules could set about discovering the weight of a principle from society's institutions; by 'noticing how the concept is used by those to whom it is important'; by 'collect[ing] his sense of the concept from its life [in the context of its use in certain precedents]'. Now, Dworkin's example as we have seen, is not altogether a clear one, for thinking the concept unimportant is not the same thing as thinking it of no value at all, and to raise our problem clearly we must talk of a 'principle' that Hercules regards as of no value at all. What in this case could Hercules notice or collect from its alleged life in society?

There might be, for instance, a number of court precedents. Let us assume there are ten decisions in which the courts have come to certain conclusions on the stated basis that the principle against people being called Harold outweighs all other relevant principles in the case. Can a judge 'notice' anything here? Does this give him any information at all about the weight of the principle? Of course, if the facts of his case are identical with the facts of any of the precedents, he can apply the precedent without (much) difficulty. But this is not a matter of weighing anything, for the precedent is in this event applied as a rule. We must assume therefore that the facts are different. What could the fact that there are ten precedents in which a certain principle has outweighed competing ones tell a judge? That it has ten times as much weight as a principle with only one such precedent? Obviously not. That it has more weight than a principle which, in the precedents, it has always outweighed (assume that all ten precedents are based on the same two-principle contest, with the same result)? No, because, as we have seen in our promise/Samaritan case, a principle's weight is not an absolute thing, but is dependent upon the facts of the case, and we have assumed that the facts of the case are different from the facts of the ten precedents. Thus there is no reason to think that the eleventh case is to have the same result as the first ten. I can see nothing at all that can be 'noticed' in the precedents about the weight of the principle against being called Harold (and *a fortiori*, nothing that could be noticed in a statute or a constitution, which are even more limited in this regard than the court decisions, since they operate only by language and not also by example).

How is the principle requiring respect for human dignity different? In contrast to the first one, I can understand this principle, and thus attribute weight to it. Perhaps I can notice something in the precedents which indicates that I should attribute more weight to it or less weight. Well, as before, the number of precedents will not be significant, nor the number of occasions on which the principle has outweighed a certain other one (the number of precedents will be significant for a different principle, *stare decisis*: see IV.9). Perhaps, however, where there are a number of precedents in which the principle has, say, outweighed principle X, and as a matter of speculation I can see that on the facts of those cases if it had been my duty to decide them I would in all of them have decided the opposite, I can rather tentatively infer that I am underweighting the principle. And so, in a case involving competition between the same two principles on different facts from the precedents (if the facts were the same I would usually be deciding by rule, not principle) I could say, perhaps, that I should give more weight to the principle of respect for human dignity than I would otherwise have been inclined to do. How much more? The whole of the problem arises again in that question. How much more would be impossible to say. I should have to guess (my judgment would thus be arbitrary). But perhaps if I would otherwise have judged that there was a slight balance in favour of principle X I could reverse that judgment and decide that the balance was in favour of the dignity principle. But this is a very tenuous possibility. Analysis along these lines looks pedantic, over-calculated and quite unpromising; untrustworthy, as Hare might have put it (IV.6). All it has done, really, is to have minimized the space in which I have had to guess arbitrarily. I shall take Socrates's word for the profundity of this problem of the transference of wisdom and suggest what seems a more promising approach, able to match this profundity. We shall treat the problem as one of education rather than of the transference of information. To learn the weight of principles is to learn how to weigh them (learn *how*, not learn what), and this is to be taken as a matter of education. The wool of Socrates is education.

IV.6

How do I learn to dance? R. M. Hare once attended to the theoretical aspects of this problem (1957, 741). One of his conclusions was that 'we can know something (e.g. how to dance the eightsome reel) without being able yet to say what we know'. The analysis was related to the problem of the amenability of language to description.

> This analogy points to a way of thinking about our use of language which is a valuable corrective to the more orthodox representational view, in which 'facts', 'qualities', and other dubious entities flit like *untrustworthy diplomats* between language and the world. We do not need these intermediaries; there are just people in given situations trying to understand one another. Logic, in one of the many senses of that word, is learning to formulate the rules that enable us to make something of what people say. Its method is to identify and describe the various sorts of things that people say (the various dances and their steps) such as predication, conjunction, disjunction, negation, counting, adding, promising, commanding, commending, – need I ever stop? In doing this it has to rely on our knowledge, as yet unformulated, of how to do these things – things of which we may not even know the names, and which

indeed may not have names till the logician invents them; but which are, nevertheless, distinct and waiting to be given names. Since this knowledge is knowledge of something that we have learnt, it has, as I have said, many of the characteristics of memory – though it would be incorrect, strictly speaking, to say that we remember how to use a certain word; Plato's word 'recall' is perhaps more apt. As in the case of memory, however, we know, without being, in many cases, able to give further evidence, that we have got it right. And often the only test we can perform is: trying it out again. In most cases there comes a point at which we are satisfied that we have got the thing right (in the case of speaking, that we have formulated correctly what we know). Of course, the fact that we are satisfied does not show that we are not wrong; but if once satisfied, we remain satisfied until we discover, or are shown, some cause for dissatisfaction. (749; my emphasis)

In the matter of law, which is not so very far from the matter of language, we might say: we can know how to weigh principles without it being the case that any judge or legislator is able to say (in a precedent case or a statute) what it is that we (or he) know (or are to know). To require or admit sources for legal principles is strictly impossible.

IV.7

Of course, Socrates knew that education was possible. Though I cannot exactly say how to dance the eightsome reel, and nobody else can either, somebody can teach me. I *can* learn it. And I can learn the law, too. In particular, I can learn how to weigh (legal) principles. Nobody can say in a statute, or in a court's reasons for decision (or in a hundred courts') exactly how I am to do this, but I can learn to do it. It is an accepted fact that judges and lawyers do often have this ability, and we may take it that some time or other they did learn it.

Legal positivism, and in particular the thesis of the separation of law and morals, is not able to accommodate the idea of legal education. Education is not the simple conveyance of information. Education and moral ability are logically connected concepts.

Legal positivism sees law as something the existence of which can, in principle, be conveyed as a matter of information. The positivists, therefore, are committed to the view that there is no such thing as legal education. Lawyers may be given information about the existence of rules, but if they are actually, in the strict sense, educated, it follows from the positivist definition of law that they have been educated in something other than the law. But the moral concept, education, clearly solves the problem of the relationship between principles and institutions. My legal education is, amongst other things, an exposure to legal institutions and this education produces in me the ability to weigh (legal) principles. That it is education which produces this means that the ability is a moral ability, and this confirms our conclusion in IV.5 that to weigh a principle one must be committed to it. It is not possible to weigh a principle uncommittedly. To do that a judge would have to be able to describe its weight, and that cannot be done. The metaphor of weight is a little misleading here, for obviously real weights and real balancing processes can be described. The unique point about weighing principles of the legal or moral sort is that there is no external balance, for the judge himself is the balance (this fact does not lead to moral relativism, but only to the truism that moral decisions must be made by individual moral agents). That legal principles must be weighed committedly is inconsistent with the thesis of the separation of law and morals. It is not possible, as proponents of that thesis would want to have it, for a judge to weigh legal principles and then separately to consider the moral bindingness of the result of the balance. If a judge did that it would follow that he was not committed to the principles; his (legal) decision could, therefore, only have been an arbitrary one. Legal *judgment* in these matters is moral judgment (although it might be wrong judgment; but that is always a truistic possibility in the case of any sort of judgment, legal, moral, or whatever).

Education is no guarantee of truth, and the best teachers never claim it is. To learn the law might, morally speaking, be a mistake. That, however, would not deny the moral nature of the undertaking. To learn to be a revolutionary has the same status, or an artist. The violent incompatibility of these things makes tragedy.

Dworkin's earlier articles used predominantly the metaphor of weight and weighing to show the way judges deal with principles. In 'Hard Cases' (now chapter 4 of 1977) this changed, and the metaphor became gravitational force. Now, gravitational force is closely related to weight in physics, but is it in Dworkin? Has the metaphor really changed? This is a difficult question, partly because 'Hard Cases' represents a radical change in Dworkin's approach to the problem of principles and legal obligation.

In the earlier articles Dworkin started with principles, and we found ourselves immediately confronted by the problems examined earlier in this chapter. What is the place of institutional history? How can principles be affected by institutional history? The problems proved to be intractable. Now, although Dworkin's jurisprudence is regarded as anti-positivist, institutional history is near to the heart of his theory. For on the moral significance of institutional history turns much of the idea of rights, and Dworkin's theory of law is a theory of rights.

Institutional arrangements in a community represent a positively established set of rights by virtue of which own things can be done, own choices made; a set of spaces to live in. Positive establishment is obviously a matter of institutional history. And without this positive establishment a rights thesis is diminished, for whilst space is natural and our requirement of space is too, spaces are not. Your space and mine need to be marked-off by our institutions, or there will be only space. Of course, rules mark-off spaces and the rights thesis can therefore offer an explanation of rule cases, but Dworkin regards hard cases as more important than do most.

So, in 'Hard Cases' we see a radical reversal of approach (Dworkin, 1977, ch. 4). Instead of trying to show how legal principles might be shaped and controlled by institutional history, Dworkin will start with institutional history itself, and see what principles (amongst other things) can be squeezed out of it. But is this reversal of the problem philosophically sound?

To start with principles is clearly justified in moral philosophy since principles are universalized reasons for action and reasons for action have an immediate practical force. There can be no better methodological justification than this. To start with institutional history, on the other hand, is not so clearly justified. Unless it is loved it has in itself no moral power. Dworkin does not rely upon any argument of love, but instead seeks to establish the moral significance of institutional history by the argument of fairness. The difficulty with this is that fairness is a principle; and unless there is a justification for isolating it from other principles, i.e. making it absolute, and none is presented, the reversal has failed, for we are back with principles, all of them, and their infinite contest.

Dworkin's theory in 'Hard Cases' is that institutional history exercises a complex system of gravitational force to which legal decision must respond. Briefly, this means that a judge must look at the relevant parts of institutional history and seek to construct that theory of principles which best explains it (justifies it). Having done that, he is in a position to apply the theory to his problem. But how is the theory to be constructed? If it is to be a theory of institutional history capable of application in hard cases, it must be able to show how institutional history has established or affected the weight of principles. It seems, however, that it must encounter the same set of problems considered in IV.5. Unless the theory-constructing judge already values a certain principle, what could he make of its mention in a piece of institutional history that would enable him to assess its gravitational force? He could perhaps understand the words used by the court, the statute or the constitution, but, as we saw in IV.5, understanding the principle is a different matter, and unless he understands the principle he will not be able to make any theory about it in terms of either gravitational force or weight. To understand a principle he must himself value it, and so the question presents itself here, as before: what *is* the significance of institutional history?

Dworkin gives various examples of the way his theory-constructing judge, Hercules J., is to work. Most of these, however, are not examples of the construction of a theory at all, but examples of a set of decisions that Hercules makes (1977, 118–21). Hercules, we may take it, is the perfect judge, and by definition, therefore, he can construct a complete set of correct legal decisions, which might certainly be used in subsequent cases. But their use would be as rules. The set would stand as a complete set of perfect decisions and rules of law. There is no reason to think that it would convey information about the weight of principles any more than there is reason to think it in the case of any decision by any judge. Hercules's construction of this set of decisions will in a sense use the sort of theory that Dworkin wants (in that it will not view any legal problem as an isolated one). But using a theory to construct a complete set of decisions is not the same thing as constructing a theory; and there is very little that Dworkin says that pertains to the latter. The distinction is crucial. We have not denied in this chapter that judges can make judgments of principles, and there is no reason for us now to doubt that the perfect judge can do this in the best possible way, and over the whole law, viewed as a whole. What we have denied is that it is possible to state what is done by this practice in a theory which will inform of the effect that institutional history itself has on the weight of principles. Hercules knows the weight of all principles, since he is the perfect judge (the perfectly educated judge), and neither institutional history nor a theory about it can, except by education, change this weight.

One example which Dworkin gives of the way his theory-constructing judge is to operate is *MacPherson* v. *Buick Motor Co.* ([1916] 217 N.Y.382), where Cardozo J., held the plaintiff entitled to recover damages for injuries caused by the negligent manufacture of a motor car. To construct a theory of the gravitational force of this decision, Hercules, according to Dworkin, must determine what set of principles best justifies it consistently with all other relevant cases and statutes. He must assign a scheme of principles to the whole of institutional history (1977, 116). Dworkin asks us to suppose that Hercules considers justifying the MacPherson case by an 'abstract principle of equality which argues that whenever an accident occurs then the richest of the various persons whose acts might have contributed to the accident must bear the loss' (1977, 116). Now Hercules, says Dworkin, will find this an unacceptable justification of the decision; and we (lawyers) agree, for it *is* a weak principle. But can Dworkin show that institutional history is able itself to bear a significant (or any) part of the burden of this conclusion? We know the conclusion is right. But if we did not, could institutional history enlighten us? One of Dworkin's arguments (*loc. cit.*) is this, and we may take it as typical: Hercules cannot show that the principle has been respected (presumably meaning: has determined cases) in the law of contract, where it could be expected to have had great impact if it were a principle of sufficient weight to have determined the

MacPherson case. It has had no impact in the law of contract (determined no cases), therefore it is not a principle of sufficient weight to have determined the MacPherson case. Now, this looks all right to us (lawyers). We might well, if we were considering the weight of the principle of equality in a torts case, consider how it would fare in the different contract cases – this is absolutely typical of lawyers' reasoning. But nothing here turns on institutional history. We might have done exactly the same thing before any of the contract cases had been decided and reflected on hypothetical cases. What we are doing here is reflecting on the weight of one principle in a contest with a second by considering its weight in a different context where it is in contest with a third. As we are (necessarily) committed to all three principles we are able to compare the weight of the second with the third and thus able to establish a basis for thinking that the contest between the first and the third is relevant to the contest between the first and the second. This is done easily by us (lawyers) who have become by our education committed to these principles. But what if we had not? Let us try to remove the element of our valuing these principles from the problem.

Call the principle of equality *A*. Call the principles supporting the defendant's case in MacPherson *B*. And call *C* those principles of the law of contract which in the supposed contract cases *A* would outweigh if it were a strong principle. Dworkin is saying that because *C* outweighs *A*, *A* cannot outweigh *B*; and that, of course, is, in the abstract, a totally fallacious argument. But if institutional history itself is to bear a significant part of the burden of Hercules's theory the argument must be statable in the abstract. The argument remains totally fallacious no matter what institutional facts we inject into it: for instance, '*C* outweighed *A* in 1,000 cases, therefore *A* cannot outweigh *B*' is no more plausible. And it is fallacious whether it is required to establish a complete answer to a case or merely a threshold answer (1977, 342, 360): in neither case can it establish anything.

Now, Dworkin has rightly rejected the view that his theory is that these matters turn on ordinary factual judgments about institutional history (1977, 339–42). A judge brings his principles to institutional history and judges it by them or through them, just as we (lawyers) a moment ago judged the MacPherson case by our understanding of the weakness of the principle *A*. But what

Dworkin has not shown, and what he logically cannot show, and what is crucial, is how bringing these principles to institutional history and then to court is different from bringing them straight to court. Of course, Dworkin can show that at institutional history certain facts can be picked up which have weight under the principle, *stare decisis*. But this does not affect our problem which is of the weight, not of that principle, but of the weight of the substantive principles themselves (see IV.9).

One who is committed to the principle of fairness, as Dworkin is, need not be too concerned about these conclusions. Legal education is mainly an exposure to institutional history; and this has its effect not only in producing a calculable knowledge of its rules, but also an (incalculable) capacity to weigh its principles. This latter capacity, we must suppose, is different from any capacity to weigh principles produced without the same exposure to institutional history (lawyers do seem to be morally different from revolutionaries). So, by way of education, institutional history will have its effect in the direction of the fairness that Dworkin wants.

But there is a very great difference between the strictly incalculable effects of education and the calculable effects of institutional history which Dworkin supposes Hercules might perceive; a difference which Dworkin, despite his recognition that 'any official's sense of the game will have developed over a career, and he will employ rather than expose that sense in his judgments' (1977, 359), fails to see. For he regards as absurd the 'view that the law is always morally sound' (1977, 341), and he clearly means this to apply to hard cases as well as to rule cases. In other words he thinks that in hard cases (where there are no rules) a judge may sometimes be forced to decide in a way which is legal but not moral. But the principles by which he decides will have to be moral principles in the fullest sense if the judge is to use them. To use them he must be able to weigh them. To weigh them is to make a passionate response to the facts on which they obtain (for only the passions can account for the possibility of indefinite graduation of weight noticed in IV.3). But the judge has only one passionate capacity. Dworkin's view suggests that a judge has two passionate capacities, one legal and one moral. Thus he envisaged the possibility of a case where the judge is pulled one way by his legal principles and another by his moral principles (1977, 327, 341).

But the basis of this distinction is the supposed effect of institutional history which we have seen fails to stand up to analysis (IV.5).

Of course, within a judge's one passionate capacity there will be a difference between the moral situation in a certain state of institutional history and the situation in its absence. Thus if a certain precedent case has been decided, respect for peoples' reliance on it (*stare decisis*) may require a decision in a subsequent case different from what would be required if the precedent had not been decided. But this does not distinguish legal judgment from moral judgment, for on any definition of 'moral' it, too, requires that weight be given to peoples' reliance on precedents.

The two senses of justification distinguished in II.8 are involved here. The precedent decision may be justified in a sense that were its deciding again in issue a judge would be justified in deciding it in the same way. The important sense of justification relates to the more practical question of whether it would be justified to follow the precedent. And obviously it can be justified to follow a precedent not justified in the first sense. A trivial interpretation of Dworkin's thesis of the separation of law and morals would be that (legal) institutional history is not necessarily (morally) justified in the first sense. But Dworkin (as we are) is concerned principally with the practical business of deciding cases where only the second sense of justification is relevant. Here there is no distinction to be drawn between legal and moral. A judge has only one passionate capacity to bring to this practical business.

A judge's passionate capacity is (at least partly) the result of his education; and of course his education might be a moral mistake (education is no guarantee of perfection, and, more basically, it might be a moral mistake for anyone to learn to be a lawyer). In that sense his principles are not necessarily morally right. But this is an ordinary possibility in any education – it might be a mistake to learn to be a revolutionary, too, or an artist. Legal judgment is moral judgment because for the lawyer there can logically be no difference. Nor can there for any one, whatever he is; for we must all, if we speak morally, speak through our education. We are, necessarily, not able to notice any educational contingency in our capacity to judge for there is no way to get outside our education. Superficially it sometimes seems that we can. But when we think we reject something we have been taught what are we rejecting it by? Answer: in rejecting it we are using our capacity to make judgments, which cannot be separated from our education. Actually what we reject when we reject what we have been taught are rules: the idea of rejecting principles is logically impossible in the same way as is the idea of institutional history imposing principles; and in the same way as weakness of the will is impossible (V.13).

We conclude that the reversal of the problem of institutional history fails. One is no more able to squeeze the weight of principles from institutional history, however firmly grasped, than establish that weight by a simple connection of argument. The metaphor has not changed. In Dworkin's theory gravitational force is a simple function of weight, and a simple function of its problems, too.

IV.9

Dworkin has tried to attach institutional history to principles. But it can only be attached to principles positively established, that is to say, to norms.

This does not save Dworkin's theory, for norms do not have weight (or gravitational force). Either they are applied internally as rules (inference (D) in IV.2), where they operate absolutely, not by weight; or they are applied externally (inference (C) in IV.2), where what has weight is not the norm itself but the fact that a certain institution or person has laid it down. This is certainly a very complex question of weight. We have called the various principles involved by the package name, *stare decisis*, after the common lawyers' term. Dworkin talks in this regard mainly of the principle of fairness, and fairness between earlier and later litigants is certainly part of *stare decisis*. But the principle of *stare decisis*, or fairness, if we limit ourselves to Dworkin's argument, will not carry Dworkin's theory. First, no explanation can be given by it of what weight the fact of a norm having been laid down is to have (what weight the principle of fairness is to have). All the problems discussed in this chapter arise there. And second, in all cases of competing norms the weight of the principles that stand behind the norms are in issue as well as the weight of the facts of the laying down of the norms (in lawyers' terms this means simply that the merits of competing precedents are in issue as well as the principle that precedents be respected, *stare decisis*). This fact would, of course, be critical where the precedents were of equal value in terms of *stare decisis* or fairness. Certainly, where there is a legal precedent relevant to a case, weight by virtue of the principle of *stare decisis* is added to one party's argument; but this does not distinguish legal judgment from moral judgment, except in the trivial sense noticed in the last section, for precisely that weight is added to what would on anyone's definition count as a moral judgment on the matter (in Dworkin's terms the fairness which supports precedents is no less a moral than a legal principle).

The major truth in Dworkin's work is a conception of (moral) objectivity: there is no contrast, he holds, between legal judgment and personal judgment. As lawyers when we make legal judgments they are necessarily personal judgments, but they are objective (and therefore legal) in the sense that they contest an objective legal position. Dworkin was right to say there was no contrast between personal judgment and legal judgment.

But he was wrong to say there was a contrast between (personal) legal judgment and (personal) moral judgment. He recognized the importance of weight in the analysis of hard cases; but failed to take the analysis through, with the result that institutional history was allowed much more significance than it could really bear. This significance was critical for his whole theory; for it forced him to say that there was a difference between legal judgment (influenced by institutional history) and moral judgment; and this placed him in the camp of the legal positivists whose principle tenet is precisely that.

A possible explanation of why Dworkin made this mistake is offered in VIII.5.

IV.10

In chapter II we argued that legal judgment was necessarily moral judgment. We can now give further support to that argument. Principles do not have categories – legal, revolutionary, political, religious and so on. There is only one sense in which I can have a principle; for to have it I must have a passionate commitment to it, and there is only one way to have a passionate commitment.

The Weight of Reasons

We know empirically that, say, lawyers and revolutionaries typically come to different decisions. But this does not establish that there are legal principles and revolutionary principles. For a lawyer looking from within his form of life will not be able to see any difference between his principles and others. And nor will a revolutionary from within his. There will simply, in each case, be principles.

There is no way out of the form of life into which one has been educated except by the exercise of moral freedom (an account of which is still owing). But freedom does not distinguish one category of thought from another. How could freedom distinguish the legal from the revolutionary or the religious, or any of these from the moral? Which one would be the free state? Moral freedom does not even guarantee the existence of more than one category of moral thought for it is a perfectly plausible account of it that it be exercised within just one category (I am free to become a better or worse or merely different lawyer). Not even the psychologically implausible view that moral freedom is freedom to choose absolutely anything distinguishes the legal from the moral in a significant way: those who have insisted upon such a distinction have required more than that these simply be two categories amongst an infinity of possibilities.

IV.11

Rules and principles were distinguished by Dworkin in the 'Model of Rules' article in 1967 (reprinted as ch. 2 of Dworkin, 1977). But he was widely criticized, not least by Raz (1972a, 823). However, in *Practical Reason and Norms* (1975) Raz, whilst ostensibly adhering to his rejection of Dworkin's distinction, goes on to re-establish the distinction, elaborately and with much development and insight, under other names. This is not surprising given the interchangeability of reasons and their harmless universalization, principles (IV.2).

Dworkin's distinction was first rejected by Raz in favour of the following one, according to which:

Rules prescribe relatively specific acts; principles prescribe highly unspecific actions. . . . The distinction between rules and principles is, on this analysis, one of degree, since there is no

> hard and fast line between acts which are specific and those
> which are unspecific. (1972a, 838)

This is in this context an uninteresting distinction, and it is no surprise to find that Raz in the later work mentions it only by the way, and with no emphasis (1975, 49) – he has much more interesting things to attend to.

Practical thought is analysed by Raz in terms of reasons for action. Reasons have a dimension of strength: 'Some reasons are stronger or more weighty than others. In cases of conflict the stronger reason overrides the weaker. This feature of strong reasons is their defining characteristic' (1975, 25). So reasons have to be weighed.

But there are norms which, Raz argues, are exclusionary reasons; that is, not only primary reasons for action in their own right but also second-order reasons to exclude from consideration other competing reasons (1975, 35–48, 73–84).

> For the most part the presence of a norm is decisive. . . . The whole purpose of having norms is to achieve this simplification. The facts that norms are exclusionary reasons enables them to achieve this purpose. Since a norm is an exclusionary reason it does not have to compete with most of the other reasons which are likely to apply to situations governed by the norm, for it excludes them. In this way norms simplify practical reasoning. *Once it is established that a norm applies to the case at hand we need not be concerned with the weight of the conflicting reasons affecting the case.* They are in most cases excluded and their exclusion is not a matter of weight. It is determined by the fact that the norm is a second-order reason. Thus norms have a relative independence from the reasons which justify them. (1975, 79; my emphasis.)

This corresponds with the concept of a rule. The emphasized passage is in almost precisely the terms in which Dworkin describes that logical feature of a rule which distinguishes it from a principle, the rule's all-or-nothing application. I would not want to underrate the subtlety and interest of Raz's analysis. But the contrast between first-order reasons for action and norms which are given a relative independence from other reasons by exclusionary reasons seems to me to be nothing in substance more than the original distinction between principles and rules. If we take the step of making a harmless universalization of the reasons (IV.2), the correspondence is exact.

It follows that Raz's theory has all the problems of Dworkin's, but Raz is not concerned to tell us about the strength or weight of reasons relative to one another, or how a source of law can determine or affect that weight, nor to answer the ontological problems that these questions pose. There is analysis of the various logical types of reasons and their respective entailments (1975, 25–8), but nothing on the basic, simple, by far more important questions of how why and when one reason of a certain logical type outweighs of its own force (i.e. with no help from rules) another reason of the same logical type.

This is a major gap in Raz's account of practical thought (the same gap which we have perceived in Nagel and Dworkin). In the case of law, however, Raz has a way of avoiding it:

> According to the source thesis the weight or strength of legal reasons is, just like their content, totally determined by social facts [sources]. Those do for the most part provide enough indications as to how to resolve conflicts of legal reasons. (1979, 74)

Where they do not, where a conflict is not resolved by a source, Raz says there is a legal gap, i.e. no law. Thus the problem of weight, of *actually* weighing a principle or reason, does not occur in law; lawyers weigh principles and reasons in accordance with the directions of a source of law, and if they are not directed the problem is not a legal one. The trouble with this account is that only rules can make this direction. The account amounts to the thesis that law is only rules.

I think what Raz has in mind when he says that sources may determine the weight of a legal reason are examples like these:

1 In Australia when you have inconsistent federal and state laws the federal law provides one legal reason, a state law a conflicting legal reason, and a (third) source (the constitution) directs how this conflict is to be resolved.

2 A statute might say that in contract cases of type X the principle of equality is to outweigh the principle of freedom of contract. When a case of type X arises the conflict

between these two legal reasons (or principles) is resolved by a (third) source, the statute.

3 A statute of family law might say that in certain cases the interests of a child of a marriage are paramount; meaning that in these cases the legal reasons for judgment constituted by the proper interests of a parent are to be over-ridden by the legal reasons constituted by the proper interests of a child.

Now, in all these cases no reasons are weighed; on the contrary, decisions are made by rule. None is a case of a source directing how reasons are to be weighed; rather, they are cases where a rule is interpolated. In case 1 it is the rule that federal laws over-ride state laws. In cases 2 and 3, depending on their details, it is either a wide and substantive rule ('in X cases the consumer is entitled to rescission', 'in Y cases the father is not entitled to custody') or a narrower almost procedural rule directed to the judge ('when in the process of your judgment you come to a conflict between the two principles decide for the (specified) one'). In none of these cases does any principle or reason have to be weighed against another; a rule, insulated from the flux of reason, determines the matter.

A positivist, of course, might claim not to be perturbed by this. Law, he might say, *is* a thing of rules.

IV.12

The following judicial statement might be thought typical and in need of explanation; it is quoted by MacCormick in support of the view (which this chapter argues is false) that a legal system's principles as well as its rules can be both described and changed (1978, 154):

My Lords, by enacting the Race Relations Acts 1965 and 1968 Parliament introduced into the law of England a new guiding principle of fundamental and far-reaching importance. It is one that affects and must influence action and behaviour in this country within a wide ranging sweep of human activities and personal relationships. In the terms decreed by Parliament, but subject to the exceptions permitted by Parliament, discrimination against a person on the ground of colour, race or ethnic or national origins has become unlawful by the law of England. In one sense there results for some people a limitation on what could be called their freedom: they may no longer treat certain people, because of their colour, race or ethnic or national origins, less favourably than they would treat others. But in the same cause of freedom, although differently viewed, Parliament has, in statutory terms now calling for consideration, proscribed discrimination (on the stated grounds) as being unlawful. (Lord Morris in *Charter* v. *Race Relations Board* [1973] A.C. 868, 889)

Lord Morris (and MacCormick) make the same mistake as Dworkin has made about the significance of institutional enactment of principles.

Rules may be changed (statutory offences and torts created, boards set up, and so on). But apart from the imperceptible beginnings of a change in the weight accorded to the anti-discrimination principle by people in a community which the Race Relations Acts as educative acts might effect, nothing else changes. No principle (reason) changes. Lord Morris is only able to prognosticate far-reaching effects for these acts because he understands (i.e. values) the anti-discrimination principle; and that means that he valued it, that it was a principle for him, prior to the enactment of the Race Relations Acts. Had it been a principle that he did not understand, for instance our principle against people called Harold, he could make nothing of it as a principle to be weighed and prognosticate no effects of its enactment. Of course, that Lord Morris accepts the anti-discrimination principle does not mean that he does not accept counter-principles, too – as his reference to loss of freedom shows.

Perhaps it is a principle which he feels more able to use after the Acts. This could only mean that the Acts repeal a rule which previously required that the principle be not applied (weighed). What this rule was in this case, or typically is, is difficult to say. One possibility is that English lawyers, notwithstanding the abolition of the forms of action by the Judicature Acts, have a rule (operating, to be sure, *very* selectively) that no claim can be made in a court of law or defence offered except on the basis of a rule from precedent or statute. This would exclude an unprecedented, pre-Race Relations Acts claim on the anti-discrimination principle. Such an exclusionary rule is possible even though after the abolition of the forms of action in the Common Law legal systems there are just the facts of any given legal case and legal entitlements based upon those facts (*Letang* v. *Cooper* [1965] 1 Q.B. 232); it is possible because the idea of legal entitlements includes rules as well as reasons, and there is no reason in theory why it should not include this sort of exclusionary rule. The rule's origins, however, would be difficult to comprehend. The system of forms of action contained exclusionary rules, but they were jurisdictional and procedural, rather than substantive (see Maitland, *Forms of Action at Common Law*, Lecture I). Thus the answer to a plaintiff raising facts which were inadequate in law would always have been the partly procedural, partly jurisdictional 'not in this form of action', never the substantive 'not in law': the substantive question of limits to law would never have arisen. We can say, therefore, that prior to the abolition of the forms of action there could have been no substantive rule stipulating such limits; no substantive rule, therefore, excluding the anti-discrimination principle. How it arises after the abolition of the forms of action is difficult to see. Nevertheless, some, even most, English lawyers may hold it (perhaps mistaking the nature of a legal system of forms of action, and in consequence mistaking the situation that obtains on their abolition). And for those who do, statutes such as the Race Relations Acts could operate as partial repeals of this rule, and thereby free the anti-discrimination principle.

This is not the only explanation of judicial conservatism. The difficulty of judgment is always a reason not to act, whether the action is a legal one (by a judge giving judgment) or some other more ordinary one. And the independence of others is always a reason not to act so as to impinge upon them (for instance, by giving judgment against them). Thus there are standing reasons always supporting defendants in law suits, only to be outweighed by strong plaintiffs' reasons (see IX.3, note 7). Judicial conservatives may differ from others in that they accord greater weight to those sorts of standing reasons (and, of course, to certain other reasons as well, e.g. *stare decisis*). However, statutes such as the Race Relations Acts cannot (except educatively) make any difference here. Only as acts repealing previously restricting rules can we explain an immediate significance of such statutes for principles (reasons).

IV.13

The modern philosophers and judges discussed in this chapter think that legal institutions can provide information capable of determining the weight of reasons in hard cases. This is a variation of the mistake in moral philosophy which Hume exposed. There is no escaping, in law or wider moral thought, the necessity of passionate commitment, for only passionate commitment can provide the weight of reasons and principles; and without this weight no hard judgment can be made.

The dilemma mentioned in IV.3 remains to be resolved: does not the introduction of the passions into moral thought make moral judgment (including legal judgment) psychologically contingent and hopelessly subjective (as Kant thought)? Does it not annihilate moral freedom (of which Kant is the magnificent champion)?

IV.14

Consider the parable of the labourers in the vineyards, which illustrates agape, the last stage of love:

> The kingdom of heaven is like this. There was once a landowner who went out early one morning to hire labourers for his vineyard; and after agreeing to pay them the usual day's wage he sent them off to work. Going out three hours later he saw some more men standing idle in the market-place. 'Go and join the others in the vineyard,' he said, 'and I will pay you a fair wage'; so off they went. At noon he went out again, and at three in the afternoon, and made the same arrangement as before. An hour before sunset he went out and found another group standing there; so he said to them, 'Why are you standing about like this all day with nothing to do?' 'Because no one has hired us', they replied; so he told them, 'Go and join the others in the vineyard.' When evening fell, the owner of the vineyard said to his steward, 'Call the labourers and give them their pay, beginning with those who came last and ending with the first.' Those who had started work an hour before sunset came forward, and were paid the full day's wage. When it was the turn

of the men who had come first, they expected something extra, but were paid the same amount as the others. As they took it, they grumbled at their employer: 'These latecomers have done only one hour's work, yet you have put them on a level with us, who have sweated the whole day long in the blazing sun!' The owner turned to one of them and said, 'My friend, I am not being unfair to you. You agreed on the usual wage for the day, did you not? Take your pay and go home. I choose to pay the last man the same as you. Surely I am free to do what I like with my own money. Why be jealous because I am kind?' (New English Bible, Matthew 20: 1–16)

The particularity of the labourers is decisive; comparison, necessarily by universals, is excluded. Agape knows only particulars.

But if it is particular facts which constitute reasons for action (I.10) how can one particular fact be weighed against another? It seems that in any moral case one reason can have more weight than an opposing reason. That implies a comparison. But if reasons are based upon particulars, how can there be such a comparison?

One can only distinguish particulars by virtue of their (attached) universals. Stripped of its (universal) properties and relations all we can say of a particular is that it is pure existence. How can one item of pure existence have more weight as a reason for action than another? (And why should it? Each particular contains the whole mystery of existence. Taking our Samaritan/promise case (IV.3), the promisee and the injured person each contain the whole mystery of existence. Keeping one's word or stopping a flow of blood seem utterly beyond significance in such a context.)

We have to say in the first stages of moral thought that the weight of a particular fact as a reason for action depends (at least substantially) upon its universals.This is not at all the same as the view rejected in I.10. We are not in practical judgment weighing universals. We are weighing particulars with certain universals particularly attached.

I think you are right to be uneasy about this last answer. But which way will you move? Not back to universals in themselves, for there moral judgment cannot be practical (I.10). The movement must be towards agape, where pure particularity, the mystery of existence, dominates. Plato spoke in the *Symposium* of the movement between stages of love, of which agape is the last. Movement is a metaphor. The concepts at this point become metaphors, such as are not open to precise analysis: certainly the point has been reached where the philosophy of law must give way to the philosophy of love.

V

THE FREEDOM AND OBJECTIVITY OF REASONS

V.1

Do judges have discretion? The positivistic conception of law divides it into rule cases and hard cases, and holds that in rule cases judges are bound by an established objective order, but that in hard cases they are not bound, being free to exercise their discretion (either *in vacuo* or in the interpretation of an uncertain rule).

Hard cases are decided by reference to the reasons that obtain on each side of the case, and there are two questions of objectivity involved here. The first is the one already asked: do judges have a discretion as to their judgment of the existence or force of these reasons? The second is a more important question, and one not so easy to identify. It might be the case that a judge has no discretion as to whether to give judgment this way or that, being bound by the reasons that obtain, but it might nevertheless also be the case that each judge's bound state is a subjective one, in that there is no objective connection between the reasons that obtain in the mind of one judge and those in the mind of another. Of course, the use of the word 'reason' tends to suggest that there is this connection.

We shall ask first: is there discretion? – the first sense of objectivity.

V.2

To say that judges do have discretion in hard cases asserts too much if it asserts that judges are permitted to decide hard cases arbitrarily, for example by the toss of a coin. They are not, and positivists do not dispute this. Thus the word 'right' or one of its equivalents ('good reasons', 'for the general good', 'just', 'best', 'balance of argument') is to be found in positivistic formulations of a judge's duty in hard cases. But these words are usually qualified to suggest the idea of discretion: thus a judge's duty in a hard case is to decide it according to what *he thinks* is right. For instance Raz (1972a, 847) says: 'What is "unjust" or "for the general good" is a matter of opinion and the courts or officials concerned are instructed by law to act upon their own views. [A judge] has discretion when the law requires him to act on reasons which he thinks are correct.' There are many formulations. I shall take the formulation 'decide the case according to what he thinks is right' as typical. Giving judgment is an action. Thus 'what he thinks is right' is 'what he thinks it is right to do'. Now, the qualification 'what he thinks' either states too little or is meaningless.

There are two meanings it might have. First, it might define the *power* of the judge. Power and duty are logically distinct concepts. One might have the power to do something, but the duty not to. Thus we might say that a judge has discretion in the sense that he has the power to choose an answer to a hard case which his duty does not allow him to choose. We would mean by this only that his wrong decision is to be accepted as law by subsequent courts; and this makes a perfectly meaningful contrast between 'what the judge thinks is right' and 'what is right'. But it does not distinguish hard cases from rule cases, and therefore cannot be the discretion that the positivists have in mind. For it is precisely the power that a judge has in rule cases where, on any account, he is objectively bound to make a certain decision: it is a very firm rule that courts (including all the relevant appeal courts) have power to make a settlement of any single case notwithstanding that the settlement is contrary to a legal rule (*finis litium*).

So far as a judge's duty is concerned (putting aside his power) the qualification 'what he thinks' might have an adverbial force, meaning something like 'conscientiously' or 'to the best of his ability', perhaps in the strict sense of the word 'responsibly' (Raz sometimes means this; see 1972a, 847). But of course all cases, where a judge is in any sense bound or not bound, must be decided conscientiously and to the best of his ability. Thus this interpretation, too, fails to produce a significant idea of discretion.

Between these two inappropriate meanings of 'what he thinks is right' it looks as though there is another which can support a significant idea of discretion, but there is not. We shall seek to demonstrate this by the dialogue in V.4; but first it is necessary to say something about a judge's duty.

V.3

Obviously a judge in a law case has a duty, or perhaps we might say several duties. In the first place he has a duty to decide the case. This duty is not really any more difficult or philosophically controversial than anyone's duty to do their job. More problematical is his duty what to decide. Where the law is clear we may say without difficulty that he has a duty to decide in accordance with law (I mean this is no more complicated a way than we might say of a workman employed to build a wall that he has a duty to lay bricks rather than to compose poetry). Where the law is not clear, difficulties arise.

Sometimes a constitution will state what it is a judge is to decide in a hard case – not what answer the judge is to give to the case, but what standard he is to decide by: right, for instance, or the interests of the state, or by reference to the requirements of a specified social policy (project). But constitutions do not usually state this, and when they do not, we have to say that it is an unsettled question by what it is that the judge is to decide a hard case. It must be a question, otherwise it would have made no sense to suppose the constitutional provisions just mentioned. And it must be a legal question in the way that any unsettled question of constitutional law is a legal question, that is, a question to be answered (when relevant to any case) by lawyers and judges. This last may seem a trite claim, but in fact it is most important; for it is the answer to the question which defines the judge's duty; and actually having a definition of the duty in hand is the key to dispelling much philosophical confusion about what it is that a judge is to decide in hard cases.

For example, Raz, who, as we have seen, is a proponent of the existence of judicial discretion in hard cases, says that 'in a legal system which contains a rule that whenever the courts are faced with a case for which the law does not provide a uniquely correct solution they ought to refuse to render judgment . . . there would be no judicial discretion' (ibid., 845). But the same would be true, i.e. there would be no discretion, if the proposition contained in Raz's rule (where there is no uniquely correct solution courts ought to refuse to render judgment) were the answer to the unsettled question of constitutional law just posed. Of course, now Raz could say there is discretion as to this constitutional issue. But the ground for the argument of discretion has been much diminished.

This progress with the problem is produced by insistence upon an answer to the question of what it is that a judge has a duty to decide by in a hard case (not, we say again, what specific answer he is to give to the case, but what standard, what branch of human thought he is to decide by). The following dialogue attempts to illustrate the necessity of continually insisting upon an answer to that question.

V.4

Judge: Good-day to you both. I think we have not met since my elevation. I have a case to decide, and there is no clear law on it. Its importance and difficulty is such that I want to be sure to decide it in the correct manner. What is my duty here? I would be grateful for your help, and I'm afraid I must trouble the two of you for precise answers to this constitutional question which unfortunately is not settled by any statute or precedent. Its time for decision has come; it must therefore be settled now with the precision always required of the answer to any legal question.

Robert: I would say that since your case is not governed by clear law you have discretion; that is, you must decide it according to what you think is right.

Judge: What sort of right is that? I must tell you that my hobby is Roman Law, and it so happens that Roman Law has an answer to the case. You don't mean *any* sort of right do you? I mean, I can't decide the case by what I think is right according to Roman Law, can I?

Robert: No. Certainly not. You could only decide that if you thought the Roman Law answer was the right one. But you are free to decide whether it is or isn't.

Judge: But decide that by reference to what? Islamic law? You see, I must know what sort of right it is according to which I am to decide.

Robert: Well, I would say you must decide what you think is right all things considered.

Judge: Yes. I'm familiar with that notion. I think I understand now what it is I am to decide.

Harold: I don't think you do. I shall follow Robert and by 'right' mean 'right all things considered'. What Robert says you are to decide is what you think is right. If he meant by that simply that *you* were to decide what is right I would have no quarrel. Of course *you* must decide it. But what is right is a standard independent of what you think. And this Robert wants to deny.

Robert: Yes. The judge is to decide what he thinks is right.

Judge: I have followed your discussion with interest and I now see some difficulty with Robert's view. You see, I have already spent a lot of time thinking about the case and have reached an impasse. The arguments for the plaintiff and the defendant seem to me to be of equal weight. My difficulty is to know what my duty requires of me now.

Harold: I should now state my view. It is that your duty in a hard case is to decide it according to what is right. To get beyond your impasse you will have to think a little harder about what is right. Of course, you may fail.

Robert: And my view too is that you will have to think a little harder about the problem.

Judge: I think I understand what Harold is saying, but I am not sure about Robert, who seems to have changed his formulation of my duty. Now he says I am to think about the problem. Well, Robert, *what* am I to think about the problem? Do you now agree with Harold?

Robert: No, I didn't mean to change the formulation of your duty. I meant that you are to think what you were

thinking before, but a little harder and a little longer.
You are to think about . . . what you think is right.

Judge: My dear fellow, I have already told you that I think the
arguments are evenly balanced. I know that is what I
think. I don't need to think any more about what I
think to know that. I don't think that thinking about
what I think will get me anywhere. I therefore cannot
see how that can be my duty.

Robert: Why do you take it that I am saying that what you think
is the subject of your reflections?

Harold: Well, what is, then? Either the subject is what the
Judge thinks is right or it is what is right. There is no
third possibility.

Robert: Why should there be a subject? The judge must reflect
on how to exercise his discretion.

Harold: Another reformulation! But I don't object at all to the
word 'discretion'. Reflecting on how to exercise his
discretion can mean nothing more than reflecting on
how to decide the case, and that leads inevitably to the
problems we have been discussing; 'how to decide the
case' means 'what is the right solution of the case'.
Judge, you are at an impasse you say. How fortunate it
is that I see my friend Socrates approaching, who will
be only too happy to discuss your case with you at
length and may offer new insights.

'What he thinks is right' is, if intended in a strong sense,
vacuous: the qualification 'what he thinks' is meaningless. A judge
with no opinion on which way to decide a case (or an incomplete
opinion) can look nowhere else for guidance as to how to proceed
than to his duty. But a duty to decide what he thinks is right is, if
taken literally, vacuous, for it contains no guidance on the matter
of what sort of opinion he should have or seek to develop. And
that is what he requires if he is to proceed.

V.5

Obviously the lawyers in a hard case are not to argue the case
according to what the judge thinks is right. For one thing, they

speak first. For another, they would have no need to persuade him of anything. Nor is each arguing about what he himself thinks is right. Why should the judge be interested in that?; and it would have the unacceptable consequence that opposing counsel would be arguing about different things. The only way to make sense of their arguing is to suppose that they are arguing about what is right. And if this argument is not to be irrelevant then the judge's concern too must be with the same thing.

V.6

If a judge's duty in a hard case is to decide by what is right then he has no discretion in any significant sense (he still has discretion in the other senses mentioned – for instance, the *power* to make a wrong decision). This is clear as long as there is only one right answer in his case. But what if there were in truth more than one right answer to the case? Would there then be discretion? What if 'judgment for the plaintiff' were a right answer and 'judgment for the defendant' also? We might ask how this could be.

If the reasons on the plaintiff's side were equal in weight to those on the defendant's side there would be two equally good answers, though not necessarily two right answers. We might think this an unlikely possibility, for in any hard case the competing arguments are likely to be complex and profound, and thus the likelihood that they are equally balanced is slight.

Perhaps, to follow a different line, they are incommensurable. Perhaps the reasons supporting the plaintiff (or some of them) are incommensurable with those (or some of them) supporting the defendant (see Mackie, 1977, 3). In this case there would be at least two answers and their incommensurability would mean that there was no way of choosing between them (of saying that one was the right answer). In the end (XI.1–XI.7) we argue against the possibility of incommensurability.

For present purposes it is sufficient to say that both possibilities, equal balance and incommensurability, can be ignored, for even in the case of two best, right or incommensurable answers a judge has no discretion. How could he decide such a case? He could not decide *which* answer is right because either both are or neither is. So how could he choose between them? We cannot say that he is

114

to choose what he thinks is right, for we have already ruled that out, and the reasons for so doing still hold. So what are we to say his duty is? It seems that in this case there can be no reason at all for a decision on the merits of the case, and if we are to insist that a judge's duty requires such a decision then it will have to be a decision on the basis of whim or chance. If it is on the basis of chance there is still no discretion. Only gods can choose or direct chance. And if it is on the basis of whim the same is true, for our judge must decide the first thing that comes into his head, or the second, or the thirteenth, and there is no discretion about that (were he to try to choose between these first, second and thirteenth things, he would no longer be deciding by whim, and all the problems about right decision would arise again). Now, if this case of equal or incommensurate balance did arise, most judges, I think, would find it unacceptable to suppose that their duty was to decide by chance or whim, and would judge it best to make no decision in the case except to reject the plaintiff's claim. This would be no exercise of discretion. Such a judge would be judging that this was the right decision in the case. Anyone who wishes to argue that there is discretion about this faces all the problems we have been discussing.

V.7

As Socrates approached (V.4), our judge was in a predicament which in all important respects is similar to one which has fascinated philosophers at least since Plato. Our judge seemed locked into his case by his judgment as to the respective weights of the competing reasons in the case. There was no obvious way out. We have seen that no *a priori* principle can give the weight of reasons for action (IV.3 and IV.4), and that it is thus necessary to look to the passions for that weight, only they being able to account for the required indefinite graduation. Thus, if our judge is locked in, his passions are his gaolers. But then, where is freedom? That is a question (Kant's fundamental question). Unlike discretion, freedom raises a real philosophical issue.

Our judge's predicament is a variation of the problem of akrasia, or weakness of the will, which can be stated thus: if I judge that such and such an action is required of me is it possible

115

(logically, biologically, psychologically . . .) for me not to do it? Is moral backsliding possible? Am I free to be wicked?

Once moral judgment is defined as conclusive or final judgment, judgment all things considered (II.9), and all the passions are thereby admitted to that judgment, it seems clear: akrasia or weakness of the will is not possible, for there is nothing left to be wicked by or for. On the other hand, if another definition of 'moral' obtains whereby the word marks an area of thought or passionate susceptibility which is in some way limited, then, by definition, there is something left outside the moral realm capable of activating what would now be defined as weakness. But there is no semblance of a philosophical problem here, either. So, where is the puzzle? What is it that lies at the bottom of this question of akrasia which has so interested philosophers for so long?

Two things, it seems, are at the bottom of both akrasia and the problem of our judge at an impasse. One is freedom. And the second is the one mentioned at the beginning of this chapter, objectivity: if I am locked in by my passions and you by yours, as well as there seeming to be no moral freedom, is not moral thought hopelessly subjective?

There is an explanation to be advanced which at once gives an account of both freedom and objectivity. The freer I am (it will be claimed) the more objective is my judgment: freedom is a form of discipline.

V.8

One explanation, one solution of this philosophical predicament, is Kant's:

> These fundamental principles [of morality] must originate entirely *a priori* and thereby obtain their commanding authority; they can expect nothing from the inclination of men but everything from the supremacy of the law and due respect for it . . . in morals the proper and inestimable worth of an absolutely good will consists precisely in the freedom of the principle of action from all influences from contingent grounds which only experience can furnish. (*Foundations of the Metaphysics of Morals*, 425, trans. Beck)

Moral principles are objective (available to all) because they are *a priori*; and man is free because he is not the prisoner of his contingent passions. But this explanation will not do in practical philosophy for it is impractical. It is not able to account for the indefinite graduation that characterizes moral judgment (IV.3 and IV.4): at best it can support an enterprise such as Nagel's to establish the mere existence of (moral) reasons for action, or Kant's to establish the mere existence of moral maxims, an enterprise which remains purely theoretical because it is the indefinitely graduated weight of reasons not their existence which has practical significance (IV.3 and IV.4).

Hume said: reason is the slave of the passions, thereby constructing the problem of freedom which so troubled Kant. But Hume distinguished between calm passions and violent passions. Passions certainly have the quality of indefinite graduation sufficient to constitute the practical element in moral judgment. But in the possibility of movement from violent passions to calm passions (from a state of violent judgment to a state of calm judgment) there is also freedom; and, further, there is in this freedom the possibility of a real objectivity.

Hume's doctrine of the calm passions is not very clearly or consistently worked out. But it is possible to identify four types of calm passions (four ways in which passions can be calm): (i) when they accord with the real qualities of their objects independent of a special consideration of these objects, (ii) when they accord with these qualities as the result of the agent forming an adequate conception of them, (iii) when they accord with the real qualities of their objects as constitutive of or a means to happiness without the agent considering them as such, (iv) when they accord with these qualities as constitutive of or a means to happiness as a result of the agent forming an adequate idea of them in this relation (see Kydd, 1946, 149, from which this classification is taken). Now, at the basis of all these passions are their objects, and what makes them calm (or calmer) is a clear (or clearer) conception of the object. Suppose I am angry at an injury you have done to someone for whom I am responsible. I have a hard case of what to do. I have reasons (let us say) to take steps to rectify the injury; and doubtless I have all sorts of reasons against it (perhaps the injury was not entirely unjustified, perhaps it is better in the interests of peace to let the injury lie). Now, if I remain angry at the injury the reasons to rectify it are likely to outweigh those against. In this situation I would be the prisoner of my anger. But am I not free to escape?; free to control myself in order to take a calmer view of the facts? And if I do, is that view not also more objective? There is a deep mistake in much moral philosophy about the nature of freedom. Moral freedom (discretion, in the thought of the legal positivists) is not freedom to choose this solution or that to a given practical problem; rather it is a freedom that the agent has about himself. Fundamentally it is because Robert in the dialogue in V.4 has a mistaken conception of freedom that he is unable to make sense of a judge's duty in a hard case.

V.9

The mistaken conception of moral freedom pictures the individual will as leaping uncontrolledly in a void. Its adherents divide into a Kantian and a surrealist wing (see Iris Murdoch, 1970, 35). For the surrealists the will leaps from one mocking joke to another; for the Kantians it is from one universal norm (maxim) to another. This appears heroic, and is perhaps attractive for that quality. But when you think that to account for the complex graduation in an ordinary moral problem (our promise/Samaritan case: IV.3) an indefinitely large number of universal norms is needed and therefore correspondingly an indefinitely large number of leaps of the will, heroic freedom begins to look tedious and implausible. Freedom is more gradual, less heroic than the Kantians or the surrealists allow. It is the process of seeing the world clearly (seeing the objects of the passions); the infinitely difficult attempt to penetrate the tissue of dreams, projects, consoling fantasies, rules and violent passions which envelop us:

> Freedom is not the sudden jumping of the isolated will in and out of an impersonal logical complex [this or that universalised principle serving as the major premise of a syllogism such as A in IV.2], it is a function of the progressive attempt to see a particular object clearly. . . . When M is just and loving she sees D as she really is. One is often compelled almost automatically by what one *can* see. If we ignore the prior work of attention and notice only the emptiness of the moment of choice we are

118

likely to identify freedom with the outward movement since there is nothing else to identify it with. But if we consider what the work of attention is like, how continuously it goes on, and how imperceptibly it builds up structures of value round about us, we shall not be surprised that at crucial moments of choice most of the business of choosing is already over. This does not imply that we are not free, certainly not. But it implies that the exercise of our freedom is a small piecemeal business which goes on all the time and not a grandiose leaping about unimpeded at important moments. The moral life, on this view, is something that goes on continually, not something that is switched off in between the occurrence of explicit moral choices. (Murdoch, 1970, 23, 37)

Let us say I use you as a means to an end, where the end is a project of mine. Which of us is free? You are my tool, certainly. But I am the prisoner of my project. I am not free, for my project blocks me from seeing you as you really are, as beautiful, as an independent (particular) being (there is irony here: when I fail to see you as independent and free I myself am dependent and unfree). Or let us say I buy a forest for newsprint. Can I see its beauty? Not if I see it as newsprint. I am then also a prisoner, cut off from a part of the beauty of the world, that is to say from part of the world as it really is. Or let us say I am angry or jealous or smarting from a personal hurt; or, recalling Kant's distinction between Affekten and Leidenschaften (*Metaphysics of Morals*, 408–9), possessed of a deeper, more vicious hatred. When I look at you to try to judge about you what do I see? How am I free? My violent passion holds my attention inward. It is not free and ranging about the world where you are as you really are. A striking image of this state in a striking account of its tragic moral failure is Achilles sitting in his tent on the plains of Troy cherishing his wrath (*Iliad*, bk 2, 769).

And perhaps the most corrupting thing of all, the most constricting of my attention to the world as it really is, is a 'smart set of concepts' (Murdoch, 1970, 33). The respectable corruption of lawyers is in point here: those who possess monopoly rights to a language so easily used to generate the delights of power and esteem may become the pimps, or themselves the libertines, of these delights. Such indulgence is not to be confused with

119

freedom. Nor, though pimps and libertines often pretend to be worldly-wise, is it to be thought a relationship with the real world, for my freedom to project my attention out to the world as it really is is in correspondence with reality.

Another way of defining this freedom is to say it is my capacity to control those parts of me which restrict my attention to the world. Plato's metaphor of the parts of the soul is obviously in order here. And also the theological idea where freedom is not freedom to choose between this or that, but freedom to turn towards God.

V.10

The capacity to undertake calm as opposed to violent passions is beyond doubt the principal judicial virtue. The best judge is the freest.

V.11

The world as it really is is the object of attention and the point of freedom. If there is no world-as-it-really-is but just my solipsistic consciousness about which no question of untruth arises, no question of distortion by fantasy or violent passion, there is no point to freedom, for there is nothing to be free about. On the other hand if there is a world-as-it-really-is, there is freedom and at the same time an objective connection between your consciousness and mine. Contrary to the idea that the legal positivists have about discretion, freedom and objectivity are mutually required.

It is clear that those philosophers who have worried about objectivity in moral thought have been concerned primarily with this problem of establishing a connection between your moral judgment and mine. Emotivism has been found wanting as a moral theory precisely because it pictures moral agents as huffing and puffing their emotions independently of each other. However, if you manage to pull me through my hatred or fantasy away from a certain moral judgment will I not say something like?: Oh, you were right, I now see what really happened (she was not doing this out of spite, he is not the wicked person I thought, she really was hurt by what I did, I now see what the consequences really are . . .). What more in point of objective connection could be required? The weight of the reasons which activate your and my judgments is objective in that it is open to objective influence in the way stated. There could be no other sort of objectivity of weight: for as we have seen in chapter IV it makes no sense to suppose that there is a certain weight attaching to a certain reason which is in any sense communicable. And at the bottom of all this there are particulars, the most clearly objective things of all, making for the most purely objective determination of the will (I.10). There are many ways open to you to display the (objective) particularity of the world to me and thereby affect my judgment (you would be Eros). Of course, it is distinctly possible that you will not persuade me to change my mind. No objective reference, however, creates the certainty of agreement, merely the possibility.

V.12

If it be accepted that the whole world is beautiful from the stars in the sky down to the merest speck of dust then the correspondence between the correlative relationships freedom/reality and love/beauty is very close. In fact the argument of the last three sections could easily be translated into the terms love and beauty; and correspondingly the argument of I.2 could be an argument about freedom and reality.

That we don't see the whole world as beautiful (correlative: that we are very selective lovers) is evidence of our lack of freedom (correlative: our inability to cope with much reality).

V.13

The problem of akrasia can now be dissolved, and with it our earlier interpretation (E) of a judge's sentence (II.4).

If the definition of moral judgment is a conclusive judgment, i.e. a judgment dependent upon all the passions, weakness of the will is not possible because by definition there is no further passion by which to act. Any action contrary to the original judgment by definition means a change of that judgment; and such a change of mind is obviously a trivial possibility, not the ground of a philosophical puzzle.

If a more limited definition of moral judgment is taken then weakness of the will is clearly possible, but trivialiy so. Obviously whatever kind of passion is excluded from the definition of moral judgment is still available to determine judgment against the (limited) moral judgment. If this happened in a particular case our definitions would require us to call it moral weakness, but we would not be entitled as philosophers to be puzzled by it.

The word 'passion' in this argument can be interpreted as wide as you like, even to include susceptibility to a Kantian categorical imperative; but the argument still holds.

This all seems very obvious. Why has the problem of weakness of the will puzzled so many philosophers? The answer is: moral freedom has puzzled them.

Where there is no moral freedom exercised, as where the will is subjectively determined (III.13), there is no question of knowingly doing wrong, for there is no question of knowing, no question of reality – the exercise of the will is simply the working out of a programme.

VI

REASONS AND RULES

VI.1

Suppose there is a rule: promises ought to be kept. This means (assuming it is a public rule) that it is the fact that there are at least two people with internal attitudes to the norm 'promises ought to be kept'. And suppose that I have to make a decision in a certain case whether to keep a promise. If I make a rule decision I, also, display an internal attitude to the rule in question. In our analysis this means that I assume the bindingness of the norm 'promises ought to be kept'. Now, it may also be the case that as well as the rule there is a reason to keep promises. But my decision is a rule decision not a hard decision, thus it is not a decision based upon this reason or any reason. The norm is assumed to be binding, not judged to be binding. Of course, it is not necessary that I make a rule decision, that is, that I make my decision on the basis of this assumption, for I may remain or become external to the rule and make a hard decision. Such a decision would be based upon reasons, and there may be any number on either side of the case. There would be the reason to keep promises, and there would also be the fact (viewed externally) that there is the rule. This latter is an *additional* reason to keep promises because it introduces into my case over and above what can be said for promise-keeping in itself what can be said against rule-breaking (expectations disturbed, uncertainty sown, difficulties raised, etc.). To rely on this reason is *not* to make a rule decision as we have defined it – the distinction is between inferences (C) and (D) in IV.2. For the purposes of our example, (C) becomes:

(C)(1) There is a rule that promises ought to be kept.
　　(2) That there is a rule . . . is a reason to keep promises.

And (D), the rule decision, becomes:

(D)(1) Promises ought to be kept.
　　(2) This is a promise.
　　(3) ∴ This ought to be kept.

Reasons are for action. Taking or rejecting a rule is an action (at least, some parts of that process are actions); and thus there may be reasons for or against rules. Thus (C2) might be: that there is a rule in the community that promises ought to be kept is a reason to take the rule. Of course, this fact is rather vague and would be better broken up into more brute facts such as the expectations raised, the certainty achieved by the rule, and so on. Such reasons since they are about a rule and put it in issue one way or another are external to the rule.

The distinction between what we shall call ordinary reasons and reasons for rules is very like that at the basis of the old common lawyers' terms, *malum in se* and *malum prohibitum* (wrong in itself and wrong because prohibited), and raises similar conceptual difficulties. Indeed, our very example may be thought a bad one; for it is a fairly common view that there is nothing to be said for promise-keeping in itself; that any moral constraint comes solely from the fact that there is a social rule on the matter. I don't believe this; but all I wish to say to those who do is to invite them to choose their own example and make the same distinction. Only thorough-going moral sceptics will be unable to do this.

External reasons for rules must not be confused with the reasons that might be said to obtain in internal rule decisions. Joseph Raz's theory of rules (in *Practical Reason and Norms*) fails largely due to this confusion (VI.8). Reasons in internal rule decisions are actually only reasons in a weak sense. If I make an internal rule decision and you ask me what my reason was, I might well say my reason for decision was the rule. But I could only mean this in a weak sense where the reason is subject to the assumptions which constitute the rule; a reminder of the rule and nothing more. If I mean reason in a strong sense, that is reason whose weight I am prepared actually to consider, my statement is not an internal rule statement, for I am not making the requisite assumptions (it takes the form of inference (C)). A further point is that if I make an internal decision my will is determined subjectively (III.13); whereas true reasons are objective (V.11).

VI.2

When I confront a community's custom or practice (a rule, no doubt, for at least some), I have reasons of at least some weight to do as is done. But there are two distinct types of reasons here. The reason that I have merely to follow the norm implicit in the practice is quite different from the reason to make it a rule; a rule is a quite different thing from merely following a norm. I might decide on the balance of reasons to follow the norm; in which case I will do as they do (not yet as we do). But if I decide to take the norm as a rule I do more than this, for I commit myself to it, and this means become internal to it, thereby making it a rule. 'As *we* do' is now appropriate. My future decisions will until I abandon it assume the norm's bindingness rather than each time recalculate its claims. The distinction can be seen clearly when I visit a community (let us say Rome). I will have good reasons to follow Roman norms (the ordinary benefits of co-operation, not giving offence, keeping out of gaol, and so on). But my following their norms is not following them as rules, for I do not assume their bindingness; indeed I don't regard the norms as binding at all, but only as things the fact of whose existence constitutes the aforementioned reasons (the reasons are in their way binding). Of course, I might adopt them as rules, but that is a different matter, and generally, if I am only visiting Rome, there would be no reason to go that far.

Typically of a number of modern fairness-based political and legal theories, Ronald Dworkin, in *Taking Rights Seriously*, fails to draw this distinction. He sees well enough that reasons can justify following a norm, but he fails to see that a further step is required to constitute a rule. When Dworkin's moral man considers a social norm (let us take one of his examples, a norm requiring the removal of one's hat in church) he considers it from the outside. It is like visiting Rome. There is no sense of his submitting to it. And the norm is accepted only in so far as it is reasonable to accept it; questions of fairness are considered, questions of people's reliance on others, questions of the harm done by broken expectations, and so on, with no limit to the questions. I shall quote a little from *Taking Rights Seriously*.

> It is true that normative judgments often assume a social practice as an essential part of the case for that judgment; this is the hallmark, as I said, of conventional morality. But the social rule theory misconceives the connection. It believes that the social practice constitutes a rule which the normative judgment accepts; in fact the social practice helps to justify a rule which the normative judgment states. The fact that a practice of removing hats in church exists justifies asserting a normative rule to that effect – not because the practice constitutes a rule which the normative judgment describes and endorses, but because the practice creates ways of giving offense and gives rise to expectations of the sort that are good grounds for asserting a duty to take off one's hat in church or for asserting a normative rule that one must. . . .

> If a community has a particular practice, moreover, like the no-hat-in-church practice, then it will be likely, rather than surprising, that members will assert different normative rules, each allegedly justified by that practice. They will disagree about whether babies must wear bonnets because they will differ about whether, *all things considered*, the fact of the practice justifies asserting that duty. Some may think that it does because they think that the practice as a whole establishes a form of insult or disrespect that can be committed vicariously by an infant's parents. Others may disagree, for a variety of reasons. (1977, 57–8; my emphasis)

To summarize, whether we are concerned with a clear case or a difficult case (such as the baby's bonnet), the difference between an internal view of a rule and the unrestricted view of a social norm is this: An internal point of view sees a class of practical decisions as being governed by a norm whose bindingness is assumed, or not considered. It is internal to the norm. *All things are not considered*. The unrestricted view on the other hand proposes to assume nothing. Dworkin's own words are: *all things considered*. Every moral decision to which a norm is relevant places that norm in issue and requires an appraisal of it. Of course, the powerful principles which support norms ('the practice creates ways of giving offence and gives rise to expectations of the sort that are good grounds for asserting a duty [to follow the practice]') will be part of that appraisal. But these principles will be weighed in the balance not assumed to hold. The whole issue, literally the whole issue, is open to rational argument. Dworkin's moral hero is indeed a hero. Perhaps, however, he is not a saint. And, more mundanely, perhaps he is a creature of Dworkin's imagination.

We do adopt rules. Moral questions occur a thousand times a day; whether to stop at a stop sign, whether to keep an appointment, whether to say hallo. Now, these are not trivial questions, although we treat them as trivial for we answer them under rules. If we treated them with full seriousness (each is if you really think about it a profound question) we wouldn't get very far in the world. We would never get past the front door; business would be impossible; we literally couldn't carry on. So, for the sake of business there are reasons to exclude questions, i.e. reasons for rules. There are reasons to go further than Dworkin's (rational) hero is allowed.

Are they reasons for my own rules or are they reasons to adopt the rules of one or other of my communities? The moral hero might accept the necessity of rules, but still treat social practices externally, relying on his own legislation, as it were (making private rules, constituted by the first assumption in rules, but not the second). Whose legislation should I submit to: my own or my community's?

There is some plausibility in the heroic stand in single moral cases, for the thrust of the individual, isolated, responsible conscience is strong. But moral legislation raises a case of strategy. Here the question is what commitment to project into the future to cover a limitless number of cases. The commitment must be to the continuing moral validity and appropriateness of a rule; one whose reconsideration in special cases cannot be guaranteed, for when something becomes a rule for us we cannot be sure that we will only apply it in appropriate cases. It will in time become more or less habitual and we will have cut off questions which might indicate the rule's inappropriateness in a particular case. Reconsideration cannot be guaranteed because we have no foolproof moral filing systems. All of this follows as a practical consequence of the character of rules. The moral hero's dilemma is that he wants to decide moral issues as they come up rightly and fully, but, opposed to this aspiration, there are reasons for rules. Now, whether they are to be his community's rules or his own makes little difference so far as his heroic aspirations are concerned, for in either case rule pre-empts heroic judgment. What could be the point then, of his insisting on legislating for himself? Confronting a community norm the thrust of his heroic conscience against submission is by this consideration much diminished; and if the hero is to have rules at all they might as well be his community's as his own. Confronting a community norm, therefore, given that he must have rules, he is no less a hero by his submitting to it rather than standing outside and legislating for himself. Of course, if he regarded the norm as a particularly bad one he would not submit; I mean there is no objection to submission itself.

VI.3

There are many reasons for the strategic decision of taking a rule. Rules, and pre-eminently legal rules, achieve a degree of certainty in the public realm which suits the rational arrangement of affairs; they minimize conflict because they provide a settlement which all are to look to. In this regard a rule does more than could be done by the simple establishment of a norm to be regarded externally. No community could be held together by a set of external attitudes to a norm, for there would not be excluded uncertainty and dispute about its bindingness (all citizens since they are external would be re-judging the bindingness of the norm afresh each time it arose). A rule excludes this, for the matter of bindingness is assumed by all who accept the rule. Thus the achievement of certainty and the minimization of conflict (in short, the establishment of community) can be said to state reasons for rules. On a personal level I might accept the rule of my community, or of somebody, thereby constituting them authorities, because I can see that they are wiser or more knowledgeable than I am, or have (had) more time to work practical problems out. Or I might make a rule for myself never to drive after a certain amount of beer (I require a rule rather than single judgments at closing-time, for there is reason to doubt my judgment at that time). These are reasons for personal rules.

There is, however, a major difficulty with reasons for rules.

VI.4

Let us say that a moral life is a search for moral truth. When we decide by rule we abdicate that search. The sense of abdication is clear enough. If I decide by rule I decide without a consideration of the whole issue, for I assume an answer to the question of the bindingness of the rule. Now, in the case of some games this usually won't matter very much (though it is easy to think of cases where it might matter – an illegal game, for instance). But in law there often seems to be a considerable moral difficulty with the abdication entailed by rule decision. Judges, sheriffs, executioners take on a responsibility, discharged sometimes to the point of taking life, often liberty, and if they decide by rule they decide these matters without considering the whole moral question which each raises. Can it ever be justified to go so far as to take life, or property, even, on the basis of a moral assumption?

The more basic formulation of this question is: Can there ever be a good moral justification for adopting a strategy whereby decisions of importance go by assumption?

One view (G. J. Warnock's) is that abdication of this sort cannot be justified morally:

> [S]hould it occur? . . . It is tempting, and I think ultimately right, to say that it should not occur. For to "follow a rule", as we have seen, is, at any rate in this sort of case, as it were to turn away from consideration of the particular merits of particular cases; and it does not appear that in the sphere in which moral judgment is exercised, there is any particular consideration to justify doing so . . . if the exercise of moral judgment, the holding of moral views, is to be the reasonable affair which it is surely ideally supposed to be, there should not occur any simplifying, undiscriminating, rather childlike acceptance of rules; for there is nothing to make such acceptance really reasonable. Rather, there should occur the constantly repeated attempt to achieve the best judgment on the full concrete merits

of each individual case. One should thus consider what there is reason to do or not do, or what view there is reason to take, rather than, less discriminatingly, what is required by some rule, or permitted or ruled out by some rule. (1971, 66–7)

But love is something which occurs in 'the sphere in which moral judgment is exercised'. And is it not the case that I can love my various communities? – most obviously my family and my country. And if I do, is not love a reason for submission to their rules?

There are two points to be made here. First, if I love you I respect your works; and its rules are amongst a community's works. And second, and more deeply, its rules are at the very heart of a community's being. Warnock contrasts conditional and unconditional reasons for rules (1971): he has no difficulty accepting that there are conditional reasons for rules (if I want community, there are reasons for rules) – it is unconditional (or moral) reasons which give him the difficulty. But love is unconditional. It certainly does not propose a conditional reason – I mean it is not a means to an end: if I am your friend only for a purpose my friendship is corrupt.

Aristotle regarded friendship as an aspect of political obligation. An important part of his treatment of friendship (in *Nic. Ethics*, Books 8 and 9) is in fact devoted to an analysis of forms of state as cases of friendship:

Each of these forms of government exhibits a form of friendship coextensive with what is just under that government. The friendship of a king for his subjects expresses itself in benevolence. . . . The affection between husband and wife is the same as that which exists between the government and the governed in an aristocracy. . . . As for the friendliness between brothers, it is like what we get between the members of some club or association. You have equality of rank and age. . . . This is the kind of sympathy one finds between the citizens of a timocracy. For the timocratic ideal is that all should be equal as well as good. Hence political power is shared among the citizens equally and in turn, and the result is that the friendship between them is friendship upon terms of equality. But in the perverted constitutions friendship like justice goes but a little way, and least in the worst; for under a tyranny there can be little or no kindness between ruler and ruled. They have nothing in common so there can be no friendliness between them, just as there can be no justice. The relations between them are those of the skilled workman to his tool . . . there can be no friendship or justice in our dealings with inanimate things. . . . There can be no friendship of a master for a slave as such, though there may be for him as a man . . . friendship is possible with any man so far as he is a human being. We cannot maintain that there is much room for friendship and justice between rulers and ruled under a tyranny. They are most adequately realized in democracies. (*Nic. Ethics*, Penguin edition, 248–9)

Thus, according to Aristotle, friendship as well as justice controls the relationship and mutual obligations of governors and citizens.

Aristotle recognized that the obligation of friendship was a special obligation that exceeded, or perhaps we might say transcended, the obligation of justice.

There are therefore different ways in which those who make such friendships may violate their obligation to one another, and the wrong thus done is aggravated in proportion to the closeness of the tie uniting them. Thus it is worse to swindle a comrade than a fellow citizen, to refuse to go to the aid of a brother than to the aid of a stranger, to assault your father than someone else. And with an intensification of friendship there naturally goes an increase in the sense of obligation between the friends, because the same persons are involved and their obligations of friendship are co-extensive with their obligation in justice. (*Nic. Ethics*, Penguin edition, 244)

The last sentence in the translation is a little unclear, but it is not difficult to see the sense. Aristotle does not say that justice is sufficient to support my whole obligation in these matters, but that where there is friendship the requirements of justice are augmented. Friendship carries the moral problem of obligation a great deal further than justice by itself would have gone, 'Worse', says Aristotle, 'to refuse to help a friend than a stranger', and worse therefore to refuse one's country and its laws. On this view some injustice to a stranger must be tolerated. If there is a moral choice to be made between friend and stranger my friend is to be preferred, for 'worse to refuse to help a friend than a stranger'; the

131

interests and just requirements of the stranger are to the extent of my friendship excluded or at least diminished.

This exclusion makes a correspondence between what I do out of love and what I do under rules. Where my loves and my rules are merged, as they are in the case of my obligation to my various communities, we can merge the respective justifications, and if love is a justification for action or judgment it can be taken as a justification for action and judgment under rules. In particular it is a justification for the moral abdication characteristic of rule judgment.

We are, it seems, inveterate lovers. Our loving attachments are numerous and various, and though in ordinary, everyday moments the erotic power of these attachments may be only faintly perceived it is liable to be more than faint in times of crisis. Then, when moral problems present themselves clearly and acutely, love will often seem the best reason that we have for staying in a community or other attachment and thus preserving its rules (in its own way such a reason is an internal one).

We have said that the taking of a rule is an action; and on this basis that there are reasons for rules. But strictly the submission involved in accepting a rule is not an action. Thus I cannot have a reason *to accept a rule*. Similarly, I cannot have (in a strict sense) a reason to love. In each case the most that I can do (and have reasons for) is perform various prerequisite actions. In the matter of love I can act so as to make myself available. I can direct my attention; but in the end, as the mythology has it, I can but await eros. In the taking of rules I can familiarize myself with the norm to which I wish to submit; I can make external single-case decisions to apply the norm, but the actual submission, actually becoming internal, where I assume the bindingness of the norm for a class of cases, is beyond my rational contrivance. I need to programme myself (III.13). The assumption in rules is an assumption of *bindingness* – not a provisional assumption such as we often make, suspecting that for some reason or another the point will turn out not to be critical for action; but an assumption which really controls action. The acquisition of this programme of action is not at all unlike acquiring a habit: often this will be the best way of describing it (I.10): the acquisition of a habit is not an action that I can actually perform.

Thus the strategic reasons for rules of which we have spoken and shall continue to speak are really reasons for the various actions prerequisite to rules. The whole process of becoming internal can be referred to as an act, like the act of falling in love.

When confronted by the object of our love do we step back to consider? (as Kant did, confronting Christ: 'even the Holy one of the Gospel must be compared with our ideal of moral perfection before he is recognised as such' (*Ground Work*, 408). If we do how could love survive, for we would have moved from the real to the ideal? The quickened reality (the particularity) of the loved one is annihilated. A rational assessment of love is destruction, for it is destruction of eros. And the problem for the lover of his community is the same. When faced by the laws of his community (as judge, executioner, soldier, citizen or whatever) does he accept them (assume their bindingness) or step back to consider the matter?

VI.5

Explanation of practical thought in terms of reasons for action is something that a number of philosophers have attempted. None, however, has attended so closely to the problem of rules in this regard as Joseph Raz has in his *Practical Reason and Norms*. It will be necessary to examine in detail his attempt to explain rules as reasons.

Rules we have said (VI.1) are reasons for action and judgment only in a weak sense for they are reasons insulated from other reasons by certain assumptions. Raz accounts for this insulation by proposing that rules should be explained by the idea of their being, as well as first-order reasons for action, also second-order exclusionary reasons whose function is to make the insulation by excluding other reasons.

The idea of exclusionary reason is introduced by a consideration of the case of a tired person (Ann), who is forced by her tiredness to reject an offer of a certain investment. Her tiredness makes her unable effectively to consider the reasons for and against the investment; Raz says that her tiredness is a reason to exclude the ordinary reasons from her decision. This is not a reason which outweighs these ordinary reasons, for Ann freely admits that the balance of reasons might be in favour of the investment; they are excluded, not outweighed. Much of Raz's book develops this idea in detail, through various other examples, to the major conclusion that rules (norms, as he calls them) are to be explained as both (ordinary) first-order and exclusionary reasons for action. The distinction between first and second orders is important. Tiredness is also a first-order reason not to weigh reasons just as it is a first-order reason not to go to the theatre. But in Raz's argument tiredness is taken as a second-order reason.

Now, if Ann is too tired to consider the offered investment, is she not also too tired to consider the exclusionary reason? Raz's exclusionary reason is and must be presented as *a* reason amongst other possible supporting and opposing second-order reasons (although there is no contest with first-order reasons, there must be with other second-order reasons). So the judgment of the second-order issue might be very tricky indeed; in which case Ann's tiredness will be a third-order reason to exclude the second-order reasons (including the reason to exclude), which leaves her with her original problem. If this were ordinarily the case, Raz's theory of exclusionary reasons would fail. The theory depends, therefore, on the question of the exclusion of exclusionary reasons.

Let us divide all reasons into two classes relative to Ann's tiredness, excluded reasons and not-excluded reasons. Raz says that Ann has a reason not to act on the balance of reasons (1975, 38). This must mean that she has a reason not to act on a balance of reasons which includes excluded reasons. There is no reason to suppose that all reasons are excluded and thus she is left with a balance of not-excluded reasons on the basis of which she can decide (if tiredness had been simply a first-order reason not to take a decision, that may have been an end of the matter; but Raz's idea is much subtler than that). Let us suppose for the moment that Ann's exclusionary reason is a not-excluded reason (i.e. it does not include itself within its scope) and follow her case through.

On the balance of not-excluded reasons she decides to accept or reject the investment – a non-rule (hard) single case decision. On the following day when she is not tired she might consider whether to adopt a rule on the matter for future cases. The exclusionary reason is now a reason for a rule; it is not now an exclusionary reason in Raz's ordinary sense for nothing is excluded from *this* (strategic) calculation; it is a reason to exclude in the sense that it is a reason to adopt a strategy of exclusion in future cases (i.e. a reason for a rule). Now, let us suppose that Ann considers the reasons for and against the previous night's investment proposal (none are now excluded), the reasons for and against other typical proposals, the other reasons for and against possible rules in the matter, and adopts the following rule: after 10 o'clock at night reject proposals of type *A* and accept type *B*. Now suppose that next night after 10 o'clock another proposal of type *A* is made. What is her position?

She is tired. Her exclusionary reason returns. She has a reason not to act on a balance which includes any excluded reasons. Her rule is now, according to Raz, a first-order reason to reject the proposal which is of type *A*. But is *this* first-order reason an excluded reason? It might be. However, if Ann has devised the rule carefully (not made it too complex, for instance) it won't be. The exclusionary reason of tiredness excludes some reasons and leaves others. Ann therefore has to make her decision on the basis of the not-excluded reasons, including her rule. Suppose the other not-excluded reasons give one answer and the rule another. How would she decide? Raz would say here I think that the rule is now a *second* exclusionary reason. All will be well for Ann if the rule as this second exclusionary reason excludes the remaining, otherwise unexcluded, first-order reasons, for this would leave the rule as the only first-order reason. But does it? That question may be difficult. Tiredness is no reason to prefer the rule to the other not otherwise excluded first-order reasons, for her capacity to weigh not-excluded reasons is *ex hypothesi* not affected by tiredness. Both possible decisions (under these reasons or under the rule) are approximations to truth; the one because it is a decision on only some of the whole balance of reasons, and the other because it is a rule decision and therefore a limited decision too. Perhaps there is reason to prefer the rule. If so the rule excludes the otherwise not-excluded reasons and Ann's decision is clear. But this question of preferring the rule (or as we might put it, this question of the rule as an exclusionary reason) is difficult; and the question itself might be excluded by the first exclusionary reason of tiredness (there is no reason why one exclusionary reason should not exclude a second exclusionary reason – an unimportant amendment to the definition of orders would be required.)

Clearly, sometimes Raz's analysis will survive these difficulties, but is it enough to provide a theory of rules?

Whenever a reason to accept a limitation on my freedom to decide the merits of a practical question, and thus to exclude certain reasons, is of a scope that includes the merits of the reason itself the idea of exclusionary reason breaks down. And exclusionary reasons of wide scope tend to be cases of rules, or at least cases where it would be appropriate to have a rule. We may therefore say that the nature of rules tends (to put the point, for the present, at its least) to be incompatible with the idea of exclusionary reason.

General incapacities like tiredness, drunkenness, illness and lack of time clearly produce exclusionary reasons that may include themselves, as in Ann's case. What about ignorance? My ignorance is a reason for adopting a rule that I accept the directions of a wiser more knowledgeable person (who would thereby be constituted an authority). If I am very ignorant, let us say maximally so, then clearly a second-order reason to exclude reasons about which I am ignorant would include the second-order reason itself. If I have a selective ignorance (say an ignorance about reasons X, Y and Z but not about reasons to exclude reasons, then perhaps the exclusionary reason analysis works. But such a selective ignorance is implausible. My recognition of my ignorance is much more likely to turn on the degree of difficulty attaching to the reasons, and there is no reason at all to think that more difficulty will always attach to reasons X, Y and Z than to reasons to (and not to) exclude them. Further, authority typically claims to govern not only matters X, Y and Z but also its own incidence; in other words, authority typically (let us instance a legal system) claims to govern reasons to (and not to) exclude reasons. The exclusionary reason analysis cannot explain that, for if I have a reason to exclude a reason I must, if I am really to be acting for a reason, *myself* be able to weigh it.

Another way of putting this last point is this: one of the main reasons for the rules of a system of authority such as a legal system is that the rules are a means of settling a common way; of ending questions which might otherwise continue to be disputed to the detriment of community. Raz would say that the rule of recognition of a legal system is a reason to exclude the reasons that would otherwise activate the settled questions. But the settlement is a reason also to end questions about the settlement itself. If, therefore, the rule of recognition is an exclusionary reason it is one that includes itself. This suggests that the principal exclusionary reason in a legal system always includes itself in its scope, and therefore always excludes itself.

VI.6

If an exclusionary reason includes itself within its scope we might say (as we did) that it is excluded and thus out of account in practical thought. On the other hand, we might say on logical grounds similar to those that arise in the case of Xeno's paradox of the Cretan liar (a Cretan says: all Cretans are liars) that the exclusionary reason cannot include itself.If so we are forced to postulate a third-order exclusionary reason that excludes the second-order exclusionary reason and thus reasserts the first-order reason. Of course, that third-order exclusionary reason is itself excluded by a fourth-order exclusionary reason; but that commences an infinite regression.

VI.7

Suppose:

(i) There is a class of cases of a certain practical question. Call the class *A*. There are 100 members *A1* to *A100*. *A* might be a question for decision by a court of law, or a wider moral question, indeed any practical case at all.

(ii) on the basis of all the relevant reasons which you accept (excluding for the moment exclusionary reasons) the right decision of the question is *X* in cases *A1* to *A99* and not-*X* in case *A100*.

(iii) you are required to decide case *A100*.

(iv) *A100* is the first case of *A* which you or anyone else have considered, and

(v) the question is difficult.

Now, (v) gives force to a typical exclusionary reason. If a question is difficult there is a reason to exclude reasons and decide by some simpler standard. Does this reason operate in case *A100*? The force given by (v) to an exclusionary reason is simply that the difficulty of the problem presents a risk of making the wrong decision. Obviously this is of no significance given (iv), for there is as yet nothing to turn to to minimize that risk. Let us then amend (iv):

(iva) You have already decided *X* in cases *A1*, *A2* and *A3*.

Does (v) now operate to give force to a reason in case *A100* to exclude consideration of reasons and decide as you have done in cases *A1*, *A2* and *A3*? The answer is clearly no. For if you do not exclude consideration of reasons you will have at least some chance of getting the right answer in *A100*. If you exclude reasons and follow your previous decisions, then, given stipulation (ii) that not-*X* is the right decision, you *ensure* that you get the wrong answer, and the point of the exclusionary reason is to minimize that risk. The point of the exclusionary reason is not applicable in case *A100* and so the reason is not applicable (alternatively it is defeated). Of course, you might think it is applicable or not defeated. But that on *your own reasons* would be a mistake (the stipulation in (ii) that we are concerned with your own reasons is crucial). You would have confused *A100* with *A1–A99*, where it is applicable. This would be a perfectly ordinary mistake of no interest to the theory of rules, for rule decisions are clearly not simple cases of mistake even in the special (*A100*-type) cases.

What if your community had a rule on the problem?

(ivb) There is a rule in your community that *X* is to be decided in all cases of *A*.

Do you now in the case of *A100* have a reason to exclude your calculations? You are given by (ivb) various reasons to decide *X* (you might be put in gaol if you don't, etc.). But that does not require that you exclude other reasons. Does (v) now give force to an exclusionary reason? The answer here, too, is no. The point of the reason which (v) constitutes is much the same as before: it is that the difficulty of the problem is such that you ought to accept your community's judgment in order to minimize the risk of error (it has the experts and the time, etc.). But here too that *ensures* error in case *A100*, and the point of the exclusionary reason is to minimize error. On *your own reasons* you have here too no exclusionary reason (though, as before, you may be mistaken about this). Alternatively, the exclusionary reason is defeated by the chance that you have of getting the right answer to *A100* if you do not exclude. No matter how small this chance is it is still preferable to the ensured wrong answer if you follow the rule.

Perhaps these conclusions appear to be applicable only to a limited class of exclusionary reason: those defined with a view to a right decision. Let us amend (v):

(va) the problem is controversial and, without settlement, provocative of violent confrontation.

This combined with (ivb) suggests an exclusionary reason of a different sort: a reason to follow the community's rule for the sake of harmony and stability. Nothing (yet) of rightness or truth.

I think we have to say that unlike (v) this reason can stand: as a reason it is not nullified or rendered pointless, as (v) was, by the fact that it leads to a wrong answer. However, one would not be justified in acting on this reason alone. There are opposing reasons (not on the first level, of course, for these are excluded or may be, but on the second). Most importantly, there is the reason not to exclude any first-order reason because of the possibility of exclusion leading to a wrong decision (the fewer reasons I exclude the greater the likelihood of my making the right decision in my practical problem). I don't see how one can avoid this counter-reason. The argument is not that the need for harmony and stability is not a reason to exclude reasons, but simply that the partial obliteration of truth is a cost of the exclusion and therefore a reason against it (not necessarily an overriding reason, just a reason, something to be weighed in the balance). So we have a second-order contest between these two reasons, the reason to exclude and the reason not to exclude. How is it resolved?

We are examining case *A100*, and our stipulation is that the right decision in this case is not-*X*. Now, if you recognize that the need for harmony and stability is a second-order exclusionary reason it seems necessary to say that on your reasons this same need is also a first-order reason against the decision not-*X* (for the rule is *X*, and the decision not-*X* would therefore tend to instability and disharmony). Let us now set up the two balances.

139

On the second order there is the reason of harmony and stability for exclusion and the reason of obliteration of truth against it. On the first order there are the various ordinary reasons (whatever they might be) in favour of *X* (call them *ABC*) and the various ordinary reasons against it (*PQR*), and in addition there is the further reason in favour of *X*, the need for harmony and stability. Our stipulation is that the right decision is not-*X*. Thus *ex hypothesi PQR* outweighs [*ABC* plus the need for harmony and stability]. Now, the exclusionary reason analysis will only work if on the second-order balance the need for harmony and stability outweighs the obliteration of truth; and it must do this despite the fact that it (with *ABC*) is outweighed on the first-order balance by *PQR*. It is, of course, perfectly possible that this be so: there is no reason why the reason of harmony and stability should not be on the winning side of the second-order balance and the losing side of the first-order balance. But we are not able to say it is likely. At the very least we have to say sometimes it will be, sometimes not. And it is obvious that this is insufficient to support a theory of rules.

The argument has proceeded on the basis of the reasons which you accept. It would hold just as well if 'which you accept' were deleted from (ii).

It would substantially fail if (ii) were:

(ii) on the basis of all the relevant reasons which you accept and *at the relevant times you have in mind* . . .

But what are reasons generally or for you does not vary with passing states of mind. A drunk, for instance, has a reason (his reason, as he would admit when sober) not to attempt to cross a busy road, though at the time of his cups he may be quite beyond recalling it.

The argument shows that a rule cannot be an exclusionary reason (or an undefeated exclusionary reason) in most cases where it gives the wrong answer to a problem. It is obvious that no theory of rules can be acceptable which tends to be limited to otherwise right decisions. Thus Raz's idea of exclusionary reason can provide no theory of rules.

If reasons to exclude reasons are seen as reasons for rules, that is as reasons for the strategic decision of accepting a rule, rather than as single-case reasons the problems of the last three sections are avoided.

Ann will not be tired on the following day when it will be reasonable for her to plan her future rule strategy; so all reasons can be considered. Most general incapacities which argue for exclusion (tiredness, drunkenness, illness and lack of time) can obviously be avoided in strategic situations; thus there is no problem of the exclusion of these exclusionary reasons. The problem of authority's typically seeking to govern my reasons to exclude as well as my first-order reasons is not applicable in strategic situations, for I am, *ex hypothesi*, out of the game and beyond the jurisdiction of the authority (Joyce was unjustly hanged).

Strategic cases are by definition cases where a class of cases is to be considered. Thus the problem examined in VI.7 with the single case of *A100* is not encountered: the rule is adopted or not adopted in respect of the whole class, *A*.

The adoption of rules can be supported by reasons (strategic) but this does not mean that, when adopted, rules stand in single-case situations as reasons to exclude reasons. In strategic situations reasons for rules can be regarded in a sense as reasons to exclude reasons; for I know that that is what I shall be doing when I assume the bindingness of a rule (assumption excludes reasons) – I can say I have a reason to adopt a rule, which will effect an exclusion of reasons. But a continuing single-case reason to exclude reasons is quite a different matter. Of authority Raz says:

> Authority can secure co-ordination only if the individuals concerned defer to its judgment and do not act on the balance of reasons, but on the authority's instructions . . . it requires that people should regard authoritative utterances as exclusionary reasons. (1975, 64)

The last part of this passage is crucially different from the first. For the point is that I can regard something as a reason (or it can in truth be a reason), but not act on it (there might be a stronger opposing reason). And what authority requires for co-ordination is

141

my act. Of course, providing a reason for an act is often a way of securing that act. But even here the point would still be the act that the reason secures, rather than the reason. The first part of the passage from Raz gets it right: co-ordination requires the act of deference. And when that act occurs, that is when I adopt the rule of authority, it makes no sense to talk of a continuing reason to exclude reasons. This is not only for the reasons already discussed in the previous four sections, but for a simpler reason too: I have no reason to exclude reasons for the simple reason that by my adoption of a rule, by my *act*, I have already excluded them.

VI.9

Both Dworkin and Raz in their differing ways see rules as reasons. But the consequences of submission to rules are real not ideal.

The ideal conception of morality is a very common one. It holds that in principle a flat catalogue of the whole of morality could be prepared; all possible changes in reality could in principle be listed, and their moral consequences calculated and itemized (as reasons for action, or in some other system). But the erotic power generated by a real submission such as to rules, or in love, governs thought; thought is a thing of liability to that power, rather than the power being an item in a calculus of thought.

A strong theory of fairness, such as Dworkin's is the most obvious case of a theory's trying to explain rules as reasons. Fairness or justice is presented as the standing, main, reason in any case for doing as a rule requires (it is fair, since I have taken the benefits of a community's rules and facilities, to follow its rules to my otherwise disadvantage, and so on). Moral thought under this theory is of the flat catalogue sort. This is because fairness is a concept, subjecting reality to its reason but possessing no reality itself. In VI.2 we saw that a strong theory of fairness is not a theory of rules at all; what is missing is the act of attachment or submission or commitment.

Raz's theory of rules, although it is a theory in which rules are expressed in terms of reasons for action, which Dworkin's is not, is in fact less of a theory of rules as reasons than the latter's. It is not flat like Dworkin's. For Raz's theory of reasons allows different levels; exclusionary reasons are second-order reasons and do not compete with first-order reasons. And movement between orders requires an act. No account can be given by this theory in its terms of reasons, of movement from one order to another. Clearly in some cases I must refuse to follow a rule *for first-order reasons*; for example, a judge will not follow a rule of a previous decision where it is shown to be grossly unjust. This injustice is in Raz's terms a first-order reason normally excluded by the second-order reason which for him constitutes the rule. But in this case the first-order reason eludes the grasp of the exclusionary reason. No account of this movement from the second-order to the first (or of the opposite movement) is available in terms of reasons, and the theory is therefore forced ultimately to admit acts. These acts and their real consequences are what constitute rules.

VI.10

Acts create discontinuities in moral thought. When I submit to a rule its norm controls absolutely the area of thought it defines. There is no rational relationship between an internal attitude and anything outside it. The same discontinuity is evident in my projects and erotic loves.

When I adopt a project there is a similar area of absoluteness in which the various reasons conditional on the project operate. There is no rational relationship between a reason conditional on one project and one conditional on another (III.12).

In the case of erotic loves there is a sort of fixation, a violent passion in Hume's terms, which tends to absoluteness: 'my country right or wrong' is only an extension of Aristotle's 'worse to swindle a friend than a stranger' (VI.4).

Any mind at ordinary moral levels is full of rules, projects and erotic loves, which inevitably clash. Because they are absolutes, this is quite unlike the meeting of reasons of competing weights.

A number of philosophers have seen that it is necessary to give status to the losing side in moral conflicts (Mounce and Phillips, Searle, Williams). If I ought to do *A* and I ought to do *B*, but cannot do both, judging that, all things considered, I ought to do *B* does not mean that it was never the case that I ought to do *A*, as some have thought (Ross, Hare). Searle's suggestion (1978, 87) is that the obligations in such a conflict have to be regarded as reasons for action; and this solves the problem as far as it goes. That one reason is stronger than another carries not the faintest implication that the latter was never a reason. But it does not go very far; and in particular it gives no account of tragic conflict. The simple ontological preservation of a defeated moral reason, whilst it might explain my regret at my failure to follow it does not explain a case of tragedy, which is a meeting not of reasons of competing weights, but of absolutes.

The paradigm of tragedy in western moral thought, one that we shall come back to, is the account that we have of the war 3,000 years ago on the plains of Troy. A more domestic example is: a criminal is convicted and sentenced to death, and his wife, who loves both her husband and her community, wonders what moral view to take of the matter. If moral thought were simply a flat catalogue of reasons she would have to judge the reasons and accept the result. If it is in favour of the sentence she is to accept it. Any struggle against the result must on the catalogue theory be moral weakness. She is, reasonably, to accept the result and that, morally speaking, is that. This is inhuman, of course. The flatness of the catalogue is really a profound lifelessness.

Whether the wife chooses her husband or the law, it will be no solution to her predicament; at best it will make a new life for her; her choice will be a revolution, the annihilation of one and possibly both her games (projects, rules, loves). It is this, the meeting and breaking of absolutes, which makes the tragedy of her situation.

The moral force of tragedy is its reassertion of the particulars of the world previously disregarded because of the hold of normative absolutes: excluded by erotic loves, used by projects (if I use you as a means to an end I fail to respect you) and subsumed into norms by rules. Thus the vivid particularity of the poetry of the *Iliad* is no mere decoration. It is the particulars of the world that make its mystery (recall Wittgenstein's 'the mystery is not how but that'). Thus tragedy reasserts the mystery of the world:

> Lear: No, no, no, no! Come, let's away to prison;
> We two alone will sing like birds i' the cage:
> When thou dost ask me blessing, I'll kneel down,
> And ask of thee forgiveness: so we'll live,
> And pray, and sing, and tell old tales, and laugh

At gilded butterflies, and hear poor rogues
Talk of court news; and we'll talk with them too,
Who loses and who wins; who's in, who's out;
And take upon's the mystery of things,
As if we were God's spies . . .

(King Lear, V iii 8)

St Thomas Aquinas's solution to the domestic tragedy just discussed distinguished between the formal and the material willing of good. The judge who passes the sentence and the wife both will the same formal good (they both give moral answers to the problem), but the judge, who wills the criminal's death and the wife, if she wills his life, will incompatible material goods. *But both act rightly*. Willing the formal good establishes this.

> The judge has care of the common good, which is justice, and therefore he wishes the [criminal's] death, which has the nature of good in relation to the common welfare; whereas the [criminal's] wife has to consider the private good of the family, and from this point of view she wishes her husband not to be put to death . . . hence . . . it is that various wills of various men can be good in respect of opposite things. (*S. T.* 1a2 æ 19.10 (trans. Pegis))

Only God, according to St Thomas, is able to will the universal material good (transcend tragedy, we might say). Creatures cannot: our will conforms to the divine will only inasmuch as it wills the formal good. St Thomas said, a man 'wills what God wills him to will'.

Man's willing what God wills him to will is not the same thing at all as man's willing what God wills. God's will, we may take it, is not discontinuous. But St Thomas recognizes that so far as creatures are concerned there are discontinuous absolutes.

No theory of rules makes an adequate account of the human condition if it proposes them as parts of a continuous moral discourse. The theories of rules as reasons discussed in this chapter fail in this way.

They are lowly violent things, rules; as are erotic loves and projects. Our methods of survival, nothing more. Ultimately, if we believe in moral freedom, there is agape, which we might call perfect freedom. The movement from eros to agape is the progressive release of the mystery of the world from appropriation, the release of absolutes: no fixations, no schemes, no binding norms – just a clear free attention to the particulars of the world. The wish to survive is replaced by the acceptance of death. Agape, attention to particulars, is said to be God's love. Lear became God's spy.

VII

LAW-GAME

VII.1

Legal decisions entail the corresponding moral judgment (II.2). To be committed to a legal rule is to be committed to its moral bindingness (III.4). To weigh reasons in legal hard cases it is necessary to be committed morally to those reasons (IV.5). The unity of moral thought is implied by these theses.

Legal positivists, however, have thought it important to maintain a thesis of the limits of law, implying a separation of law and morals. It is not hard to see why they have wanted to do this. The world is mysterious and difficult to live in, and its difficulties are compounded by the fact that we must live in it with others who can be expected not to see it quite like we do. So we try to make it simpler, more obvious, more settled and more public. One result of this, the main one, is that we minimize the incidence of hard decisions by making rules, whose logical character is calculated towards simplicity (the assumption of bindingness in a rule excludes all the difficulties of the questions it covers). This simplification is rightly thought to be important by legal positivists, and they mark this importance by insistence upon the thesis of the limits of law as the limits of that public settlement which people may look to as they set more confidently about their business. But there is a mistake here. This argues only for a thesis of the limits of rules, which is not the same thing as the limits of law.

Law-Game

VII.2

The limits of law is not the same thing as the limits of laws. The words 'legal system' are apt to cause confusion here.

A legal system, if the term is taken literally, is a system of laws. This means the system constituted by a certain set of norms, for it is obvious that only norms can be laws (reasons could not be laws). It is not implausible to suppose that such a set is definite, that is that there are limits to the laws of a community, thus limits to a legal system. And once that is established it is easy to move from 'legal system' to 'law', and say there are limits to law.

The confusion in this line of argument stems from a failure to see that there is another, less literal, but far more important meaning of the phrase 'legal system', where it simply names a case of law.

We really need another phrase here. Law is that human activity which we are discussing in this book. We need a phrase for a case of this activity, this legal system rather than that. . . . You see that I have to use the phrase 'legal system' where I don't want to. I can't say this law rather than that, because the phrase used like that means a certain type of norm. I don't want to say a legal system because that suggests a set of laws (its strict meaning), and that is misleading because a case of law is not just a case of a set of laws. We shall have to content ourselves with 'legal system', but use it in the non-literal sense.

VII.3

Are there limits to a legal system? Can we mark off what is law from what is not? Consider the position of a judge. Can we make any sense of the thought that he is bound by law up to certain limits but not thereafter?

Proponents of what we shall call the thesis of the limits of law commonly hold that we can make sense of that thought by referring to the concept of discretion. According to this view judges are bound by law up to a point and beyond that point they are free to exercise their discretion. That point becomes the limit of law.

But we have seen (V.1–V.6) that judges do not have discretion in a significant sense in any cases at all. They have power and responsibility (weak meanings of 'discretion'), but there is simply no area of thought in clear cases or hard where the judicial will is unbound, free to leap this way or that. The mistaken view that there is such an area is, we have argued (V.8), based upon a mistaken conception of moral freedom.

If there is no judicial discretion in the strong sense in any case at all what could be the point of the thesis of the limits of law? Let us for the purpose of argument postulate those limits. There will then be what we may call inner cases (within the limits) and outer cases.

If judges are to decide both inner and outer cases in accordance with binding considerations about which there is no discretion what could be the point of insisting that the former are legal and the latter are something else? Someone might want to attach those names, but there would be no importance in this. There are both rules and reasons on each side of the postulated limit which are binding in their respective ways, and there is no point at all in arguing here about the application of the word 'law'. If there were a significant difference in the quality of the thought on each side of the limit, as there would be if there were discretion in outer but not inner cases, then the thesis would certainly have an importance. A criticism which Raz makes of Dworkin is instructive here. Dworkin (according to Raz) maintained that in the case of some legal systems judges may decide some cases at least by reference to principles for which there is no source in any simple correspondence. And Raz in reply to this, defending both a sources and a limits thesis, suggested that Dworkin was missing the point:

> [What Dworkin says] is of course possible. The point of the sources thesis is not that courts never rely on sourceless considerations, but rather that when doing so they are not relying on legally binding considerations but exercising their own discretion. (Raz, 1979, 58)

The thrust of this argument depends on the existence of something like discretion beyond the limits of law in order to make significant the distinguishing of outer cases from inner. When the last five words of the extract, or something like them, are not available the argument that there are limits to law is merely verbal.

The argument of this section has turned on the strong sense of discretion. But the point is the same with the weak senses, too. For both the power that a judge has to make a legally binding wrong decision and the fact that it is his responsibility to make the decision are applicable in both inner and outer cases. Thus these weak senses of discretion don't distinguish inner cases from outer such as to require limits to law.

VII.4

What else could there be that would make the thesis of the limits of law worth maintaining? There is certainly a distinction between rules and reasons such as would make a thesis of the limits of rules worth maintaining, and certainly a distinction between a rule of recognition, such as Hart conceived it, and other types of rule sufficient to make a thesis of the limits of a rule of recognition and rules valid under it maintainable. But reasons as well as rules bind judges. They do not have discretion about reasons (V.4). Thus a judge's duty binds him to reasons as well as rules. What could be the point of saying that one part of a judge's duty, rules, was law and another part, reasons, was not law? It would seem that a thesis of the limits of law as rules must fall at the same time as the thesis that the limits of law are drawn at the point where discretion begins.

Of course, the limits of rules might mark the limits of laws. But this is not the same thing as the limits of law (VII.2). Compare two cases. In the first there is a legal rule which determines that Harold must perform a contract. In the second there is no rule but the clear balance of (legal) reasons is in favour of the same conclusion (you may add if you like that all lawyers are agreed on this). In each case Harold is bound to perform his contract. We might wish to say that in the first case but not the second he is bound by *a* law. But in both cases he is bound by law (or bound in law, or legally bound).

VII.5

There is an old question which relates to these matters of limits and discretion: do judges make the law? If there is no discretion in either inner or outer cases there is a sense in which judges cannot make anything. They are to find the right answer to a given problem, not make it. Hart has said of another theory which has argued against discretion (Dworkin's) that:

> [Bentham] would undoubtedly have thought it was an extension of Blackstone's theory of the common law, according to which judges' decisions do not make the law but are merely evidence of what the law is. (1976, 551)

When a court makes a decision in a hard case its decision may create a rule (more strictly it creates the possibility of rule decisions in subsequent cases). Since it is a hard case, there is by definition no rule pre-existing the decision. The case effects the transformation of a matter of reasons into a matter of rule. Can this not be said to be a form of creation?

It is true to say that the correct decision of a case is implicit in pre-existing reasons (reasons are the units of hard decisions, and are therefore whatever it is that makes the decision right or wrong). In a sense, therefore, it might be thought that the correct decision pre-exists. But the decision of a case is not the same thing as the rule created by that case. And second, the decision in any case is not necessarily the right one. Let us put this second matter aside for the moment and assume that a right decision has been made. A decision is not the same thing as the ensuing rule, thus it would not follow from the fact that there was no discretion as to the decision that there was no discretion as to the rule. It is conceivable that a court might have discretion as to the width of the terms in which it formulates its decision and this might in some sense entail discretion as to the width of the ensuing rule. There are several difficulties here.

The first is that what is the rule of a case is principally a matter for a subsequent court, not for the deciding court. The norm in such a rule is constructed by the subsequent court rather than found by it in the precedent case (IX.7). The width of language chosen by the deciding court cannot therefore be regarded as determinative of the width of any ensuing rule. A second difficulty is that it is not obviously true to say that a deciding court has discretion as to the width of the language of its decision. Consider *Donoghue* v. *Stevenson*, a prominent example of a rule-creating decision. Had the House of Lords stated that the rule that followed from their decision was that people were liable to their neighbour when their acts injured him (or had they stated their decision in these terms) they would have been wrong, for the reasons which justify the decision require a lesser degree of generality, namely, that the rule concerns negligent acts, not acts. There is no discretion here, though, as always, the possibility of error. At the other extreme, their language might not have been general enough. For instance, if the Lords had stated that the rule that followed from the relevant reasons was that when any Scotsman allowed a snail into a ginger beer bottle so as to injure a shop assistant, whose friend had purchased the bottle in a cafe at Paisley . . . they would plainly have been wrong. Here too, as in the case of over-generalization, we have to say there was no discretion. Reasons seem to dictate a definite level of generality. Whether there is a limited area of discretion around the middle ground, neither very over-general nor very under-general, is hard to say. But if there is, then, given the fact that the determination of the rule is principally for a subsequent court, it is not a discretion of any great significance.

The case of error has to this point been put aside. Error is a common possibility, and there is perhaps a sense in which erring courts make the law. We must distinguish two kinds of error.

A court's decision may be wrong in a weak sense, meaning wrong but not wrong in a way that justifies a subsequent court's not following it. Or it may be wrong in a strong sense, in which case subsequent overruling is required. Sometimes courts take it on themselves to deny this second category, e.g. the House of Lords in *London Street Tramways* v. *London County Council* [1898] A.C. 375. But this is a logical error, for the declared absolute bindingness of court decisions can always be subverted by questioning the bindingness of the declaration itself (a decision by a court that its precedents were absolutely binding could be logically in order only if there were a supervening rule of recognition authenticating (recognizing) such declarations; but there is no rule of recognition of court decisions (IX.10). The two senses of wrong can be illustrated as follows: Suppose *ABC* are the reasons for a plaintiff and *XYZ* the reasons for a defendant and that *ABC* outweighs *XYZ*. Suppose, however, that there is a precedent case on all fours supporting the defendant (since *ABC* outweighs *XYZ* it follows that this precedent case was wrongly decided). The defendant now has in addition to *XYZ* an argument of *stare decisis* based upon the precedent. Call this argument *S*. The case therefore becomes *ABC* for the plaintiff against *XYZS* for the defendant. If *ABC* outweighs *XYZS* the precedent is wrong in the strong sense, but if it does not it is wrong only in the weak sense.

Now in the case of a court's decision, wrong in the strong sense, we cannot say that the court has made the law for future decisions, for it has made nothing at all. (It has, of course, even when wrong in the strong sense, made a binding settlement of the issue between the parties to the litigation. That is a relatively unproblematical aspect of a court's decision. We are here concerned only with a decision's wider law-creating character.And though such a court has made nothing at all, a subsequent court might (mistakenly) take it to have made a binding rule; in which case we simply transfer our analysis of mistake to that subsequent decision). But where the court's decision is merely wrong in the weak sense it is possible to say that it has made the law, and in a sense made a rule for the future (strictly, as we saw, whether there is a rule is for a subsequent court to decide, and this applies in this case too; but we shall talk more loosely). What the judge has made will be limited and narrow, for his decision, being wrong, will need to be distinguished where possible; but it can certainly be viewed as a case of law-making.

It is a mistake to think that the possibility of law-creation by a judge entails the existence in him of discretion. It entails only his power. I may have the power to do something but not the discretion. The sense of discretion which we have been examining relates logically to duty rather than to power, and a judge's duty is to make the right decision. That his decision creates something which did not exist before says nothing at all about his duty or his discretion.

VII.6

Those philosophers who think there are no objective values are right. There is only the world, and no reason to think that objective values are to be found in it (what would an objective value look like, sound like, or feel like?). But respect for the world is required, and this is a sufficient foundation for moral thought, which is objective in the sense established in V.11. We have been talking in this chapter of judges being bound by reasons. They are objectively bound in the sense just mentioned.

To say with the old common lawyers that the law is found and not made does not commit us to objective values, to the existence of some 'brooding omnipresence in the sky', as Oliver Wendell Holmes thought it did (or in the more recent metaphor, some Aladdin's cave where there is hidden the Common Law in all its splendour – Lord Reid, 1972, 22). The old common lawyers usually spoke of the common law as custom; and of course it would be absurd to suppose that a customary answer to every legal question was waiting somewhere to be found. But when they speak of the law's being found not made they speak, or must be taken to speak, not of the Common Law customs, strictly conceived, but of the logical structure of the thought that goes into and surrounds these customs. The point that is being made must simply be the logical one established in Chapter V concerning discretion and objectivity in legal decisions. Their talk does not imply the existence of some extra entity in the world corresponding to their judgments. And to say that there is no discretion is quite compatible with affirming that there are no objective moral or legal values. It might be right to say, as one philosopher has recently done (Mackie, 1978), that we have invented moral thought (I should want to say we have invented it because of our respect for the world). But the invention (if it is that) has a logical structure; and the arguments we have made against the existence of discretion in a strong sense are based only upon an analysis of that structure; they are not dependent upon the existence of some extra 'uninvented' entity in the world. It is possible to say: there is only the world.

What actually lies behind Holmes's point is a claim about the responsibility of judges. Judges are responsible for their decisions, Holmes implies, and cannot pass that responsibility to 'some brooding omnipresence in the sky'. But it is legal positivism which is defective here, for it is positivism which claims that a judge can make a legal judgment separated from moral considerations; it is positivism which allows (indeed requires) a judge to say: it is the law which makes this decision, not me (II.2–II.3). The unity of moral thought guarantees that there is moral responsibility for legal decision.

VII.7

Kant distinguished law and morality by the nature of the constraint or sanction that applied: law constrains by natural means (fear of punishment, love of the comfort of community, for instance), morality by simple consciousness of duty.

However, we have seen that this conception of morality cannot stand because it cannot account for the weight of reasons for action (IV.4). Morality itself constrains by natural means (the exercise of the passions); and the unity of morality, where law is an undifferentiated part of the whole flux, follows.

VII.8

Law in the unity of moral thought has two modes. So far as rules are concerned, it is the totality, the absoluteness, of the appropriation of moral thought by rules that constitutes the unity. If a rule judgment is made the whole field of moral thought is appropriated; there is no ground left for further questions. In hard cases, on the other hand, it is the requirement of indefinitely graduated weight that determines the unity. I have only one capacity to weigh reasons; legal reasons are therefore indistinguishable from moral reasons. These are two rather distinct modes, and to reflect them we might say: law in the unity of moral thought is everything or nothing.

In this it is like a game.

VII.9

In analysing rules and rule systems we move easily between law and ordinary games like chess: the structural or logical similarities are considerable. The most important of these similarities is the characteristic claim to absolute supremacy by the rules of each (the appropriation of the whole of moral thought). Three aspects of this claim can be distinguished.

(1) Law claims the power to override the rules of a game: to say for instance whether and when the game shall be played. This supremacy of legal systems is sometimes regarded as one of their

distinguishing features. However, it is not a distinguishing feature of legal system at all, but a defining feature of all rules and rule systems (all games). Games claim the same power over law. I still lose a game if I decline to make my move in response to the law's direction. Let us assume that a certain game, perhaps of chance or violence, is prohibited by law but that I play it. At any particular moment in the game its rules tell me that I may do one thing and the law that I may not. *Neither defers to the other.* Each claims to appropriate the whole of moral thought. What I do (what I am bound to do) in this situation of conflict (not straightforward conflict because there is no direct confrontation; each purports to occupy the moral field to the exclusion of the other and all others) depends simply on which game I happen to play, the law game or the chess game. Of course, the rules of the chess game might prescribe that actions in breach of the law are not permitted. But this is no real deference; for the rules of the game, saying what might and might not be done, are still supreme. The logical situation here is similar to a constitution's deference to religious practices: though some norms which would otherwise be laws have to give way to the requirements of religious freedom, it is still the law which provides this (and which might provide otherwise), and which is logically supreme (for its players, we must add).

(2) Law recognizes no limits to its power: it may deal even in death. And it is possible to play Russian Roulette, or duel, or throw Christians to lions.

(3) Law claims the power to conscript; to say whom and what falls within its jurisdiction regardless of their consent. And so do games: Forcible Hopscotch, Christians and Lions.

Sometimes games are less complex than legal systems. Often they do not have the rules of recognition or hierarchies typical of legal systems. But some do: it is not unusual for a game to have an authoritative text and a controlling body with legislative power, and there is still one university in Australia which plays a game called Roman Law, which, because it is derivative, is actually more complex than the former legal system on which it is modelled.

Plato thought that life was play (*Laws*, VII, 803). A game is something which while it continues has no point except its own self-contained, self-constructed point. That is what Plato meant to bring out when he said life must be lived as play. The game is necessary (who is ready to die?), but unworthy (morally point-less), and that is our misfortune (our predicament when we consider our place in the world and our difficulty in seeing through our games):

> And notwithstanding that human affairs are unworthy of earnest effort, necessity counsels us to be in earnest; and that is our misfortune . . . a man ought to be in serious earnest about serious things, and not about trifles . . . the object really worthy of all serious and blessed effort is God, while man is contrived . . . to be a plaything of God . . . What then is the right way? We should live out our lives playing. . . . (loc. cit., trans. Bury)

Plato himself was not unwilling to play. The passage in *The Laws* concludes with a brisk re-entry into the game, in which Plato, as ever, catches the tone as well as the substance of the moral problem:

> *Megillus*: You have a very mean opinion, stranger, of the human race.
>
> *Athenian*: Marvel not, Megillus, but forgive me. For when I spoke thus, I had my mind set on God, and was feeling the emotion to which I gave utterance. Let us grant, however, if you wish, that the human race is not a mean thing, but worthy of serious attention.
>
> To pursue our subject, – we have described buildings for public gymnasia as well as schools in three divisions within the city. . . .

> (*The Laws*, 804 BC)

Games are constituted by the internal point of view (I cannot play a game without accepting the rules). This is one of the senses in which games are pointless. Once I start wondering about the point of a game I become external to it, and am no longer playing. The game has gone. In this sense games are necessarily pointless. Of course, I can become external and think about the point of the game. And, returning to Plato, I can think about the point of law or life. Usually I do not: I hide from revolution and I hide from God. When I do think about it the deeper sense in which all games including life are pointless becomes apparent: our attempts to survive (win) are but passing events.

Law-Game

VII.10

The legal philosopher who best understood bindingness in rules was Hans Kelsen. Kelsen wrote:

> From the point of view of the normative science of the game of chess a rook differs from a piece of ivory in the shape of a castle by the fact that only the rook is the subject of a normative order assumed to be valid.

Actually, what Kelsen wrote was:

> From the point of view of normative jurisprudence, the order to pay taxes differs from the gangster's threat . . . by the fact that only the tax order is issued by an individual who is authorised by a legal order assumed to be valid. (1945, 176)

Kelsen's whole theory of the basic norm, his most important single idea, was a response to the problem of distinguishing the demand of a tax collector from the demand of a gangster. It is sometimes misunderstood. The basic norm is not the ultimate norm in a legal system, whose bindingness is presupposed or assumed. Rather, it is the (normative) assumption of bindingness itself. The ultimate real norm of a legal system is the rule of recognition, which is in Kelsen's terms the historically first constitution. This is, in the presupposition of the basic norm, assumed to be binding; upon which event (i.e. the making of the assumption) the whole set of subjective meanings operated on by the basic norm become objectively binding, including the demand of the tax collector. In outward manifestations there might be no distinction at all between a tax collector and a robber; the words used in each demand might be identical, and all other facts might be, too; hierarchical support, a system of enforcement, and so on. But our (lawyer's) internal way of regarding the tax collector is what makes the difference. We assume the bindingness of the system of which he is part, and the whole structure of objective legality follows. Now, all of this applies exactly to games. There is an equivalent problem: what is it that distinguishes a piece of ivory in the shape of a castle from a rook? This is the equivalent of the problem of the robber and the tax collector, for the outward manifestations of the two objects are identical. And the solution of the problem is equivalent too. As soon as we (chess-players) have assumed the

158

bindingness of (become internal to) the relevant set of rules the whole normative structure of the game follows, and our piece of ivory in the shape of a castle becomes a rook. We are now bound, and amongst other things cannot move our rook diagonally. But as soon as we finish the game (abandon our assumption, annihilate our rule) we may move our piece of ivory as we like. In both cases, law and games, bindingness is explained by Kelsen's theory of assumption.

The idea of annihilation must be examined further. The sense of annihilation in the case of a legal system is obvious enough. When a revolution comes (wholesale, or in just one lawyer's talk) the previously binding rule of recognition is regarded as normatively destroyed. The former institutions (taken now, necessarily, in a descriptive not normative sense) might remain, but they have become mere collections of reactionaries, capitalist gangs, or other items of behaviour significant only for their muscle. For normative theory, this transformation resembles closely the transformation by normative annihilation of a rook into a piece of ivory. Of course, revolutionary transformation in chess is a rather commoner event than in law: it occurs as frequently as we play a game and finish it or finish it prematurely. But the frequency of an event does not necessarily make a difference to its logical character. And the annihilation in chess looks more provisional than the annihilation of a legal system, for the pieces are likely to be there waiting for tomorrow's game. But so, often, are deposed prime ministers and generals, whose muscle might in the event win out.

The radical transformation involved in this movement into and out of games is beautifully caught by Plato in the passage from *The Laws* quoted earlier:

Megillus: You have a very mean opinion, stranger, of the human race.

Athenian: Marvel not, Megillus, but forgive me. For when I spoke thus, I had my mind set on God, and was feeling the emotion to which I gave utterance. Let us grant, however, if you wish, that the human race is not a mean thing, but worthy of serious attention.

To pursue our subject, – we have described buildings for public gymnasia as well as schools in three divisions within the city. . . .

(op. cit., 804 B–C)

Nevertheless, it is not uncommonly thought that there is an important difference between games, which are for fun, and more serious pursuits like law (and life). Mary Midgely, for example, complains of the profligate way in which modern philosophy attaches the name 'game' and its associates (in 'The Game Game', 1974, 231. A revealing title, actually. Philosophy is a 'serious' business. Why do philosophers play the game game?):

> The word institution [the point applies to 'game'] would be best saved for things which were once instituted and could at a pinch be disinstituted again without taking the entire human race with them. (1974, 252)

And Joseph Raz (1975, 122):

> The uniqueness of games as normative systems depends on the special nature of their values. They are artificial values because they are not inherently connected to wider human concerns . . . games are merely games.

Law is more serious than games (the heavy view). What is one to say to that? That it overrates law? Or that it underrates games? Both answers are required. As to the first, think of Plato's words. And if it is thought that law is distinguished by the seriousness of the things with which it deals, think of the game of Christians and Lions. As to the second, think of a world without games. This last reflection exposes a fallacy in the heavy view. This fallacy is to confuse game in general with particular games, and law with particular legal systems.

Certainly, chess or Russian roulette might be disinstituted 'without taking the entire human race with them'. But not *all* games, for then there would be no fun or play, and the survival of the human race without fun or play is inconceivable. Equally, *this* legal system might be disinstituted. This would not take the world with it or even our world for we might substitute another legal system just as in the case of a game we might substitute another game. And Raz is partly right to say that the values of games are artificial. He is wrong, however, to say that that distinguishes them from law. The value or point in chess, which according to Raz is winning, is certainly artificial; chess constructs by its rules its unique method of winning. But the value of winning in general is an inseparable part of play (contest) and no more artificial than play itself is artificial. You and I need play; there are therefore unconditional other-regarding and self-regarding reasons to play. So far as law is concerned we might say the value instituted by the establishment of the rules of a legal system is the establishment of community. As a general value community is not artificial. You and I need community. Therefore, as with games, there are corresponding unconditional reasons for action. But particular legal systems establish particular communities; and the values constructed by the laws of this community rather than that are no less artificial than the values constructed by the rules of this game rather than that.

VIII

CASES

Practical thought is concerned with action. It seems reasonable to define a case of practical thought by reference to an action. The form of what we are calling hard cases (i.e. non-rule cases) is ABC against XYZ, where ABC are the material facts on one side, the reasons for the action in question, and XYZ are the material facts on the other and the reasons against the action (in law cases the action is whatever disposes of the case: give judgment for the plaintiff, convict the defendant, issue such and such an injunction). The form of rule cases we have seen is the practical syllogism, where the major premise states the action and the conditions of its being required:

1 Give judgment for the plaintiff where ABC.
2 A, B and C are the case.
3 Therefore, give judgment for the plaintiff.

In these cases of action each fact raises a case of belief. Each case of belief may be a simple case or a complex case. At its simplest a case of belief will take the form ABC against XYZ, the reasons for and against believing the fact (actually, it's not quite right to say 'at its simplest'; for $ABCXY$ and Z, the reasons for belief, are themselves facts, and thus if infinite regression is to be excluded the point must be reached where some facts are simply believed rather than decided to be believed. The most obvious example of this is the fact that a witness said such and such –

162

before one's very eyes.) Most cases of belief will be complexes of cases not just of belief but of actions as well. The rules of evidence will be applied in cases concerned with the various actions associated with coming to a belief: excluding inadmissible facts, calling a halt in the search for evidence, applying a presumption (these are all actions). And there may be hard cases of the law of evidence, too, where, rather than a rule being applied, a hard judgment is made between the reasons for and against actions of the sort mentioned (there is no reason to think there are fewer hard cases in the law of evidence than in, say, the criminal law).

There are, we have just seen, many cases within cases. There are as many practical cases in a law-suit (itself a case defined by the action implicit in the ultimate judgment sought) as there are actions taken, and as many cases of belief as there are facts to be found.

VIII.2

The problem of distinguishing a question of law from a question of fact arises in many forms in the law. But actually the distinction is quite a simple one: questions of fact are raised by cases of belief, questions of law by cases of action.

VIII.3

In a hard case of action *ABC* is weighed against *XYZ*. This is a matter of degree, we might say, in the sense that weight is a cardinal not ordinal concept: there are no discontinuities or orders, it is just quantity or degree which is in issue.

Some currency has been given to Lord Radcliffe's suggestion in *Edwards* v. *Bairstow* [1956] A.C. 14, 33, that a cardinal question of this sort (a question of degree, he called it) is necessarily a question of fact. But it may not be. *ABCXY* and *Z* in the form *ABC* against *XYZ* may be reasons for belief or reasons for action. Only if they are reasons for belief do they raise a question of fact. If they are reasons for action in a law case they raise a question of law. Lord Radcliffe seems to have allowed only for rule cases, where norms (laws) are applied absolutely, not by degrees. In such cases it is true that questions of degree can only arise in relation to the minor premise, the question of fact:

1 Eat red apples.
2 This apple is red (in sufficient degree).
3 Therefore, eat this apple.

VIII.4

Cases where a norm is applied are complex. They usually have to be analysed as at least two or three cases.

First, there can be a case of recognition of the norm. 'Recognition' is here used in the sense which Hart developed (1961), viz., recognition as valid or proper to be applied. Recognition can be by rule or, where there is no rule of recognition or it is not settled on this point, it can be by hard decision (in the Common Law legal systems whilst there is a rule of recognition of statutory norms there is (as we shall see: IX.10) no rule of recognition of norms from precedents; and in any case not all recognition of statutory norms is by rule: X.5). A hard case of recognition will take the form *ABC* reasons to recognize the norm in issue against *XYZ* reasons not to. If the norm is recognized it is taken absolutely. For example, statutes once recognized are absolutely valid (though, of course, they have to be interpreted): there are no degrees of validity – either a statutory norm is valid or it is not. In the case of a rule of recognition the concept of a rule gives this absoluteness. Where there is no applicable rule of recognition the concept of a practical decision assumed to be binding gives this absoluteness.

The second complication in the individuation of cases concerned with the application of a norm is that there may be cases of interpretation.

Suppose there is a statutory norm 'no vehicle shall be taken into a park'. Consider two cases that might arise: first, a motor car and second, a skateboard.

The contrast between these cases that immediately suggests itself is that the motor car case seems to raise no special case of interpretation whereas the skateboard case does. The motor car case seems to be a simple and ordinary case of the application of a recognized norm.

However, the skateboard case might be just such an ordinary case. One who regarded a skateboard as unquestionably a vehicle within the meaning of the statute would apply the norm 'no vehicle-including-a-skateboard shall be taken into a park' in the ordinary way. And although we might regard this as eccentric, it would be no answer to the eccentric to say: that is not what the statute says. For he, too, is simply reading the word 'vehicle'. And anyway, eccentrics aside, there might be in existence a binding precedent holding that within the meaning of the statute 'vehicle' includes skateboard. In this case, too, if there were no question of reconsidering the precedent, an ordinary decision applying the statute would be made. These cases would not be significantly different from the motor car case.

Usually, though, we would want to say that the skateboard case is a hard case. But what sort of hard case?

It is evident that so far as recognition is concerned there is no difference between the motor car case and the (hard) skateboard case. In each case I recognize a norm 'no vehicle shall be taken into a park'. And in neither case is this recognition an end of the matter. In each there is now a second case; namely, for the purposes of applying the norm is the particular in issue a vehicle?

This second case may be the final case where the norm is applied to the particular thing in issue, but not necessarily. Suppose there is a precedent relevant to this second case which I follow as a rule and which has held that a skateboard is a vehicle for the purposes of the statute. I apply this rule, but still I would have to decide whether the thing in issue is a skateboard for the purposes of this second rule. This might not be clear: it might be a dubious skateboard, a two-wheeled skateboard, for instance. So, there is a further case which also, in turn, might be partly a rule case. There might be another precedent which I follow as a rule and which has held that a two-wheeled skateboard is a skateboard within the meaning of the first precedent. Thus I would conclude by rule (two rules) that a two-wheeled skateboard is a vehicle. But still I would have to decide that the particular in issue is a two-wheeled skateboard for the purposes of that conclusion. It might be odd in some other way. And in the end even if it is not odd when compared with a given norm it is still a particular. In rule cases the final problem is always the application of the norm of the rule to the particular in issue. This is the decision of the minor premise in the practical syllogism (no vehicle shall be taken into a park, *this is a vehicle*, therefore this shall not be taken into a park.)

Let us take the skateboard case and assume there are no precedents on the matter. Is the particular in issue a vehicle for the purposes of the statute? To decide whether it is is a matter of weighing the reasons for so deciding against those against. But reasons at this point are not at large. As it is often put, a court has room for interpretation of the statute (recognized norm), but only a certain amount of room. A reason of justice, for example, might be relevant (to be precise, that set of reasons to which the concept, justice, reduces): a certain interpretation of a statute might lead to injustice, and so there is a reason against that interpretation. But the reason of justice is not at large. It is not as though the case is to be decided in the absence of the statute (we are not simply deciding the question whether skateboards ought to be taken into parks; whether, for instance, it is just to exclude skateboard riders). And it is not that the injustice of a certain conclusion is to be weighed against the various reasons that there are for obeying Parliament (democracy, certainty in public affairs, etc.); if that were so justice would be at large and entitled to its full weight (and, incidentally, the case would then be a hard case of recognition of statutes, not a case of the application of a recognized statute). Lawyers know that in neither of these ways is justice at large; it is limited in its relevance to the question of interpretation. How is this limitation to be presented analytically? It seems to me that the form into which our analysis requires us to put the relevant reasons answers this problem.

Roughly speaking, we said, the question was a matter of weighing the reasons on one side of the case against the reasons on the other. To be more precise we must ask what are these reasons for? They are reasons for (judicial) action, but what is the action? The action is not that which disposes of the case (if it were, the reasons would be at large), but the action of interpreting the recognized norm of the statute. Thus the reason of justice if it is relevant is not: that such and such is unjust is a reason not to convict the defendant. But rather: that such and such is unjust is a reason to interpret the statute in a way which does not encompass it (just *a* reason: there may well be stronger reasons arguing that it does). These reasons are obviously quite different.

166

Suppose some rule of a chess tournament provides that the referee shall declare a game forfeit if one player 'unreasonably' annoys the other in the course of play. The language of the rule does not define what counts as 'unreasonable' annoyance; it does not decide whether, for example, a player who continually smiles at his opponent in such a way as to unnerve him, as the Russian grandmaster Tal once smiled at Fischer, annoys him unreasonably.

The referee is not free to give effect to his background convictions in deciding this hard case. He might hold, as a matter of political theory, that individuals have a right to equal welfare without regard to intellectual abilities. It would nevertheless be wrong for him to rely upon that conviction in deciding difficult cases under the forfeiture rule. He could not say, for example, that annoying behaviour is reasonable so long as it has the effect of reducing the importance of intellectual ability in deciding who will win the game. The participants, and the general community that is interested, will say that his duty is just the contrary. Since chess is an intellectual game, he must apply the forfeiture rule in such a way as to protect, rather than jeopardize, the role of intellect in the contest.

We have, then, in the case of the chess referee, an example of an official whose decisions about institutional rights are understood to be governed by institutional constraints even when the force of these constraints is not clear. We do not think that he is free to legislate interstitially within the 'open texture' of imprecise rules. If one interpretation of the forfeiture rule will protect the character of the game, and another will not, then the participants have a right to the first interpretation. (Dworkin, 1977, 102)

Chess, we may say, has no rule of recognition. Its rules (though joint rather than several) are rules in their own right not rules because they are valid under a rule of recognition. But the problem of interpretation is the same as in a legal system where there is a rule of recognition. The problem in the chess case is to say whether 'unreasonable annoyance' in the relevant norm includes smiling.

167

Dworkin's analysis catches accurately the sense in which the interpretation of 'unreasonable' is not at large. He attacks the popular idea of interstitial legislation, and is right to do so, for that would mean that reason was at large in the gaps. He argues that one can gather from the institution, chess, that it is an intellectual game, and that this would influence one to say that the smile was unreasonable. Background convictions, as Dworkin calls them, which might argue for reasonableness (all's fair in love, war and chess), would not be controlling. Our analysis would say that whatever the facts were which suggested that Tal's smile was unreasonable were not to be taken as reasons for action at large but as reasons to interpret unreasonable annoyance under the rules of chess to include that sort of smile; and the attachment of this question to the rules of chess brings into account the fact that chess is an intellectual game, and various other things too. Dworkin's idea of background conviction is equivalent to reason at large.

This analysis of the problem says nothing about the weight of reasons. We show merely that the reason to stop Tal smiling is different from the reason to interpret 'unreasonable annoyance' under the rules of chess so as to include smiling; that the reason to keep skateboards out of parks is different from the reason to interpret 'vehicle' as including skateboard for the purposes of the statute against vehicles in parks. Now, we may take it that these reasons for actions have different weights; and can thus see how Dworkin has been led to the rather fundamental mistake discussed in chapter IV whereby he holds that institutional history can affect weight (or gravitational force). To see this we shall need a more borderline case than motor car or skateboard. We shall consider a motor-cycle.

The reason to keep motor-cycles out of parks has a certain weight. Institutional history intervenes (the statute is passed). The relevant reason becomes the reason to interpret 'vehicle' to include motor-cycles for the purposes of the statute, a reason which, since it is not a reason at large, is, we may surmise, a reason of different weight. *Post hoc ergo propter hoc*: the weight was changed by institutional history. But as we have seen (ch. IV) institutional history cannot change or in any sense determine the weight of either reason. One sort of reason can be changed to the other in the way stated. But that exhausts any senses in which institutional history might be said to affect the weight of reasons, and certainly cannot carry Dworkin's theory of gravitational force which claims for institutional history a wholesale and complex action on weight. Dworkin's theory is only plausible when analysis is conducted in terms of the loose, strictly spurious (IV.2) concept, principle. The identical (loosely conceived) principle might be thought to operate both before and after the intervention of institutional history. Let us say this is the principle of respect for the safety of children in parks. Before the passing of the statute this principle operates in favour of keeping motor-cycles out of parks. After, it operates in favour of a certain interpretation of the statute. The intervention of the statute would not change the identity of the principle. But something changes, for the case *is* different after the statute has been passed. What else could that be but weight (or gravitational attraction, in Dworkin's later way of putting it)? It is this appearance of identity of the principles combined with a change of weight which is misleading. But only the loose concept, principle, allows this false appearance. Reason for action, by contrast, avoids the error, for it requires discrimination of actions and thus allows no appearance of identity: the reason to keep motor-cycles out of parks and the reason to interpret 'vehicles' in our statute to include motor-cycles are different on the simple ground that the actions are different. Two things are essential for clear analysis here. First, that primacy be accorded to reasons for action over principles. And second, that the interpretation of a norm be seen as an action.

VIII.6

Where no question of interpretation of the norm arises the decision of the minor premise in a rule case is a pure question of fact. Related to this is a doctrine in English law that where in a statute a word is used in its ordinary sense a decision about its application is a question of fact not a question of law. Thus in *Brutus* v. *Cozens* [1973] A.C. 854, where the question was whether an anti-apartheid demonstration at the All England Lawn Tennis Club, Wimbledon, was a case of insulting behaviour under the Public Order Act, 1936, the House of Lords held that the word 'insulting' was used in its ordinary sense in the statute; it was therefore a question of fact not law whether the defendant's behaviour was insulting. But this is quite confused.

Interpretation, as we have seen, raises a case of action not belief, and in law cases this means a question of law rather than fact. And a word can be used in its ordinary sense and still raise a question of interpretation, i.e. a question of law. Thus in the examples we have been using there is no reason to think that the words 'vehicle' and 'annoyance' are used in any less ordinary a sense than 'insulting' was in the Public Order Act. Yet they still raise difficult cases requiring interpretation of the norms. The most ordinary words have peripheral as well as central cases of application; 'vehicle' is a paradigm of this.

Clearly what was troublesome in *Brutus* v. *Cozens* was not whether the defendant insulted the spectators in any simple sense. Was it, for instance, the defendant who insulted the spectators or might it have been someone else? Or was what the defendant did something other than insult the spectators (a suspected burglar may in fact be repairing locks)? The House of Lords did not hold that it was such questions as these, clearly questions of fact, that were at issue in the case. Clearly not. The troublesome question was the meaning of the word 'insulting'. And this like 'vehicle' has peripheral cases of application as well as central. The difference is that in the motor-cycle case the question of interpretation is able to be easily articulated; does 'vehicle' include 'motor-cycle'? Whereas in *Brutus* v. *Cozens* a dozen or so words would be necessary to pose the question of interpretation. This is a mere accident of language. The cases are not distinguishable by one being easier than the other. Nor do they raise questions of a different logical status. The motor-cycle case might have arisen in relation to the first motor-cycle ever made and before the word had been coined; a dozen or so words would then have been needed to describe the contraption. And there might well develop a single word for what Brutus did at Wimbledon. Clearly this has nothing to do with the distinction between fact and law. Confusion has been caused here by the fact that the words 'Brutus insulted the spectators' can be used as the conclusion of either a simple case of fact or a case of interpretation. The House of Lords failed to allow for the second possibility.

We cannot distinguish *Brutus* v. *Cozens* and our motor-cycle case on the ground that one raises a question of fact and the other a question of law. What is true about the distinction between these cases is that the process by which an appeal court's interpretation becomes authoritative is simpler where there is a single word to describe the issue. If the highest appeal court decides that 'vehicle' includes 'motor-cycle' it is almost as though the norm is amended to stand objectively as: 'no vehicle-including-motor-cycle shall be . . .'. If, on the other hand, the House of Lords had decided the substance of *Brutus* v. *Cozens* there would have been competing descriptions of Brutus's act, and thus competing accounts of what the decision was authoritative for – by no means would it have been as if the norm had been amended to read 'insulting-including . . .'.

The possibility of authoritative decision in this way does not mark the distinction between fact and law. That distinction turns on the difference between a case of belief and a case of (judicial) action (a case of believing that Brutus insulted the spectators and a case of the action of interpreting 'insulting' to include what he did). The most that can be said of the possibility of easily authoritative decision is that its absence is a reason for according to a lower court the power to make the final decision in the matter.

VIII.7

The power to make the final decision in a matter (the power to make a wrong decision) is the only substantive meaning of 'discretion' (V.2). It does not mark the distinction between fact and law: clearly there can be discretion in this sense to decide either cases of fact (belief) or cases of law (judicial action).

VIII.8

When precision is necessary we talk in this analysis of rule cases, not of rules.

This allows for human idiosyncrasy.

Where there is no authoritatively promulgated norm, as in customary rules, it is obviously possible, indeed likely, that the norm which one man applies will be at least slightly different from that which another applies (different, at least, at the peripheries of the concepts it uses). And even where there is an authoritatively promulgated norm there will be idiosyncratic conceptions of its meaning. Thus one man will think it obvious that in the norm 'no vehicle shall be taken into a park' vehicle includes motor-cycle. In effect his norm is 'no vehicle-including-motor-cycle . . .'. Another will think it not obvious and thus will require a case of interpretation. Further, no one can ever be rationally required to make an assumption. Thus no one can be rationally required to make a rule decision. One day I might decide a certain point by the assumptions that make my decision a rule decision; another day I might not, for I might decide by the reasons that relate to the point. Whether in any case there is sufficient uniformity of rule behaviour either between people or in one individual to say 'there is a rule that . . .' or 'he has a rule that . . .'. is a question which sociologists or psychologists might conceive it necessary to answer; but neither the question nor the principles applicable in the answering of it are of interest to the author of this book.

VIII.9

Hard cases at their simplest take the form *ABC* against *XYZ* where these are the unconditional reasons for and against the (judicial) action in question. But often they will be conditional reasons, reasons conditional upon a certain project (III.12). The hard case will now be a complex of cases for it must include a case of the adoption of the project. This may be a conscious hard decision in favour of the project, it may be by rule (always adopt projects of such and such a type), but most likely it will be a case of the application (by assumption) of a previous decision in favour of the project (III.12). The law is full of projects in the guise of principles. The fundamental judicial project is probably: keep the community together.

In *Haseldine* v. *Daw* [1941] 2 K.B. 343, one question was whether *Donoghue* v. *Stevenson* [1932] A.C. 562, which, to speak broadly, established the liability in negligence of a manufacturer of goods, covered the case of a repairer as well, and it was held that it did: 'a repairer of a chattel stands in no different position from a manufacturer', said Goddard L.J. (at p. 379).

Since Lord Goddard attended expressly to the question, we

have to say his decision was not a pure rule decision (he did not assume the point), but a decision on reasons; he decided that the reasons supporting the decision in *Donoghue* v. *Stevenson* applied with equal effect in the case of a repairer, or, as the point is more usually put, that the fact that the defendant in *Donoghue* v. *Stevenson* was a manufacturer not a repairer was immaterial. Now, another court might well have made a rule decision in such a case. It might have cited *Donoghue* v. *Stevenson* as authority for a norm which made no distinction between manufacturer and repairer and applied the norm by assumption. Goddard, however, considered the point. But he may not have considered it strenuously. Steps in his reasoning may have been taken by assumption. Thus, what looks like a hard case may turn out to have been partly a hard case and partly a rule case.

Conversely, what looks like a rule decision may be a decision partly for reasons. For instance, suppose another case of a repairer subsequent to *Haseldine* v. *Daw* which accepted it as authority for the extension of *Donoghue* v. *Stevenson* and decided accordingly. This would be a rule decision. The strenuous processes of reference to all the reasons would be absent, giving the appearance of a simple rule decision. But these strenuous processes might be absent only because of the immediate intuitive plausibility of treating manufacturer and repairer alike in their responsibility for negligence. This immediate intuitive plausibility is, of course, a matter of reasons, and so this case too would be partly a hard case and partly a rule case.

The author is not aiming to encourage anyone to examine the complexities of these amalgams in any depth or to develop principles for the finer individuation of cases. The point is just to show how complex practical thought is, and to set the rather simple, ideal analysis of the rest of this book in its proper context.

IX

PRECEDENT

IX.1

When one of the higher courts decides a case its decision is authoritative not just for the disposition of the case itself but for future cases. Its facts, its decision and the reasons that the judge gives for decision are reported and it stands as an authoritative precedent.

The problem of how it is authoritative in this way is called by lawyers the problem of *ratio decidendi*. The special difficulty of this problem is caused by the fact that any decision of a case is a decision on particulars not universals (I.10); and it is not at all clear how a decision on one particular (or set of particulars) is authoritatively applied to another.

There is no such difficulty in seeing how a decision in universal form can be applied authoritatively to a particular. Thus there is no equivalent problem with the authority of statutes. Statutes usually lay down norms in universal form, and the problem is simply one of membership of the class proposed.

IX.2

Suppose I am a waiter and am told by my employer: all white wine is to be served chilled. A customer asks for unchilled white wine and I say: I'm sorry, sir, my orders are that all white wine is to be served chilled. I shall be sacked, and I shall not be able to claim that I was following instructions. I was not, for I misunderstood my instructions, which were general rather than absolute. Compare to this instruction a statute which says: all white wine shall be served chilled. Because there is a rule of recognition of statutory norms this is absolute, not general. Of course, the statute might make exceptions, but the norm with its exceptions would still be absolute. Take another case: Suppose I watch you planting vines every three feet in a straight line across a vineyard. I follow, I say, and begin planting. You see that I have learnt, and leave me in charge. I come to a fourteenth-century stone cross in the vineyard right on the three feet of my progression. I demolish the cross to plant the vine. My mistake here is worse than in the restaurant for my vine-planting instruction was only by the example of single cases. At least in the restaurant it might have been the case, though it was not, that my instruction was intended to be an absolute norm; but to infer absoluteness from the example of single cases would always be a mistake.

Norm and example are incompatible: if I turn an example into a norm I lose the example. But example cannot be dispensed with in moral and legal thought. We are out walking. You doff your hat to some girls, but not to some others, and teach me by your example. But what if you now say: always doff hats to girls, except such and such, attempting to put your teaching into the form of a norm. Where now is the example? Has the norm which you have stated taken it over? In which case the example is lost, for an example is not to be found in a norm (consider of any norm: what is the example?). If the norm has not taken the example over, we must ask why not. Answer: because there is something in example which cannot be taken over by a norm.

There is here proposed a dichotomy between norm and example. At a certain simple level, however, norm and example are compatible. Suppose you propose a norm to me: do not doff your hat to girls with red hair. To apply that norm I need to know the meaning of the word 'red', and I only learn that by example. But that is not a case of learning the norm by example; rather, of learning the language by example. And the case of language confirms the present thesis. For the fundamentals of language are learnt by example not norm, and furthermore these language-learning examples are not reducible to norm.

Hare's position is as follows:

It is hardly necessary to point out that principles of driving, like other principles, are normally not inculcated by their verbal repetition, but by example, demonstration, and other practical means. We learn to drive, not by precept, but by being shown how to do particular bits of driving; the precepts are usually only explanatory or mnemonic of what we are being shown. Thereafter, we try to do the particular manoeuvres ourselves, and are criticized for failures, commended when we do them well, and so gradually get the hang of the various principles of good driving. For although our instruction is far from being purely verbal, nevertheless what we are being taught are principles. The fact that the derivation of particular acts (or commands to do them) from principles is normally done non-verbally does not show that it is not a logical process, any more than the inference:

> The clock has just struck seven times
> The clock strikes seven times at seven o'clock only
> ∴ It is just after seven o'clock

is shown to be non-logical because it is never made explicitly in words.

Drivers often know just what to do in a certain situation without being able to enunciate in words the principle on which they act. This is a very common state of affairs with all kinds of principles. Trappers know just where to set their traps, but often cannot explain just why they have put a trap in a particular place. We all know how to use words to convey our meaning; but if a logician presses us for the exact definition of a word we have used, or the exact rules for its use, we are often at a loss. This does not mean that the setting of traps or the use of words or the driving of cars does not proceed according to principles. One may know how, without being able to say how – though if a skill is to be taught, it is easier if we can say how. (1952, 63)

But there is not an analogy with the clock inference; for there is no difficulty at all in stating the principle on which the clock inference is based ('the clock strikes seven times at seven o'clock only'). But often where I have learnt by example the principle (norm) is unstatable. When Hare says 'one may know how without being able to say how' I don't think he is pointing to a certain state of ignorance such that if I knew more I would know how to say how;

on the contrary, if I knew how to say how I should probably know less, for I should probably then have a rule, the norm of which is whatever it is that I know how to say, and I should be deciding by the assumption of the bindingness of that norm, i.e. without a consideration of the truth. I would know less because truth would be out of account.

Hare believes that universalizability is a necessary feature of moral thought. If he were right it would follow that moral examples of the sort we are discussing could be universalized, that is reduced to norms. Hare's arguments, however, apply only to statable things, and such things by no means account for the whole of moral thought; indeed we might go further and say that Hare's arguments apply only to stated things, i.e. norms:

> Suppose then that we find ourselves in circumstances which fall under the principle, but which have certain other peculiar features, not met before, which make us ask 'Is the principle really intended to cover cases like this, or is it incompletely specified – is there here a case belonging to a class which should be treated as exceptional?' Our answer to this question will be a decision, but a decision of principle, as is shown by the use of the value-word 'should'. If we decide that this should be an exception, we thereby modify the principle by laying down an exception to it. (1952, 65)

The words used in this passage are very revealing: 'intended', 'incompletely specified', 'decision', 'modify', 'laying down'. These words suggest that the 'principle' is really a norm, i.e. something actually formulated. Perhaps Hare's whole moral theory is a theory of norms, i.e. principles actually formulated: this would tend to explain his views about universalization, for there are many norms that would be morally objectionable for lack of universalization. His conception of 'exception' suggests this, too. I should say that you can only have an exception if you have a norm. A counter-example to an example is not an exception; just a counter-example.

The inadequacy of a theory dealing only in norms is that it cannot tell us anything about the movement between norms; in Hare's terms, between formulated principle and formulated exception. But the whole of moral substance is contained by such movements (they are hard cases in our terms). Of course, there

177

may be a (third) normative formulation to account for the movement. But not always. The time must come when normative formulations run out. Another way of putting this is that when I am programmed subjectively to make responses of the will to universals (III.13) the time must come when the limits of the programme are reached. And what then? Hare's idea of freedom is that I am free to choose absolutely anything. But what can this mean? Absolutely any programme?

There are three reasons why a norm cannot replace an example.

First, there is the inexhaustibility of description (Hampshire, 1978, 30 ff.): in any moral case the significant facts can never be exhaustively described. Thus in any moral example the description upon which a corresponding norm might be constructed can never be completed.

The second reason is related to this. If we take a case such as Hare uses of learning to drive by the example of a teacher we can see that the requisite bodily movements, their strength and their timing, are so complex that in the end if I have succceeded in learning, all I shall be able to state, apart from a few very broad principles, is that I have learnt how. I shall not be able to say I have learnt that . . ., and then set out what it is I have learnt in sufficient detail to construct a norm that can stand as a complete account of the exercise. And in hard moral cases where I learn by the example of another I learn a certain passionate response which seems even further beyond description than the bodily movements requisite to the driving of a motor car. This, of course, is the thesis of ch. IV that the weight of reasons for action (my passionate response to facts) can be learnt but not stated.

The third reason why a norm cannot replace an example is perhaps at the bottom of it all. A norm, at least the sort of norm in issue, deals in universals; whereas an example is a particular or a set of particulars. And particulars, though they have properties and relations, which are universals, cannot be reduced to universals.

The idea of learning by practice corroborates these points. There is a close relationship between learning by example and learning by practice, but none at all between norm and practice. The idea that I might learn the application of a norm by practice is a nonsense. Suppose the norm is 'x ought to be done'. If I apply it I apply it by syllogism (x ought to be done, this is an x, therefore this ought to be done) and there is no sense to the idea of practising this.

Of course, there is sense to the idea that I might need practice in logic or language but that is not the same thing as practice in the application of this norm. And there is sense to the idea that I might need practice in the decision of hard cases of interpretation of the norm, but this is precisely because they are hard cases, not cases decided by the application of a norm. When, on the other hand, I am shown something by example there is every point in my practising it for myself, to get the hang of it, as Hare puts it. This connection to practice which obtains for example but not for norm shows that examples and norms are not substitutes.

The first function of a judicial precedent is to stand as an example. The example is the decision of the case and the particulars on which it is based. There is a temptation to think that one reads a law report merely to learn of the (universal) properties and relations that obtained in the facts of the case with a view to constructing an appropriate norm; that one's interest in and knowledge of the particulars is irrelevant. But this is a mistake. One can know particulars as well by reading about them as by seeing, touching and hearing (in *all* cases one might be misled). And since it is particulars that give the intrinsically practical response which constitutes reasons (I.10), it is to the particulars of the precedent that I must attend if I am to learn the practical business of judging hard cases.

This is clearly the most important function of precedents. The weight of reasons is unstatable (ch. IV). If I am to learn how to weigh reasons in law cases it can only be from the example of precedent cases. Thus does institutional history educate (IV.8). Of course, the main part of my ability to weigh reasons in law cases is learnt as a child; there, too, by example rather than norm.

IX.3

Suppose an authoritative precedent case where a court has made a decision in favour of the plaintiff on facts *ABCXYZ*. Let us say that *ABC* are the facts in the plaintiff's favour and the reasons that they raise, and that *XYZ* are their equivalents for the defendant (we say nothing for the present on the question of who or what determines this set of facts). Suppose further that we (or a court) have a case to decide which is identical with the precedent in its properties and relations (its universals) except that D is the case rather than A, and that we decide this case also in favour of the plaintiff. There are various ways of deciding this.

In the first place we might ignore the precedent, refer to it perhaps, but not allow it to figure significantly in our reasoning:

   1 (i) DBC outweighs XYZ
       (ii) therefore judgment for the plaintiff.

The ways of giving the precedent a significant place in the reasoning are more various. But before examining them some preliminary remarks are in order:

(a) 'DBC outweighs XYZ' and its variations, as well as its primary assertion about the outcome of a balance of reasons for action, is to be taken to assert the particular facts that D, that B, etc. These facts are particulars though what is predicated in them are universals. They are particulars in that the universal properties and relations predicated are asserted particularly to obtain. For example, suppose the facts are:

D Jones ran Smith down.
B Jones was negligent.
C Smith was injured.
X Smith was contributorily negligent.
Y Smith was an alien.
Z Smith was unemployed.

What are predicated here (which we might say are all either properties or relations) are universals suitable to stand in the following norm in universal form: 'a person is liable to another when he negligently runs him down and injures him notwithstanding that the other was contributorily negligent and was an unemployed alien'. This norm we would abbreviate as 'liability where $DBCXYZ$'. In the following schema norms shall go in quotes

(b) Also asserted in DBC outweighs XYZ is that the particular facts are reasons for action: that DBC are reasons for giving judgment for the plaintiff and that XYZ are reasons against it.

(c) The conclusion of a balance of reasons for action is action or a decision to act. The conclusion '(ii) therefore judgment for the plaintiff' stands for the action of giving judgment for the plaintiff. Of course, there are many other actions that conclude law cases, and many philosophical problems about the individuation of action which we do not go into, despite the fact that it is the action which individuates cases (VIII.1). For example there are in traditional litigation:

> convicting a defendant,
> imprisoning him,
> sentencing him to death,
> distraining his goods,
> awarding a plaintiff damages (a second case, after giving him judgment),
> ordering a joinder of parties
> making a declaration of rights,
> issuing an injunction,
> adjourning a case,
> ordering a specific performance,
> putting in a receiver,
> requiring further and better particulars,
> excluding a piece of evidence,
> and so on.

In the more modern trends of litigation:

> ordering reinstatement in employment,
> certifying a representative for a class action,
> deregistering a trade union,
> prohibiting the acquisition of shares in a corporation,
> restraining a restrictive trading practice,
> breaking up a monopoly structure,
> ordering a government organisation to desist from this practice or that,
> desegregating a school,
> prohibiting a certain zoning scheme,
> requiring a certain zoning scheme,
> ordering changes in the structure of an errant corporation,
> and so on.

These are complex actions, particularly the latter class; and would often have to be broken up into a set of smaller actions. But all these judicial actions, large or small, are actions to be justified by reasons; and in this analysis the form 'therefore judgment for the plaintiff' is to stand for any of them.

Precedent

Rule cases are more complex in the matter of action. Actions, though they are the conclusions of balances of reasons for action, are not the logically proper conclusions of practical inferences (cf. Edgley, 1969, ch. 4); and the form of rule cases is the strictly inferential form of the practical syllogism (IV.2). Thus in rule cases the conclusion 'therefore judgment for the plaintiff' (which is still an action) covers a philosophically difficult movement from what is really a theoretical conclusion (the syllogism is by itself theoretical) to an action. The practical content is given by a subjective determination of the will in the rule way (III.13).

(d) All cases in the schema are two-sided conflicts – *DBC* against *XYZ*, judgment for the plaintiff against judgment for the defendant. Some cases, of course, are many-sided: send a defendant to gaol or fine him or release him on a bond, for example (these have as many sides as they have possible actions); and often they don't easily break up into sides at all, because the possible actions are almost limitless: an example of this is the common problem of deciding how much to award a plaintiff by way of damages, or the not so common problem of deciding what sort of restructuring to require of an errant corporation. Such cases need more complex analysis. I think the simple analysis undertaken below will go some way here.

The rest of the schema is as follows. It identifies ways of giving the precedent case (that *ABC* outweights *XYZ*) a significant place in the reasoning.

2   (i) 'judgment for the plaintiff where *ABCXYZ*' taken as a rule on the authority of the precedent (assumed to be binding)
   (ii) therefore judgment for the plaintiff where *ABCXYZ*
   (iii) therefore *ABC* outweighs *XYZ* (the practical force of this is given by the practical force of the rule assumption. It is a tricky step in other ways as well: see note 4 following).
   (iv) no difference in weight between *A* and *D* sufficient to swing the balance in (iii) when *D* is substituted for *A*
   (v) therefore *DBC* outweighs *XYZ*.
   (vi) therefore judgment for the plaintiff.

3   (i) 'judgment for the plaintiff where *DBCXYZ*' taken as a rule on the authority of the precedent (strictly if this

norm is stated in the precedent it is an *obiter dictum*, the
common lawyers' term, meaning beside the point, which
in the precedent was *ABCXYZ* not *DBCXYZ*, but this
consideration cannot *prevent* the rule being taken)
- (ii) therefore judgment for the plaintiff where *DBCXYZ*
- (iii) *DBCXYZ* is the case
- (iv) therefore judgment for the plaintiff.

Now suppose there is a class *P* with members *A* and *D*, a very
common case in the application of precedent decisions. We now
have:

4 (i) 'judgment for the plaintiff where *PBCXYZ*' taken as a
        rule on the authority of the precedent.
- (ii) therefore judgment for the plaintiff where *PBCXYZ*
- (iii) *D* is a *P*
- (iv) therefore judgment for the plaintiff where *DBCXYZ*
- (v)   *DBCXYZ* is the case
- (vi) therefore judgment for the plaintiff.

It is commonly said that judicial reasoning typically proceeds by
analogy. When the analogy is clearly articulated the class, *P*, is
formed and 4 is appropriate. For instance a court might for the
purposes of its case see an analogy between a motor-car (*A*) and a
motor-cycle (*D*) and actually articulate the class motor vehicle (*P*).
When the class is not clearly articulated the looser type 2 of this
schema obtains.

5 (i)   the precedent decided that *PBC* outweighs *XYZ*
- (ii) *PBC* does not outweigh *XYZ*
- (iii) But *PBCS* does outweigh *XYZ* (where *S* is the fact
        stated in (i) constituting the reason of *stare decisis* – the
        reliance of people on the precedent, the uncertainty if it
        were disturbed, etc.)
- (iv) therefore judgment for the plaintiff.

A variation of 5 would have 5(i) as: the precedent laid down the
norm 'judgment for the plaintiff where *PBCXYZ*'. The rest of the
reasoning would be the same. Of course, the important contrast
between 5 and 4 is that in 4 the norm is taken internally in the rule
way and in 5 is it taken externally, merely as a fact constituting one

reason for action amongst others (this distinction was discussed in IV.2). It is, of course, perfectly possible that *PBCS* does not outweigh *XYZ*; in which case the precedent is not followed.

Note 1 XYZ, the facts supporting the defendant, have consistently been included in any norm: e.g. 'judgment for the plaintiff where *ABCXYZ*'. It would be more common for this simply to be 'judgment for the plaintiff where *ABC*'. And this would have the same effect, for the norm would apply no matter what other facts there were. With *XYZ* in the norm it would be commonly stated in something like the following way: 'judgment for the plaintiff where *ABC* notwithstanding that *XYZ*'. But stated in this way, this latter part is strictly unnecessary.

Note 2 The schema displays these movements of thought:

(a) *Logical necessity* The reasoning is by syllogism when it moves from *PBCXYZ* to *DBCXYZ*. In 4, for example, it would be a contradiction, given (ii) and (iii), to deny (iv).

(b) *Rational necessity* The reasoning where reasons are weighed is not logically necessary. For example, in 1, it would not be self-contradictory to affirm (i) and refuse to give judgment for the plaintiff, but it would be irrational, for it is irrational to act other than in accordance with the weight of reasons. The point can be made stronger than this. It is impossible, for weakness of the will is impossible (V.7).

(c) *Rule application* Rule applications, though they are in part syllogistic, are supported as a whole by no logical or rational necessity. For example, in 4, (ii) does not follow rationally or logically from (i). The reason for this is that (i) is an act (the taking of an internal attitude to a certain rule, or the submission to it or acceptance of it – there are many ways of putting this). But there is a logical connection, for if (ii) is denied by the acting subject (i) is undone.

Note 3 In a hard case such as 1 there is no normative proposition which we could add to the reasons *DBC* or *XYZ* to make the plaintiff's or defendant's cases any stronger. If I have made a promise then the facts of the promise (including the facts of the consequences of breach) are my reasons for keeping it. I add nothing at all to the moral or legal situation in a hard case if I add the universal: one ought to keep promises. This is discussed in IV.2. Of course, in rule cases there is nothing but the universal in the form of a norm.

There are two further points about facts in cases.

First, they are often hypothetical, agreed on pleadings rather than proved. A little imagination is needed here on the part of judges if such facts are to constitute reasons of the same power as observed or directly experienced facts. But the situation here is not really very different from that in cases taking the ordinary course; for imagination is needed to understand proved facts, which also are not observed or directly experienced.

Second, facts include future facts. Sometimes these are very extensive. Traditional modes of adjudication have not eschewed future facts (for example, likelihood of deterrence or of a criminal's repentance in a punishment case, likely loss of expectation of life in a damages case, likelihood of an act being repeated as a ground for an injunction, irreconcilable breakdown as a ground for divorce, a threatened tort as a ground for a *quia timet* injunction), but it is equally clear that recent trends, particularly in the United States, have increased the range of future facts that courts are to look to.

> The traditional model of adjudication was primarily concerned with assessing the consequences for the parties of specific past instances of conduct. This retrospective orientation is often inapposite in public law litigation, where the lawsuit generally seeks to enjoin future or threatened action, or to modify a course of conduct presently in train or a condition presently existing. In the former situation, the question whether threatened action will materialize, in what circumstances, and with what consequences can, in the nature of things, be answered only by an educated guess. In the latter case, the inquiry is only secondarily concerned with how the condition came about, and even less with the subjective attitudes of the actors, since positive regulatory goals are ordinarily defined without reference to such matters. Indeed, in dealing with the action of large political or corporate aggregates, notions of will, intention or fault increasingly become only metaphors.
>
> In the remedial phases of public law litigation, factfinding is even more clearly prospective. As emphasized above, the contours of relief are not derived logically from the substantive wrong adjudged, as in the traditional model. The elaboration of a decree is largely a discretionary process within which the trial judge is called upon to assess and appraise the consequences of

185

alternative programs that might correct the substantive fault. In both the liability and remedial phases, the relevant inquiry is largely the same: How can the policies of a public law best be served in a concrete case? (Chayes, 1976, 1296)

All these future facts have weight as reasons for this or that judicial action (a weight which varies with their degree of probability: I.6), and no doubt they come within rules, too, when rules purport to cover them. Chayes calls them legislative facts, but this is a little misleading. Such facts might be used in legislative decision; but by courts they are usually used, even given the modern American developments, in purely single-case decisions. I might decide an ordinary moral case by reference to a wide range of extensive and future facts (decide to go to law school, for instance, rather than join a revolutionary group); but my decision is no less a single-case decision by virtue of its being influenced by such facts. And nor is a court's decision. Courts' decisions would only take on a legislative character when they were decisions not of single cases or of a set of single cases (where there is a large number of defendants), but of a class of cases (this is discussed further in X.1).

Note 4 The move in 2 from (ii) to (iii) depends upon what is meant by the assumption of the bindingness of a rule. When I apply a rule to a case I assume its bindingness in the case. Does this mean that I assume it gives the right hard answer to the actual hard case (i.e. that *ABC* does outweigh *XYZ*) or only that it gives the right hard answer in a majority or reasonable number of the class of cases to which it applies (sufficient number to justify having the rule)? If the latter, (iii) would not be entailed by (ii). If (as I think, and as I argue shortly) the former, (iii) is entailed by (ii); more accurately the assumption in (ii), being an assumption of the moral or ultimate bindingness of the norm in the case (III.2), entails (the assumption of) the truth of the corresponding moral or ultimate judgment in the case, i.e. *ABC* outweighs *XYZ*.

Now, the assumption of the bindingness of a rule cannot be merely an assumption of a right answer in a majority of cases to which the rule applies, for then no rule judgment would be logically sound. The final step of such a judgment must be 'it ought . . .' or some equivalent form if it is to justify a decision. Something like 'averagely it ought . . .' would not justify a decision unless a further norm was added to the effect that one ought to act on the average. But this further norm is not added in rule decisions. Furthermore, the assumption of a right answer in a majority of cases cannot be justified by reasons for rules. One reason for a rule is that it usually gives the right decision. This justifies me in assuming the rightness of rule decisions; it does not justify me in assuming the usual rightness of those decisions (if something *is* the case I have no reason to *assume* it is the case). Thus we have to say that the assumption of bindingness in a rule case is an assumption that the rule gives the right hard answer to the case.

Note 5 Often one party will in his argument rely heavily on the lack of a certain fact to support his opponent's case. There is no need to make any adjustment in the schema to reflect this possibility, such as by the addition of a negative fact. If in the case $DBCXYZ$ the defendant relies simply on the absence of A (as he might), this argument is given its due weight by the simple absence of A on the plaintiff's side in the balance DBC against XYZ. There is nothing needing to be added to the defendant's side of the scales to reflect his argument. The scales metaphor is helpful here, for on real scales a positive weight W on one side is exactly equivalent to the negative weight W on the other side.

Note 6 Sometimes the case in hand will be represented by $BCXYZ$ rather than $DBCXYZ$. For instance in *Barwick* v. *English Joint Stock Bank* [1866] L.R. 2 Ex. 259, a master was held liable for the wrong of his servant committed in the course of his employment and for the master's benefit. In *Lloyd* v. *Grace Smith* [1912] A.C. 716, the question was whether the absence of the last fact was significant, i.e. whether it was necessary for liability that the wrong be committed to the master's benefit; all other facts were equal. It was decided that it was not. Thus if *Barwick* v. *English Joint Stock Bank* is $ABCXYZ$, *Lloyd* v. *Grace Smith* is $BCXYZ$, where A is the fact of the master's benefiting from the wrong. The reason why *Lloyd* v. *Grace Smith* is a case of $BCXYZ$ rather than $DBCXYZ$ is that for those facts there is no natural or ordinary class P of which A (for the master's benefit) and D (not for the master's benefit) are members. Thus a subsequent case will not present D and will therefore only either have or not have A. (I say 'natural or ordinary class' because it would always be possible to invent class P).

Note 7 Let us say that a defendant without negligence or intention runs a plaintiff down and is sued. On the plaintiff's side if the case is a hard one we could say there is A, the fact that the defendant ran the plaintiff down, and B, the fact that the plaintiff was injured. There is nothing more, let us say, to constitute reasons for judgment for the plaintiff. Now, what supports the defendant? A lawyer would perhaps immediately say: the fact that there was no negligence or intention in the defendant; and this would be thought a strong defence. But this analysis is not in order, for these absences of fact are already taken into account by their simple absence from the plaintiff's side of the scales (see note 5) and they cannot be entitled to double weight.

Well, what are we to say for the defendant? If there is nothing, must we not say: AB outweighs nothing, therefore judgment for the plaintiff? This is a little puzzling. The answer, I think, is to say that for the defendant there is X, his freedom, which constitutes a reason not to give judgment against him, only to be outweighed by a strong case for the plaintiff, which AB is not. There is also Y, the social expense of litigation. (In earlier times there might also have been Z: lack of a form of action.)

X and Y with these values, are, I think pervasive general facts for defendants. There are fewer special defendant's facts than one might think. Most defendant's cases are simply assertions of the absence of special plaintiffs' facts, combined with a reliance on X and Y. An example of a special defendant's fact is in a negligence action the fact that the defendant is a barrister (as was argued in *Rondel* v. *Worsley* [1969] 1 A.C. 191, which established the partial immunity of barristers from suit).

IX.4

The Common Law doctrine of what a precedent case is to be authority for, commonly called the *ratio decidendi* of the case, typically tries to answer the problem of how to choose between reasoning of type 4 and reasoning of type 2; i.e. between taking the broad rule 'liability where $PBCXYZ$' or the narrower 'liability where $ABCXYZ$'.

The *ratio decidendi* of a precedent case according to Goodhart (1931) is the decision of the case based upon the material facts of the case. Thus we would say that the *ratio decidendi* of a precedent case is applied in a subsequent case when its material facts are found to be the same as those of the precedent and it is followed. This is the case in our type 4 (the material facts are *PBCXYZ*), and this qualifies in Goodhart's terms as a case of the strict application of a *ratio decidendi*. Type 2 is more complex, but the reasoning is based upon the judgment that there is no material difference between *A* and *D*. It is therefore a case of a correspondence of *material* facts between the precedent case and the case in hand (there is no material difference between *A* and *D*). Type 3 is a case that follows an *obiter dictum* in the precedent not its *ratio decidendi*.

Goodhart's was a successful theory of *ratio decidendi* (unlike any since) because it accounted with the greatest possible economy for both reasons and authority. The precedent has to stand for reasons (*rationes*) and it has to be authoritative. Goodhart saw that the facts of a case were the reasons for its decision; hence, the decision based upon the material facts gave the *rationes*, and in a form capable of being taken authoritatively. This seems so simple, but there are some problems lurking.

(a) Goodhart was superficially unclear about the nature of reasons. He actually held that the phrase *ratio decidendi* was a misnomer, for the reason which the judge gives is never the binding part of the precedent. This is a loose use of the word 'reason', meaning perhaps explanation. Certainly the explanation is not part of the *ratio decidendi*; it is merely a part of the judgment that one looks to to see which facts the judge regarded as material (Goodhart recognized this), and thus a part of the judgment which discloses the reasons (in the strict sense).

(b) There are reasons and there are descriptive reasons: reasons of which I speak committedly and reasons which I simply describe. Thus if I speak of a precedent court's reasons I can speak committedly of them or simply describe them. If I speak committedly of them, then, when there is an objective determination of the will I am referring to particular facts as reasons. I may take these as an example (IX.2), and that is the extent to which I (or a subsequent court) can use *the particulars*. If I describe the precedent court's reasons I am necessarily speaking of the (universal) properties and relations that obtained in the facts of its case (particulars are lost in description: they can merely be pointed to), and if I am to use these properties and relations it will not be as an example (for the particulars are the example) but as the basis for the construction of a norm which I can take authoritatively (e.g. 'judgment for the plaintiff where *PBCXYZ*'). Goodhart saw that a theory of *ratio decidendi*, being concerned with the construction of a norm for which a precedent could stand authoritatively, had to be concerned with descriptive reasons not reasons. He therefore insisted that it was for the precedent court to determine what the material facts of its case were. The subsequent court merely described them as a basis for authoritative application: it did not make a committed judgment about them. But he was not quite consistent here. For instance, of *Riggs* v. *Palmer* [1889] 115 N.Y. 506, where a precedent court held that a legatee who killed his testator could not take under the will, Goodhart says that the principle stated by the court was too wide. That principle was that no man shall be permitted 'to acquire property by his own crime', and Goodhart regards it as wrong or doubtful in its application to a large number of facts; an example he gives is where the legatee has killed the testator by manslaughter. Let murder be *A*, manslaughter *D* and criminal killing *P*. The question is whether the precedent is to be authority for *ABCXYZ* or *PBCXYZ*. Is the material fact to be *A* or *P*? Goodhart says *A*, for he sees a difference in point of reasons between *A* and *D*. And perhaps we do too. But we must be clear that it is Goodhart and those of us who agree with him who make this judgment of reasons. *The court said P*, for in various places it referred to criminal killing. Goodhart can give no reason for refusing to allow this to be a determination by the precedent court of what the material fact is. Reasons have been confused with descriptive reasons.

IX.5

Later theories of *ratio decidendi* have been less successful than Goodhart's because they have looked for norms *in* precedents rather than for material facts as a basis for the construction of norms *from* precedents. This is either because their authors have not been clear that facts are reasons, and have looked for something beyond them, or it is because they have followed Kant and Hare in thinking that practical reasoning requires a universalized major premise. These are fundamental mistakes which make clarity of analysis impossible. An example of such a theory is the following:

> The *ratio decidendi* of a case is any rule of law expressly or impliedly treated by the judge as a necessary step in reaching his conclusion, having regard to the line of reasoning adopted by him, or a necessary part of his directions to the jury. (Cross, 1977, 76)

Such theories fail because either there are no such norms (rules of law) to be found in precedents, or if there are they are not authoritative. There are only two sorts of norms to be found in precedents. If the precedent is a rule decision the norm which it takes authoritatively is likely to be revealed; but the precedent cannot be authoritative here, for no one can be an authority on something which he himself takes by authority. The operative authority would obviously be the first one from which the rule is taken. Secondly, norms which are *obiter dicta* (beside the point) can be found in precedents (in varying degrees of impressiveness: from off-the-cuff remarks to items of legislation). It is perhaps true to say that in modern times the higher courts have been rather more active than hitherto in reorganizing substantial areas of the Common Law. Sets of norms are thereby created. But they are *obiter dicta*, and though they might happen subsequently to be accepted as legislation (as in 3 in our schema), they are not authoritative in the judicial way at all (Cross's theory, just quoted, recognizes this, for it refers to 'rules of law . . . treated by the judge *as a necessary step* in reaching his conclusion'). The function of courts is to decide single cases, not legislate; legislation is making law for future cases; it is thus by definition not necessary for the decision of a case in hand (there is no dispute about this, though there is dispute about a different question of judicial legislation: whether in deciding a case a judge is to be regarded as making the law for his case or in some sense finding it: VII.5).

The idea that there might be a norm 'impliedly treated by the judge as a necessary step in reaching his conclusion' would be justified if a universalized major premise were a necessary part of practical reasoning. But it is not (IV.2). It is a necessary feature only of rule decisions. Theories like Cross's generally fail to see that 'judgment for the plaintiff where *ABCXYZ*' is not part of the precedent court's decision, which comes straight from '*ABC* outweighs *XYZ*'. It is weight which determines the will (gives the practical content of the decision) (IV.3–IV.4), thus the form '*ABC* outweighs *XYZ*, therefore judgment for the plaintiff', which is an immediate movement from weight to action, is primary.

To justify his departure from Goodhart in this matter, Cross refers to *Bourhill* v. *Young* [1943] A.C. 92, a negligence case where there were two possibly important facts for the defendant: first, the plaintiff was outside the range of the defendant's reasonable foresight, and second, the plaintiff's injury was of a special and perhaps dubious kind, nervous shock. There was judgment for the defendant. Cross regards it as necessary to look at the 'portions of the law' (meaning, presumably, 'rules' of law) in the speeches of the judges in order to know whether the *ratio decidendi* was to be limited by both these defendants' facts, or by only one of them and if so which (1977, 74). It is perfectly true that it is necessary to look to the speeches of the judges, but it is not necessary that we find rules of law there before we can construct the *ratio decidendi* of the case. The 'portions of the law' show which facts were regarded as material, and as soon as you have them you have the *ratio*. Let X be the fact that the plaintiff was outside the range of reasonable foresight and Y the fact that the injury was a case of nervous shock (the best analysis would have these as absences of plaintiff's facts, but this would complicate the example). The *ratio* of *Bourhill* v. *Young* is: no liability where *ABCXZ*. We determine that simply by determining that X was a material fact for the defendant but Y was not; and we can do that without the necessity of finding norms (or rules) of law in the precedent.

IX.6

In a well-known article ('The Model of Rules'; now 1977, ch. 2) Dworkin distinguished rules and principles on a number of logical grounds, the most important of which was that rules are absolute but principles have weight. Principles are generalized, we have been saying universalized, reasons, they therefore have weight, and the distinction as far as it goes is accurate. Dworkin, however, did not deal clearly with the question of the level of generality at which his principles are to be pitched, and this caused confusion. For example, Raz (1972a) mistakenly proposed that it was the level of generality which distinguished rules from principles. There are two problems of generality or universality involved here. One of Dworkin's examples is the principle that no man should profit from his own wrong. This, as principle, is the generalized (our term has been universalized) form of: that you committed a relevant wrong is a reason not to allow you to profit from it. But both (universalized) principle and reason are in a different and more important sense general rather than specific. Dworkin's example comes from the case of *Riggs* v. *Palmer*, where the question was whether a murderer (Elmer E. Palmer, aged sixteen, who administered poison to his grandfather) should take under the will of his victim. Now the operative reason in that case might be the one stated: that the beneficiary committed a relevant wrong is a reason not to allow him to profit from it. Or it might be the much more specific: that the beneficiary murdered the testator is a reason not to allow him to take under his will. Nothing in point of logical character turns on which of these is adopted. Each reason has weight and behaves logically in the same way, and each reason can be universalized into a principle of corresponding degree of generality:

(1) No man should be allowed to profit from his own wrong.
(2) No man should be allowed to take under the will of a
    testator whom he has murdered.

The court in *Riggs* v. *Palmer* called its principle a 'general fundamental maxim' (115 N.Y., 511), but this generality, though it raises an important issue as to the *ratio decidendi* of the case (is the *ratio* to be as general as stated or something more specific?), does not determine the logical character of the principle, which, being a reason universalized, functions by weight no matter how general it is. Raz, as we have seen, defined principles in terms of generality rather than weight, and so lost their logical character (loc. cit.).

The choice between the specific and the general versions of the reason is a choice between *ABCXYZ* and *PBCXYZ*, where (in *Riggs* v. *Palmer*) *A* is murder and *P* is the wider class, wrongful act. One gathers from a reading of the judgments of the court in *Riggs* v. *Palmer* that it thought that the more general principle was

stronger than the more specific; that *PBCXYZ* was a stronger case
than *ABCXYZ*. In fact the opposite is true: *PBCXYZ* is only as
strong as the weakest case of *P* (in *Riggs* v. *Palmer* this would be
the weakest case of wrongful act). But sometimes courts choose *P*
because *P* is strong enough (*PBC* is able to outweigh *XYZ*).
Rylands v. *Fletcher* [1868] L.R. 3 H.L. 330, may be analysed as an
example of this. There was liability for the escape of water from
the defendant's land. Negligence on the part of the defendant was
held to be irrelevant. Let *P* be escape, *A* negligent escape and *D*
non-negligent escape. Thus there was liability where *PBC*, rather
than liability where *ABC*. Obviously *A*, negligent escape, is a
stronger plaintiff's case than *D*, non-negligent escape; and *P*,
escape, is only as strong as its weakest member, *D*. Likewise, in
Riggs v. *Palmer* wrongful act (*P*) is not as strong a reason (or, if
universalized, principle) as murder (*A*), and in fact is only as
strong as its weakest member.

These are important and difficult questions of generality. It
would not be claiming too much to say that they constitute the
whole problem of *ratio decidendi*. But the other question of
generality, that of universalizing reasons into principles, is of
limited importance. Universalizing, as we have argued at some
length (IV.2), adds nothing to the weight of a reason: 'no one shall
profit from his own wrong' is in a hard case no stronger than 'that
you committed a relevant wrong is a reason not to allow you to
profit from it', and 'no murderer should take under the will of his
victim' no stronger than 'that you murdered the testator is a reason
not to allow you to take under his will'. The only significance of
the universalized form is that it is the form of a norm and can
therefore be taken as a rule.

IX.7

A subsequent court must, if it is to take a decision of a precedent
court authoritatively, construe the decision on its material facts as
a norm. Since the precedent is a decision on the particulars of a
single case this norm is not to be found constructed by the
precedent (IX.5), but must be constructed by the subsequent
court. The precedent court's decision:

1 (i) *ABC* outweighs *XYZ*
   (ii) therefore judgment for the plaintiff

must be turned into the norm: 'judgment for the plaintiff where *ABCXYZ*', and then the subsequent court is in a position to apply the norm in the rule way:

   (i) 'judgment for the plaintiff where *ABCXYZ*' taken as a rule on the authority of the precedent
   (ii) therefore judgment for the plaintiff where *ABCXYZ*
   (iii) *ABCXYZ* is the case
   (iv) therefore judgment for the plaintiff.

Now, what is the justification for this? Norm and example are incompatible things (IX.2), so what is the justification for so radically transforming the precedent? One answer is that the transformation is made necessary by the convention that judges give reasons (meaning explanations) for their decisions; if this requires reference to a precedent then the force of the precedent must be put into words; and putting an example into words, unless the words are poetry, necessarily makes a norm.

This analysis commits us in some cases to what Raz has called the tame doctrine of distinguishing, whereby when we find a new material fact in a subsequent case, say *D*, we say that the norm of the precedent case 'judgment for the plaintiff where *ABCXYZ*' simply does not apply. Raz's strong, and favoured, idea of distinguishing is that the norm of the precedent case is changed (1979, 183–5). This can only be if the norm gathered from the precedent is 'judgment for the plaintiff where *PBCXYZ*'. Here (*P* being a class which includes *A* and *D*) we would, if we thought there was a material difference between *A* (the precedent's fact) and *D* (the subsequent case's fact), limit the *ratio decidendi* of the precedent to *A*: instead of 'judgment for the plaintiff where *PBCXYZ*' we would make it 'judgment for the plaintiff where *ABCXYZ*', and the precedent would be distinguished in Raz's strong way, with the norm amended. Since the precedent court might have taken either *P* or *A* to be the material fact, both tame and non-tame ideas of distinguishing are required; it all depends on how the *ratio decidendi* norm of the precedent is constructed.

Sometimes norms are found in precedents which although they are strictly *obiter dicta* are taken authoritatively. A prominent example is *Miranda* v. *Arizona* [1966] 384 U.S. 436, where the Supreme Court of the United States laid down some rules for the interrogation of suspects by the police. These were clearly intended to be norms and not just judgments on the particulars of the Miranda case itself. Since the norms are found in the precedent no question of transformation by a subsequent court arises. No question of *ratio decidendi* arises. If such norms are to be authoritative it is as legislated norms are authoritative. There is no reason why they should not be authoritative in this way – at least no philosophic reason (there are, in fact, reasons against it, for instance that courts are not usually democratically elected, and constitutional reasons relating to the separation of powers) – what I mean is: it presents no philosophic puzzle to find a court deciding to be a legislature (wholesale or just for a small point), nor to find a community accepting this.

IX.8

Reasons and authority are incompatible concepts.

Accepting authority, according to Raz (1979, 26), involves giving up one's right to act on the balance of reasons. Raz himself would not put the matter quite as starkly as in the opening sentence of this section: to accept authority, Raz says (loc. cit.), is to accept an exclusionary reason, and thus authority is actually constituted by that sort of reason. What are incompatible, in Raz's terminology, are authority and first-order reason.

Amending Raz, as we must do if his idea, exclusionary reason, is to be rejected (VI.5–VI.8), we would say: deciding by authority is deciding by a certain sort of rule. The contrast is seen in types 4 and 5 of the schema. Type 4 follows the precedent as an authority. Type 5, although it follows the precedent to a conclusion which in its absence would not be in accordance with reasons, does not follow it as an authority. It accepts it only externally as a fact constituting the various reasons of *stare decisis*; it is like a case from Wolff's *In Defence of Anarchism* that Raz examines and rightly rejects as a case of authority (loc. cit.). Wolff says:

> For the autonomous man, there is no such thing, strictly
> speaking, as a command. If someone in my environment is

Precedent

issuing what are intended as commands, and if he or others expect those commands to be obeyed, that fact will be taken account of in my deliberations. I may decide that I ought to do what the person is commanding me to do, and it may even be that his issuing·the command, is the factor in the situation which makes it desirable for me to do so. For example, if I am on a sinking ship and the captain is giving orders for manning the lifeboats, and if everyone else is obeying the captain because he is the captain, I may decide that under the circumstances I had better do what he says, since the confusion caused by disobeying him would be generally harmful. But insofar as I make such a decision, I am not obeying his command; that is, I am not acknowledging him as having authority over me. I would make the same decision, for exactly the same reasons, if one of the passengers had started to issue 'orders' and had, in the confusion, come to be obeyed. (1970, 15–16)

Following the captain's order in this way, or the order of the passenger who has become the *de facto* captain, is not following authority. Raz says (loc. cit.)

Wolff is making two valid and important points here. (1) Because an order is always given with the intention that it be taken as both an exclusionary reason and a first-order reason, its addressee has more options than either to disregard the order altogether or to obey it as he was intended. He may hold it to be a valid first-order reason, given the circumstances of its utterance, whilst denying that it is an exclusionary reason. (2) This means that an anarchist can reject the legitimacy of all authority while giving some weight to the instructions of de facto authorities. He can take such instructions to be first-order reasons without conceding the legitimacy of the authority. For it is only by acknowledging that such instructions are also valid exclusionary reasons that one accepts the legitimacy of the issuing authority. Only such an acknowledgement amounts to submission to authority for only it contains the necessary element of the denial of one's right to act on one's own judgment on the merits.

There is another way to show that reasons and authority cannot run together. Reasons do not exist independently of their weight.

Precedent

No authority can determine this weight, for an authority can only act by communication, and weight cannot be communicated (according to the argument of chapter IV).

But an authority can state the material facts of a case it decides, and when the decision on these facts is construed as a norm the norm can be taken as a rule, i.e. authoritatively, as in types 2, 3 and 4 ('judgment for the plaintiff where *PBCXYZ*' taken as a rule, etc.). Reason has in this process become descriptive reason, constituted by described material facts; thus there is no question of weight for a subsequent court.

IX.9

Reasons and example run together (IX.4). But someone from whom I take an example is a teacher not an authority.

IX.10

There is clearly a rule of recognition of statutes ('rule of recognition' is here used in Hart's sense in *The Concept of Law*: a rule which identifies or recognizes the (primary) rules of a legal system). But is there a rule of recognition of precedents? (Hart thought there was). We mean here rule of recognition of law generally: there is clearly a rule of recognition of the norm by which a court settles a particular case. Thus we mean rule of recognition of norms such as 'judgment for the plaintiff where *ABCXYZ*' as opposed to the norm 'judgment for *this* plaintiff'.

One problem is that any rule of recognition must be at least partly constituted by precedents. But, more basically, we may ask: what could the rule of recognition of precedents be? In the case of statutes this question can easily be answered: the rule of recognition of statutes is simply a rule for recognizing as law the norms in statutes. But in the case of precedents this answer is not open, for there are no clearly authoritative norms in precedents. There is clearly in the Anglo-American legal systems no simple rule that what a precedent lays down (normatively) is the law. Some norms of this sort are perhaps the law, for instance the Miranda norms discussed in IX.7; but there is no rule of recognition saying which. And even if there were it would be exceptional and devoid of philosophic interest. For in such cases the court is simply acting as a legislature, and a rule of recognition of legislation is a commonplace. The interesting question is whether there is, as Hart thought, a rule of recognition of the law produced by courts in their adjudicative capacity.

What of the primary (adjudicative) aspects of a court's decision in which it decides its case and gives reasons for its decision? Could there, for a subsequent court, be a rule of recognition operating to recognize law in the precedent court's reasons? Those who think there could be are influenced by the fact that reasons often take the universalized form of principles, and thus look like norms capable of being recognized.

Consider the principle discussed in IV.2: (A1) One ought to exercise care towards anyone in front of his car (*prima facie*). Suppose a precedent in a running down case where negligence is shown and judgment is given for the plaintiff; and suppose (A1) is stated by the precedent court. The context will indicate whether the *prima facie* qualification is intended or not; that is, whether weight is relevant or not. If it is, then, for the reasons given in IV.2, the principle (A1) is spurious and its proper form is that of the reason (B2): That the plaintiff is in front of his car is a reason for the defendant to exercise care towards him (which translates for the judge into the reason: That the plaintiff was in front . . . and the defendant did not exercise care . . . are reasons to give judgment for the plaintiff). *(A1) is not a norm*, and thus is not available for recognition. One of the reasons for calling such principles spurious is that they look like norms, but are not. Recognition of them is inappropriate because they are a function of weight, and weight with its indefinite graduation is not available for recognition. Only norms, which are absolute, can be recognized.

If, on the other hand, there is no *prima facie* (weight) qualification to the precedent court's statement of (A1), then it is intended to be absolute. It is therefore a norm. In this case it is applied by the precedent court either externally (inference (C) in IV.2) or internally as a rule (inference (D) in IV.2). But in neither case is the precedent authority for the norm. If it applies it internally, the precedent is not authority for the norm, for the precedent court *itself* takes the norm by authority (IX.5). And if it applies it externally any authority attaching to the norm would be similarly independent of the precedent court's decision. The most that the precedent court could be authority for would be a norm of *stare decisis* (that which justifies its applying the norm in question).

Perhaps, however, not what the precedent court reasoned, but what it decided, i.e. its *ratio decidendi*, can be the subject of a rule of recognition. The difficulty with saying that there is a rule of recognition of the *ratio decidendi* of a precedent is that since a *ratio decidendi* is not a norm to be found in a precedent (IX.7), this could be no rule of *recognition* of norms. It could only be a rule to construct certain norms from certain precedents.

It is possible for there to be such a rule; though unlikely in the present state of Anglo-American legal thinking. The reason for this unlikelihood is that the principles for the construction of such norms (the principles of the construction of *rationes decidendi*) are extensively controversial, and controversy is incompatible with rule.

In the first place there is controversy as to what is a *ratio decidendi*: Goodhart proposed a definition half a century ago (1931), and it is still disputed, and disputed not at its edges like the rule of recognition of statutes, but at its heart. And in the second place, even if there were general agreement on the definition of *ratio decidendi*, its application in any case would be controversial. The question at what level of generality has a court pitched its decision? is almost always open and almost always susceptible of a number of answers. A bottle of ginger beer is a bottle of soft drink, a bottle of drink, a food, a manufactured thing, a thing sold, a thing, and so on. It would be highly unusual in any case of 'liability where *ABCXYZ*' for a subsequent court to glean all of *ABCXYZ* from the precedent without itself making (hard) judgments of materiality; and, even if it did, even more unusual for there to be general agreement about this. A statute, on the other hand, states norms rather than decides cases and so raises no such problems. That is why there can straightforwardly be a rule of recognition of statutes, but not one of precedents.

This is no small matter. Legal positivists require norms capable of being recognized if they are to be able to point to the posited laws that their theory requires. Clearly if the arguments of this section hold, they must concede that their theory cannot accommodate the Common Law.

There is a lesser sense of rule of recognition which can apply to precedents, and (apart from the recognition of the single-case norms which settle the dispute between the parties in a case) it is perhaps the only sense which can. The extraction of a norm is not the only way to use a precedent. Of the five types of decision identified in the schema, only 1 does not use the precedent case. The other types use it in various ways, and for all of them the identification of the precedent as an authentic or authoritative source of law is necessary (as different from a piece of fiction or a judgment in a moot case or a case in an unrelated legal system). This identification since it is of authority is done by rule, and we may talk of a rule of recognition of sources of law. But that is not the idea of rule of recognition of norms ('primary rules') that Hart tried to establish in *The Concept of Law*.

IX.11

The distinction between the strong and the weak senses of wrong is important for it establishes the binding power of precedent. The distinction is that only in the strong sense of wrong is it the case that a court ought not to follow a wrong precedent (VII.5). Type 5 in the schema illustrates the two senses of wrong. The precedent court has decided that *PBC* (the plaintiff's reasons) outweighs *XYZ* (the defendant's reasons). But according to the subsequent court it does not. Thus the precedent is wrong. When all the reasons of *stare decisis* arguing that the precedent ought to be followed (called *S*) are taken into account the case becomes *PBCS* (for the plaintiff) against *XYZ* (for the defendant). If *PBCS* does not outweigh *XYZ* the precedent is wrong in the strong sense and cannot be followed. If *PBCS* does outweigh *XYZ* it is wrong only in the weak sense and must be followed, that is, judgment must be for the plaintiff.

Raz says: 'If every court is entitled to overrule any decision of any other court which applies to the case before it whenever it thinks it best to do so, then the legal system does not recognise the binding force of precedent' (1979, 189). We must distinguish overruling in the strict sense from not-following. In the case of not-following, what Raz says would be true only if courts were entitled not to follow precedents wrong in the weak sense as well as those wrong in the strong sense. Whenever the reasons of *stare decisis* (*S*) are recognized the entitlement not to follow is limited to decisions wrong in the strong sense, and thus the binding power of precedent is recognized. Of course, in each case the subsequent court decides itself whether *PBCS* does or does not outweigh *XYZ* (decides what 'it thinks it best to do'); but this qualification adds nothing of significance to the analysis (V.2–V.4).

Overruling in the strict sense raises different considerations. If a subsequent court decides that *PBCS* does not outweigh *XYZ* it does not follow the precedent; it may also, if it has the authority, overrule the precedent, either expressly, or implicitly in its not following it. If, on the other hand, the court follows the precedent on the ground that *PBCS* does outweigh *XYZ* it may still overrule it, intending to cancel it as a precedent for the future (and its own decision as well) so that in the future it may not be true that *PBCS* outweighs *XYZ*. The point is, it would cancel the justification of reliance on the decisions, and thus significantly diminish the weight of *S* for the future.

The question of prospective overruling, which has been extensively canvassed in the courts of the United States and is beginning to receive attention in the United Kingdom and Australia, is confused unless the distinction between overruling in the strict sense and not following is maintained.

> What many people regard as the last relict of the declaratory theory is the current invariable English practice of retrospective overruling.

> > And if it be found that the former decision is manifestly absurd, or unjust, it is declared, not that such a sentence was bad law, but that it was not law. [Blackstone]

> This practice could be productive of great hardship and might operate as an undesirable curb on the exercise by a court of its overruling powers. For example, if the House of Lords were to overrule the decisions which most lawyers consider to have set the seal on the doctrine of privity of contract, settlements of property based on the assumption of the validity of that doctrine would lose much of their point, and the intentions of the settlor together with the legitimate expectations of others would be defeated. Such injustices could be avoided if the decision in question could be overruled with purely prospective effect. The

old law would apply to events occurring before the date of the overruling, (including those of the instant case), but it would cease to be applicable to transactions entered into after that date. (Cross, 1977, 229)

What the declaratory theory means here is simply that if a court judges that *PBC* outweighs *XYZ* therefore judgment for the plaintiff, it is logically committed to the truth of that on the same facts yesterday. Thus if it so decides a case it is logically committed to the proposition that any previous court which decided the opposite on facts materially the same was wrong, that is, that it is and was always legally correct to hold (always the law) that *PBC* outweighs *XYZ* therefore judgment for the plaintiff. Far from being something represented only by a 'last relict' this is a quite fundamental logical point which only moral relativists or subjectivists would question.

Thus, so far as following or not following a precedent is concerned no question of the time at which it might be wrong arises.

And so far as overruling (in the strict sense) is concerned, no question of time arises, for overruling can only be prospective. If a court decides that *PBCS* outweighs *XYZ*, thus making it necessary to follow a wrong precedent, it would be pointless to overrule the precedent retrospectively: that would not affect the weight of *S*, thus the precedent would still have to be followed. Indeed, more than this, it would be logically impossible to overrule retrospectively, just as it is logically impossible to decide today to knock down a wall yesterday. And the same points obtain where the subsequent court decides that *PBCS* does not outweigh *XYZ*.

Many of the problems attaching to prospective overruling have been produced by a failure to distinguish not-following from overruling. For instance, Cross says:

'Prospective overruling is not invariably the most just course. This point can be made most clearly apparent in relation to criminal proceedings. Suppose that A's conviction is affirmed by the Criminal Division of the Court of Appeal on the strength of one of its past decisions which the House of Lords holds, on A's appeal, to have been erroneous. If the overruling of the decision of the Court of Appeal is to be entirely prospective, A's conviction ought to be affirmed. (1977, 230)

Here overruling and not-following are assumed to be identical; so that if overruling is to be prospective, (retrospective) not-following is impossible. '*A*'s conviction ought to be affirmed', following the precedent. But it is quite clear that the House of Lords can overrule the precedent (necessarily prospectively) and not follow it for the purposes of the decision of *A*'s case. It may even (as we have seen) overrule it and follow it (on the ground that *PBCS* outweighs *XYZ*).

The main cause of confusion here is that if you run not-following and overruling together you run together the necessary retrospectiveness of judgments of reasons and the necessary prospectiveness of overruling. This is obviously impossible. Thus judges have tended towards absolute positions on one side or the other. On the one side Lord Reid has said: 'Judge-made law is always retrospective. We cannot say that the law until yesterday was one thing, from tomorrow it will be something different' (1972, 23). And on the other there is Lord Diplock:

> And yet the rule that a new precedent applies to acts done
> before it was laid down is not an essential feature of the judicial
> process. It is a consequence of a legal fiction that the courts
> merely expound the law as it has always been. The time has
> come, I suggest, to reflect whether we should discard this
> fiction. (1965, 17)

The truth is that with suitable modification both are right: Lord Reid is right about the logical character of judgments of reasons, and Lord Diplock is right about the proprieties of overruling.

IX.12

Courts must respect precedents, but must low courts respect them more? Assume there is a precedent of the highest court deciding *P*, and assume that this is wrong in the strong sense, i.e. wrong in such a way that it must not be followed. Now, this case is unproblematic when it comes before the highest court: the precedent must not be followed and the correct judgment, not *P*, must be made.

But what if the case comes before a low court? Must the low court decide *P* or not-*P*? Sometimes it is said (not uncommonly by

high courts) that the low court must loyally decide to follow the
high court's decision even if it is wrong in the strong sense; that it is
not for a low court to refuse to follow a high court. For example:

> The fact is, and I hope it will never be necessary to say so again,
> that in the hierarchical system of courts that exists in this
> country it is necessary for each lower tier to accept loyally the
> decisions of the higher tiers (per Lord Hailsham L.C. in *Cassell
> v. Broome* [1972] A.C. 1027 at 1054)

But this view is a logical confusion, for it reduces to contradiction.
It entails that the low court must decide *P*; and that the low
court must decide *P* entails that the law for the litigants was *P* (it
cannot be the case that the law for the litigants at the time of their
relevant actions was other than what the court must decide it was;
call this the principle of correspondence). But how could the law
for the litigants be *P*, for their case might get to the high court?
And there, *ex hypothesi*, the correct decision is not-*P*. The same
principle of correspondence must hold, and thus the law for the
litigants must be not-*P*. Contradiction.

The principle of correspondence connects the law for the low
court to the law for the high court by way of a double
correspondence to the law for citizens. The only way this
connection could be broken would be by establishing an independence of the relation of citizen to low court from the relation,
citizen to high court. But either a low court case can go to the high
court (as an alternative jurisdiction or by appeal), in which case
there is no independence; or it cannot, in which case the low court
is a high court. In neither case is the independence of the low court
relation established.

Low courts, therefore, are required not to follow high court
decisions that are wrong in the strong sense, just as high courts are
required. The most deference that can be claimed from a low court
is that where there is a possibility of stating a case to the high court
and not itself making a decision it should out of respect do so.
Where a decision is required, however, the low court can do
nothing but make the right decision; i.e. the very decision which
the high court is required to make. (Do low courts, therefore, have
an authority equal to high courts? Of course not. *Stare decisis* and
the various methods of respect strongly support the decisions of
high courts, but those of low courts hardly at all. And low courts

have no authority to overrule, as distinct from not to follow, high court decisions.)

These conclusions can be avoided if the law is *P* until the high court reverses its earlier decision and decides not-*P*. But this cannot be, for if the law were *P* immediately prior to reversal there could be no reason for reversal by a high court or any other court. The earlier decision, *P*, would be right. The only reason for reversal is that the earlier decision is wrong; i.e. that the law is not-*P*.

IX.13

Lord Hailsham in *Cassell* v. *Broome* said (loc. cit.) that it was necessary for low courts loyally to accept the decisions of high courts. Now, where high court decisions are merely wrong in the weak sense (wrong, but ought to be followed) low courts must follow them just as high courts must. Presumably Lord Hailsham wanted to say something more in the case of low courts; namely, that they must follow high court decisions wrong in the strong sense, i.e. those wrong decisions which ought not to be followed (by the High Court). Well, as we have seen, this is not so as a matter of reasons, but may it not be the rule?

The rule would have to be: low courts must follow high court decisions absolutely.

Suppose a low court has this rule. Why should it continue to hold it? More to the point, why should it apply it in any particular case? It is necessary, said Lord Hailsham, meaning perhaps that there are reasons for the rule. Perhaps there are. But it is a mistake to think that the existence of reasons for a rule covering a class of cases, even of sufficient reasons, requires that the rule be applied in a single case (a member of the class) where on the balance of the reasons that obtain in the single case, including the existence of the rule, it gives the wrong decision. No doubt Lord Hailsham can point to good and sufficient reasons for the rule that low courts follow high courts absolutely. They would be reasons for the absolute rule, not for a rule 'follow high court decisions except those wrong in the strong sense'. There would be no balance of reasons in favour of this limited rule, for two reasons. First, such a rule would be superfluous, for it would reproduce exactly the situation that would otherwise obtain on the balance of reasons. And, second, because it would require low court judges to decide themselves whether high court decisions were wrong in the weak or strong sense (something which for various reasons they are not fully equipped to do) it would tend to cause more bad decisions by low court judges than it would save (if it be objected that precisely this would be the consequence of a low court judge accepting the arguments of this section, so be it: philosophy is not in the service of the state). Thus there are good and overriding reasons for the absolute rule. But this does not entail that the rule be applied in any single case where it is wrong to do so.

This is perhaps a paradox. What we are saying is that there can be overriding reasons for a rule to cover all cases of a certain class notwithstanding the fact that when a certain member of the class of cases comes up for decision it would be wrong on the balance of reasons to apply the rule to that case. Thus when there comes up for decision a single case where a high court precedent is wrong in the strong sense, that there are overriding reasons for a rule requiring low courts to follow all high court decisions including this one does not exclude the possibility that in the single case a low court is required by the balance of reasons in the single case, including the various reasons to follow the rule, to decide against the precedent and against the rule. This is simply because in the single case the action in issue is not the taking or keeping of the rule but whatever action it is that disposes of the *single* case. These actions are not the same and that a balance goes one way for one action and another for a different action is perfectly in order. Of course, there would not be a balance of reasons in favour of the rule covering the class of cases unless it were right in a substantial majority of the single cases comprising the class to follow the rule.

This is a fundamental point about rules, and is discussed further in XI.10 (see also X.7, where the question is examined in relation to the rule of recognition of statutes).

Rules obtain by assumption. And it may, of course, be that the psychological hold that an assumption has will not be collapsed in single cases where a rule gives the wrong decision. But that should be seen for what it is. Strictly speaking, though his statement looks reasonable, Lord Hailsham is bluffing.

All authority is constituted by rules. The existence of rules depends upon nothing more than the psychological fact of their holding. Thus any authority who insists, himself, on respect is bluffing. It is rather like insisting on being loved.

IX.14

Proponents of the thesis of judicial discretion beyond the limits of law might think their thesis avoids the conclusion of the last two sections, which is given its point by a conception of rightness that is independent of any particular precedent. We have argued that the thesis is a false one (V.1–V.4); but even if it were true the conclusions would only partly be avoided. Low courts would still be bound by reasons not to follow high court decisions wrong in the strong sense in all cases within the limits of law.

X

STATUTE AND CONSTITUTION

X.1

Obviously statutes make the law: they are items of legislation, and to legislate is to make law. But in what sense are we to say they do this?

A precedent decision of a court operates in two ways: at the general level it has a complex effect which we have spent the last chapter examining, and at the level of the single case it creates a norm or set of norms which settle the dispute between the parties. The question whether the courts make the law is, at the general level, a rather murky one, and one which we have sufficiently discussed (VII.5). The level of the dispute between the parties in a case presents the possibility of a clearer analysis. A court in settling a case creates a norm or set of norms. These norms were not in existence before the court's decision; thus it is clearly in order to say that the court created the norms. Are these norms laws? Well, why not? A better question, however, is, how do these norms differ from the norms which statutes create?

The important difference is that the norms which it is common for statutes to create cover a class of cases, whereas a court's norm covers a single case or set of single cases (a set of single cases where, for instance, there is more than one defendant). This distinction between types of norms might found a definition of a law: it might well be thought suitable to say that only norms which cover a class of cases are laws; thus that parliaments but not courts ordinarily make laws. There would be exceptions: on the one hand there are private Acts of Parliament, creating single-case norms, and on the other there is a modern trend in favour of actions against a class of defendants (though most defendant class actions, so-called, are actions against a set of defendants rather than an (open) class). Of these exceptions one might say that parliaments sometimes adjudicate and courts sometimes legislate. The important distinction is between adjudication and legislation: that these processes are sometimes mixed in particular institutions is of no philosophical interest.

A traditional distinction between legislation and adjudication is that the former is prospective and the latter retrospective. For adjudication this is, at the general level, true enough: a court decides its case on the basis of rules and reasons which already exist (IX.11). But the norm which it creates to settle the dispute between the parties is clearly prospective. In fact retrospective norm-creation, whether by courts or parliaments, is impossible; no more possible than it is for me today to build a wall yesterday.

In that sense retrospective legislation is a logical impossibility. If a statute creates a set of norms and declares that they are to operate as from yesterday the norms still operate only prospectively: they prospectively require a certain chronological pretence on the part of courts and officials.

X.2

Roscoe Pound wrote:

> Four ways may be conceived of in which courts in such a legal system as ours might deal with a legislative innovation. (1) They might receive it fully into the body of the law as affording not only a rule to be applied but a principle from which to reason, and hold it, as a later and more direct expression of the general will, of superior authority to judge-made rules on the same general subject; and so reason from it by analogy in preference to them. (2) They might receive it fully into the body of the law to be reasoned from by analogy the same as any other rule of law, regarding it, however, as of equal or co-ordinate authority in this respect with judge-made rules upon the same general

subject. (3) They might refuse to receive it fully into the body of the law and give effect to it directly only; refusing to reason from it by analogy but giving it, nevertheless, a liberal interpretation to cover the whole field it was intended to cover. (4) They might not only refuse to reason from it by analogy and apply it directly only, but also give to it a strict and narrow interpretation, holding it down rigidly to those cases which it covers expressly. The fourth hypothesis represents the orthodox common law attitude toward legislative innovations. Probably the third hypothesis, however, represents more nearly the attitude toward which we are tending. The second and first hypotheses doubtless appeal to the common law lawyer as absurd. He can hardly conceive that a rule of statutory origin may be treated as a permanent part of the general body of the law. But it is submitted that the course of legal development upon which we have entered already must lead us to adopt the method of the second and eventually the method of the first hypothesis. (1908, 385)

This was a strong and influential article at a time of great Common Law complacency:

Can we say that homestead and exemption laws, mechanics' lien laws, bankruptcy laws, divorce laws, wills acts, statutes abolishing the common law disqualifications of witnesses, permitting accused persons to testify, and allowing appeals in criminal causes, had no roots? Do any judge-made doctrines rest more firmly upon principles of right than these statutes, or than Lord Campbell's Act or Lord St. Leonards' Act or the Negotiable Instruments Law? Do the refinements of equity and the ultra-ethical impossibilities which the chancellors imposed upon trustees have deeper roots or represent right and justice better than trustees' relief acts? Are any judicial decisions more deliberately worked out or more carefully adjusted to the circumstances to which they are to be applied than the draft acts proposed by the Conference of Commissioners on Uniform Divorce Legislation? What court that passes upon industrial legislation is able or pretends to investigate conditions of manufacture, to visit factories and workshops and see them in operation, and to take the testimony of employers, employees, physicians, social workers, and economists as to the needs of workmen and of the public, as a legislative committee may and often does? Failures are not confined to legislative law-making. The fate of the fellow servant rule, of the doctrine of assumption of risk, and of the whole judge-made law of employers' liability, the Taff-Vale case in England, and the fate of judicial adjustment of water-rights in America, should make lawyers more cautious in criticizing the legislature. (ibid., 405)

There were some bad judges and some good statutes; but we should try to get the analysis in order.

How might a court 'reason from a statute by analogy'? A statute is in normative form, and a norm can not be an analogy (not like a precedent, which is a case and therefore can be an analogy). What can Pound have had in mind here?

Perhaps type 2 in our schema of types of reasoning from precedents can be adjusted to apply to statutes, for it is a type of reasoning by analogy. Assume there is a statute which has enacted the norm 'judgment for the plaintiff where $ABCXYZ$'. Our case is, as it was before, $DBCXYZ$.

2   (i)   'judgment for the plaintiff where $ABCXYZ$' taken as a rule from the statute.
    (ii)   therefore judgment for the plaintiff where $ABCXYZ$.
    (iii)   therefore ABC outweighs XYZ.
    (iv)   no difference in weight between A and D sufficient to swing the balance in (iii) if D is substituted for A.
    (v)   therefore DBC outweighs XYZ.
    (vi)   therefore judgment for the plaintiff.

This would seem the only way of extending a statute by analogy. As in the case of the precedent it operates only when DBC does not on a judgment of reasons outweigh XYZ (step (v), 'therefore DBC outweighs XYZ', is simply a development of the original rule assumption). If DBC does outweigh XYZ there is no problem; judgment for the plaintiff can be decided independently of statute or precedent on the ground that DBC outweighs XYZ. Now, DBC does not outweigh XYZ, and further, there is no material difference between D and A, therefore ABC does not outweigh XYZ either. Therefore 'judgment for the plaintiff where $ABCXYZ$' is wrong. So Pound's argument is limited to the extension of a bad statute; and we may presume he did not intend that.

What is the reason for Pound's muddle? I suspect it lies in confusion about reasons and legal reasons. We have said that if *DBC* outweighs *XYZ* then the court can decide it does independently of statute or precedent. Perhaps Pound thought that there was a restriction on the court's power to act on '*DBC* outweighs *XYZ*'; perhaps he thought that although *DBC* outweighs *XYZ* the *legal* reasons *DBC* do not. But this is a confusion about the nature of reasons similar to Dworkin's (IV.8). As we have seen, no distinction between reasons and legal reasons is logically open. Or Pound might have had in mind that a court may be limited in its access to the reasons *DBC* and *XYZ*. However, the court would be equally limited in its access to the supposed analogy between *A* and *D*. (We may presume that Pound was not making the simpler mistake of basing his argument on the insignificant fact that although *DBC* outweighs *XYZ* bad judges have decided that it doesn't.)

Pound's other suggestion was that a statute might offer a 'principle from which to reason'. This raises no fresh point. Principles are reasons universalized for certain purposes. When taken for the rigorous purpose of deciding cases they reduce to reasons. Thus in our example they reduce to *ABC* and *XYZ*.

X.3

At the level of general law-making there is a radical difference between legislatures and courts. Legislatures make law by the simple enactment of norms which cover a class of cases; and the only question in a subsequent case is whether it is a member of the class. Courts make law by the decision of single cases; and the questions which arise in subsequent cases are the complex and subtle ones considered in the last chapter.

Perhaps for some cases it matters which form of law-making a community adopts. Yet often courts pass the responsibility for the amendment of the common law to legislatures notwithstanding that legislation is not the amendment of the common law at all, but the substitution of a different and in some cases unsuitable system. And the new legal institution, the law reform commission, is usually made adjunctive to a legislature; as though all law reform had necessarily to be legislative law reform (why is it not expected that where appropriate law reform commissions would make their recommendations to courts?).

The reason for this state of affairs is not hard to find. The false philosophy of legal positivism has it that courts as well as legislatures make the law by creating norms that cover classes of cases (this is what enabled Hart to hold that there was a rule of recognition of court-made rules (IX.10), and Raz to reject what he called the tame doctrine of distinguishing (IX.7)). If the end-product is much the same it can't matter too much whether law reform is undertaken by courts or legislatures. It is possible that the Common Law will expire because of this confusion.

X.4

Hart said: the key to the science of jurisprudence lies in the combination of primary and secondary rules (1961, 79). This claims too much. Primary rules, we may say roughly, are the rules that apply to citizens to regulate their conduct, and secondary rules are rules about primary rules. The most important secondary rule, and the one which gives plausibility to Hart's claim, is the rule of recognition. But there is no rule of recognition of norms in precedents, no secondary rule whose function is to recognize primary rules in precedents (IX.10). There is no doubt a rule of recognition of the single case norms which settle the dispute between the parties to a case. And there is a rule of recognition of precedents as sources of law, as sources to provide a base for the various types of reasoning discussed in the last chapter. Thus in the case of precedents at the general level a thesis of the combination of secondary rules and sources is maintainable. But this is not the interesting thesis that Hart had in mind. The problem, we saw, is that precedents at the general level are not, except peripherally and accidentally, in normative form: there can be no straightforward connection to a norm in a precedent and therefore no straightforward connection to a (primary) rule. Statutes however are different. Statutes take normative form and their norms therefore may straightforwardly be recognized as primary rules. In the case of statutes the thesis of the connection between primary and secondary rules can be maintained.

X.5

There is a rule of recognition of statutes. However, there can be hard cases of recognition. This is not only in cases of revolution where a court is required to choose by hard decision between statutes of competing regimes but in certain cases in legal systems where no rule of recognition is actually formulated in certain terms.

An example of this is the United Kingdom legal system. There is in that legal system no rule of recognition in certain terms because there is no written constitution. The rule of recognition is a Common Law rule subject to settlement from case to case; this entails that recognition is made by the variety of reasoning examined in the last chapter. 'Common Law doctrine' would be a more accurate term than 'Common Law rule' because it is able to reflect this variety.

To speak of a single, objective rule of recognition in any legal system is, though convenient, strictly inaccurate. Citizens, lawyers, judges all have individual rules of recognition; each one himself assumes the bindingness of a norm stating the conditions of recognition (and makes the second assumption that others assume the bindingness of this norm too (III.2)), and there may or may not be exact correspondence between his norm and another's. In a legal system with a written constitution one would expect correspondence to be considerable. But in a case like the United Kingdom it is certain that no two judges assume the bindingness of precisely the same norm. This legal system holds together, however. It does this because for ordinary cases there is a sufficient correspondence of norms: each second assumption ('that you accept the bindingness of the norm') whilst not completely true is true enough for ordinary cases because the norm which 'you' accept differs only in respects irrelevant to those cases. Conversations survive with only approximate agreement in assumptions; and the conversation which constitutes a legal system is no different.

X.6

A norm in its terms is absolute and when it is applied internally it is applied absolutely. Either it is applied or it is not applied: there is no question of its weight, of its being in competition with anything else. Statutory norms are applied as a result of recognition, either the application of a rule of recognition or of a hard decision of recognition (X.5). In either case they are applied internally, and even where cases of interpretation are required, the norms themselves are, once recognized, applied absolutely. In this way it is characteristic of legislation to override everything: this is one sense of the doctrine of the omnipotence of Parliament.

However, it is obvious that the absolute character of statutory norms when recognized does not entail that absolutely any statutory norms are to be recognized. Yet in the British legal systems there is thought to be a fundamental constitutional doctrine that whatever Parliament enacts is law.

Stephen held, Dicey affirmed, and British constitutional lawyers have thought ever since, that the United Kingdom Parliament is so omnipotent that it can pass a law requiring the execution of all blue-eyed babies (Stephen, 1882, 143: Dicey, 1885, 81). Whether Stephen was the originator of this doctrine in constitutional law is not clear. But its subsequent acceptance among British constitutional lawyers has been remarkable. It has become a constitutional commonplace.

One reason for this extraordinary progress of a quite extraordinary doctrine has been that it usually carried an apology, enabling readers not to take it seriously. The good sense of Parliament, or at least the practical constraints on it, it is usually said, can be relied upon to prevent such legislation ever coming about. Stephen put it thus: 'But legislators must go mad before they could pass such a law, and subjects be idiotic before they could submit to it' (loc. cit.). Well, legislators have sometimes gone mad. And what then are judges to say?

Actually the apology shows that the doctrine is vitiated by a fundamental logical mistake. Subjects would have to be idiotic to submit, and so, we may presume, would judges. Thus what is proposed by Stephen is that a judge faced by a blue-eyed babies statute would have to say: this is the law, but on moral grounds I refuse to apply it (and resign, or whatever). This is the fundamental logical mistake of legal positivism refuted in ch. II.

Legal judgment entails (conclusive) moral judgment. Thus the judgment that the blue-eyed babies statute is the law entails that it is morally (conclusively) to be applied (II.2). If a judge is not prepared to stand up to that, as Stephen, happily, was not, the only course logically open to him is to say that it is not the law, that is, that the norm is not to be recognized (II.10).

Some judges perhaps would stand up to the entailment (many Nazis did); so it is necessary to examine what justification there might be for so doing. Let us put Stephen's legal judgment in order, logically speaking, and assume that it is intended as a conclusive judgment.

But before this, let us notice how pervasive the doctrine is. It clearly obtains in Australia where the constitution is written and limits the types of legislation that can be passed. The point is exactly the same within the types; for instance, within the power to legislate for immigrants a statute requiring the execution of all blue-eyed immigrants would be thought valid under Stephen's doctrine. And it obtains even where there is a bill of rights such as in the United States. A statute which has survived all sections of the bill of rights is thought by American lawyers to be valid regardless of any residual iniquity. For those who think that the United States constitution is so wisely conceived that it guards against all conceivable iniquity the point is merely theoretical. But still, American lawyers who subscribe to the absolute bindingness of any statute valid under the Constitution are in underlying philosophy the successors of Stephen.

X.7

Let us say that *ABC* are all the reasons in a single case to recognize a statute of Parliament requiring the execution of blue-eyed babies and *XYZ* all the reasons against. These reasons are very complex. *ABC* will include all the reasons in favour of certainty in the recognition of law, all the advantages that this brings for a community, and so on. *XYZ* will include the innocence of the children, the nature of the killing proposed – all the reasons which constitute the iniquity of the statute.

Perhaps the balance of reasons is in favour of an absolute rule of recognition. These reasons (certainty in the recognition of law in a community, etc.) are not the same as the single case reasons *ABC*, though there would be a considerable overlapping. One difference is that the loss of certainty when there is no rule is far more widespread than its loss when the rule is simply not applied in the blue-eyed baby case. Let the reasons for the rule be *DEF* and the reasons against it *UVW*. That *DEF* outweighs *UVW* is no reason for thinking that *ABC* outweighs *XYZ*, for *DEF* are reasons for the action of taking or keeping the rule, and that is not the action in question in the single case *ABC* against *XYZ*. I can quite consistently decide to take or keep a rule (on the ground that it will usually give the right decision, or that it achieves this value or that) and also decide against it in a single case. I do not contradict myself because the actions are different and thus the reasons are, too (*ABC* is different from *DEF*). Suppose a judge had a case of the application of the blue-eyed babies statute. He might (not quite understanding the situation) regard the case as a case of *DEF* against *UVW* and decide *DEF* outweighs *UVW*. His case, however, is not a case of *DEF* against *UVW*. It is a case of *ABC* against *XYZ*. He would therefore not yet have decided his case. He would have decided only to take or keep a rule. Almost certainly, given his misunderstanding, he would then proceed to apply the rule in the single case. That would be relevant, for that *second* decision would be the single-case decision required of him. But our question would stand. Why is that single-case decision to be a rule decision rather than a decision on the reasons *ABC* and *XYZ*?

The reasons to adopt the rule, which he has just accepted, do not answer this question. That *DEF* outweighs *UVW* does not require that he make a rule decision in a single case where *ABC* is outweighed by *XYZ*. A judge might say that he must make a rule decision in the single case because if he doesn't the rule will tend to break down and that will lead to uncertainty and confusion, etc. But this will not do. These reasons are already part of *ABC*, the reasons to decide the single case in accordance with the rule, and *ABC* is outweighed by *XYZ*, the iniquity of the statute.

Is there not something wrong in this whole argument? Is not the action of rejecting the statute in the single case at the same time the action of not keeping the rule? Thus must not the decision of the single case necessarily also be the decision of the question of keeping the rule? No. The action of rejecting the statute is not the action of not keeping the rule. Rather, it is the action of not keeping the rule *in the single case*. And when we say *DEF* outweighs *UVW* therefore keep the rule we do not say therefore keep it in the single case where *ABC* is outweighed by *XYZ*. *DEF* outweighs *XYZ* means there is a balance of reasons in favour of a rule which by its terms is to be kept in all cases and which may as it turns out be kept in all cases; it does not mean that there is a balance of reasons in favour of keeping it in all cases – that would contradict our hypothesis that *XYZ* outweighs *ABC*, for that is one case where the balance of reasons is the other way.

In real terms this last point is as follows: there is a balance of reasons in favour of the rule 'all statutes are to be recognized' notwithstanding the risk that it may be applied in all cases (as by Nazi judges, for instance). There is this balance of reasons in favour of the absolute rule rather than a rule which makes an exception for the blue-eyed baby case for much the same reasons as there is a balance of reasons in favour of the absolute rule to follow high court precedents (see IX.13); that is, the qualified rule may cause more wrong decisions than it saves (see also XI.10). But in the single blue-eyed baby case the reasons to apply the rule are outweighed by the iniquity of the statute. The risk that a rule will be applied in all cases is a standard risk in the taking of rules. The undertaking of this risk is part of the audacity mentioned in the second chapter of this book.

The primacy of the single case, which these arguments imply, is a fundamental moral notion, discussed in XI.9.

X.8

Suppose a legal system where there are ten precedents of the highest court applying statutes like the blue-eyed babies statute (of that degree of iniquity). They may be regarded as authority for the proposition that such statutes are to be recognized as law. Harold is a judge of the highest court who holds that on the balance of all the relevant reasons including *stare decisis* (*ABC* against *XYZ*) these precedents ought to be overruled and the blue-eyed babies statute not recognized as law. This stipulation is intended to embrace all and only the reasons properly relevant in a court of law. If there are reasons relevant but not proper in a court of law (I don't think there are) they are excluded. Harold wonders what decision he should reach, and he wishes to be candid:

Robert: Come off it, Harold. You know that the law is that this statute is law. Disagree with the law, by all means, but don't pretend it's not the law.

Harold: I don't know that the law is what you say it is. I regard this as a hard case, so there is no rule which I can simply apply: neither the rule of recognition itself nor the rule of the precedents (since they may be so wrong that they ought to be overruled). I must therefore decide the case by reference to legally proper reasons. If these reasons supported your opinion as to the recognition of this statute or if they required following the precedents in this case you would be right about what the law is. But they do not. I wish to be candid, and if this sort of statute were law I would say so. But I cannot see that it is. I judge that *XYZ* outweighs *ABC*.

Robert: *Your* reasons, Harold. You are dressing your reasons up and giving them the status of law.

Harold: I am judging by reasons. I am only judging by *my* reasons in a trivial sense of 'my': that is, in a sense which emphasizes that I am the one making the judgment of reasons. I might be wrong in my judgment, of course. The truth might be that *ABC* outweighs *XYZ*. In that sense also the reasons I use might be said to be my reasons, but you are not arguing that I am wrong; indeed, you are refusing to do so.

Actually this case is fairly straightforward. Robert's last objection is very common and takes many forms, some of which were dealt with in chapter V. A more difficult case is of a legal system with a written constitution which expressly and unequivocally includes the power to pass statutes requiring the execution of blue-eyed babies. What does candour require of Harold here?

Robert: My dear Harold I don't think you will be able to wriggle out of this one.

Harold: Let us see. The question is what is the law? Is this collection of norms which you and the populace call a constitution really so? I cannot be prevented from asking that question (it is clearly logically required). By asking it, assumptions are collapsed, and the case turns into a hard case. Thus there is no constitutional *rule* in the case that the blue-eyed babies statute is valid; there is merely a norm whose status is now in issue. In the hard case which the question raises what does the balance of legally proper reasons require? The fact that there is a clearly posited set of norms that the people may look to and have in the past looked to to settle such matters as this makes a strong reason to follow all of its terms as the legal constitution. This could be nothing more than a strong reason (only rules are absolute). Although the reason is a strong one, it is actually only a little stronger than the reason to follow the precedents which we discussed earlier; and it is not strong enough to outweigh the iniquity of the enforcement of the sort of statute we have in this case. That norm which requires that enforcement, therefore, is without the force of constitutional law and may be excised from the other norms which remain as the constitution.

Robert: I can't say I didn't expect as much. But perhaps you can tell me what makes you think that you can take the written constitution selectively?

Harold: Reasons.

Robert: But how are you so free with reasons?

Harold: Where there is no rule there are only reasons.

Robert: You are out of step, Harold. The populace and your brother judges regard the norm in question as part of the constitution. Resign if you like. Refuse to accept it as your constitution. But what right do you have to say it is not *their* constitution?

Harold: I am a judge.

Robert: But your brothers are judges too. Why do you not defer to their opinions?

Harold: Because they are wrong on a very important question.

Robert: You say they are wrong, Harold. Why do you give precedence to your opinion?

Harold: I give precedence to reasons, not to my opinion. You are very confused. I dealt with this objection in our last exchange.

Robert: You are a very small minority, Harold.

Harold: Only bad philosophy could make that significant.

Robert: I can't help feeling, Harold, that you are not being candid about the rule here.

Harold: I candidly admit the following:

(a) the written document which calls itself a constitution includes the norm in question.

(b) yesterday, I accepted the whole of the document as the constitutional rule.

(c) all the populace and all my brother judges so accepted it and still do.

From none of these taken singly or in any combination does it follow that the norm is now of constitutional force such as to control my case.

Robert: But have you not by your judgment instituted a new legal system? Must you not candidly declare yourself a revolutionary rather than a judge?

Harold: I see no opposition between the two roles: I don't know what you mean.

X.9

Is Harold a revolutionary? Robert's last question by raising this problem requires consideration of the nature of a legal system.

A legal syste.n is, *inter alia*, a conversation around a certain rule of recognition (III.8). Let us say that before the blue-eyed babies case arose Harold (as he says) accepted the whole written constitution as the legal system's rule of recognition including the part authorising statutes of the blue-eyed babies sort. Let P be all the norms of the written constitution, and $P-Q$ all those norms less the one authorizing the blue-eyed babies statute. At first, therefore, given our definition of rule and the assumptions required to constitute it (III.2), Harold assumed (1) that P was binding, and (2) that others in the legal system to whom he was accustomed to address his legal statements accepted P. When the blue-eyed babies case arose Harold rejected P and accepted $P-Q$ with a corresponding pair of assumptions. Does this mean he makes a revolution? For his own part, yes. He makes a revolution because he abandons his original rule of recognition (not, be it noted, because he decides against common legal opinion).

This personal sense is perhaps the only interesting sense of revolution. Harold's impact on the whole conversation we have called the legal system might be small or great; the whole interlocking set of assumptions which create it may be little affected by Harold's revolution or much affected. But there is little point in wondering (at least for our purposes) whether there is a general revolution. Criteria for such a thing are lacking; and there would be no interest in stipulating them.

There is no getting away from this problem of personal idiosyncrasy in the matter of rules (VIII.8 and X.5). But for legal systems it usually does not matter. The conversation that constitutes a legal system will survive the fact that some have a rule of recognition (with the necessary assumptions) in terms of P and others a rule in terms of $P-Q$, so long as Q is either unimportant or does not commonly arise. Ordinary conversations survive the fact that there is only approximate agreement in assumptions. Legal systems are no different.

X.10

Where the rule of recognition in a legal system is dependent upon precedent (as it is in the United Kingdom) there is a risk of confusing generality with absoluteness.

Take a more ordinary case. Suppose a precedent decides that occupiers are liable to people who are injured on their land. This is decided in the case of an invitee. The next case is of a licensee. The general proposition of law is applied without difficulty. But the next case is of a trespasser. The general proposition is distinguished on the ground that trespassers are materially different from invitees and licensees: the decision is no liability to trespassers. There is no difficulty at all with this. The generality of the proposition that occupiers are liable to people injured on their land was not confused with absoluteness, despite the fact that trespassers are 'people'.

There is no significant difference between this case and the case of the rule of recognition. There are many precedents applying statutes and the general proposition implicit in them, and occasionally explicit, is that statutes are to be recognized. By ordinary Common Law doctrines this is general not absolute. And when a case such as the blue-eyed baby statute comes up there is no difficulty in saying that it is significantly different (on the ground of its degree and type of iniquity) from any statute previously recognized. Thus previous cases are distinguished and the statute is not recognized. The English constitutional theorists, however, have confused generality with absoluteness.

X.11

Common lawyers keep saying, like Dicey and Stephen, that they think that their rule of recognition authorizes the blue-eyed babies statute. But actually they don't think this. In the first place they are common lawyers trained to think in the way stated in X.10. And in the second place, they tend to have moral reservations which make it logically impossible for them to think it (X.6).

X.12

If a lawyer from Stephen's and Dicey's legal system reads this book and accepts its arguments, but still thinks that a blue-eyed baby case is determined by rule, what are we to say? He is psychologically possessed (by an assumption) and relentlessly prevented from seeing part of the world (to wit: *A*, *B*, *C*, *X*, *Y* and *Z*). It follows on very ordinary definitions that he is mad.

X.13

Suppose a constitution says: there shall be no interference with freedom of speech. Written constitutions are in normative form like statutes. They can therefore easily be taken as rules. The only difference is that in the case of historically first constitutions (which are the only constitutions properly so called: X.15) the norms are rules in their own right not rules by virtue of being valid according to a rule of recognition.

In the United States there have been conflicting views about the First Amendment (freedom of speech): some have thought it an absolute protection of freedom of speech and others a protection to be balanced against other principles such as danger to the state, and therefore occasionally to be overridden. Dworkin said (1977, 27) that those of the former view treat the First Amendment as a rule and those of the latter, as a principle. But it could only be a rule. As a principle (a generalized reason) it could not exist independently of its weight, and the constitution can say nothing about its weight (chapter IV); therefore as a principle it could not exist in the constitution. What, then, is the explanation of the divergence in views about the First Amendment?

The strict constructionists, we might say, take the rule 'there shall be no abridgement of freedom of speech'. They then have to apply it, and this means they have to name things in issue under it. This is the absolutist school. The loose constructionists, those who allow in other considerations, could differ from the strict constructionists in various ways:

(a) they might differ in their naming under the rule. For instance they might quite plausibly say that shouting 'Fire!' in a crowded theatre is not to be named speech. And they might say the same thing about words exciting people to revolution, or to sexual activity.

(b) they might read an exception into the rule: 'except pornography', for example, or 'except a clear and present danger to the constitution'. Dworkin was right when he showed that certain cases where a principle or reason was outweighed were not cases of exceptions to rules. But this obviously did not mean that there were no exceptions to rules. It would be wrong to overlook this possibility as an explanation in terms of rules of the differing positions taken on the First Amendment, or

(c) they might not be applying the constitution at all. They might actually be weighing the principle (reasons) of freedom of speech against other reasons. The First Amendment would not be irrelevant to this: it would operate as a repeal of any rules which might otherwise institute a doctrine of a legislative omnipotence sufficient to allow the legislature to abridge freedom of speech (compare the discussion of the United Kingdom Race Relations Acts in IV.12).

X.14

Dicey's statute requiring the execution of blue-eyed babies would be invalid under a constitution with conventional bill of rights provisions; in the United States, for instance, it would infringe the due process clause. This would mean that such a statute would not be recognized because it would be named an infringement of due process under an exception to the rule of recognition which the Constitution constitutes. In a constitution without a bill of rights the same conclusion obtains (provided that the iniquity of the statute, the main reason against recognition, outweighs the reasons for its recognition), but the reasoning is different.

In the bill of rights legal system we would say that the innocence of the babies was a reason for naming the statute an infringement of due process. A rule of recognition including the bill of rights provision would have been taken and the norm in issue in the case would have to be named or not named a statute infringing due process under it. In a legal system without a bill of rights the case would be a hard case of recognition; and the relevant reason, the innocence of the children, would be a reason at large not to recognize the norm as law, rather than simply a reason for a certain interpretation of the words 'due process'.

X.15

When is a constitution a statute? The important logical difference here is between a rule which exists in its own right (constituted by assumptions of its own bindingness) and a rule which exists because it is valid under a higher rule (where the assumptions of bindingness are of the bindingness of that higher rule). There are what *might* be called rules of recognition at different levels in a legal system: for instance, a statute, itself recognized by a higher rule, might state the power of a local government body to enact by-laws, and then the statute itself might be said to be a rule of recognition of the by-laws. But it is best to reserve the term for the ultimate rule of recognition, the historically first constitution, the rule which exists in its own right and not by virtue of its validity under a higher rule of recognition. Anything validly enacted will be called a statute. The ultimate rule of recognition is a constitution.

It is easy to go astray here. If the amendment provision of an historically first constitution is used to amend itself what is the result? Answer: the amended amendment provision is a statute; and the old provision is still the historically first constitution or rule of recognition. Though its procedure is not current, the rule of recognition must continue to exist as the source of validity of the statute. Now, this terminology might be thought odd, but it preserves the only important distinction; that between a rule which exists in its own right and a rule which exists because it is validly enacted.

The distinction assists in solving a number of problems.

Not a few have thought that the question of a parliament's sovereignty involved paradox. Parliament can legislate everything. Therefore Parliament can by legislation restrict itself. But if it restricts itself it cannot legislate everything. Paradox. An analogy with Xeno's paradox of the Cretan liar has sometimes been maintained. But Xeno's is a real paradox, whereas the constitutional one isn't; this becomes clear when close attention is paid on the one hand to what precisely the Cretan is saying and on the other to the terms of the rule of recognition of statutes.

The statement 'Parliament can legislate everything' is ambiguous. 'Everything' might be taken literally so as to include 'that Parliament cannot legislate everything' or it might not. The Cretan's statement, too, can appear ambiguous in much the same way. 'All Cretans are liars' could be meant by Epiminedes, the Cretan, to include himself or not to include himself.

If he means not to include himself then clearly no paradox exists. But if he insists on including himself as a Cretan, the paradox stands with its well-known force; it is in fact the simple paradox 'I am a liar'. But now consider the ambiguity in the rule about Parliament. On no interpretation is there a paradox. If the rule of recognition is that Parliament can legislate everything except 'Parliament cannot legislate everything' we are left with no problem of any sort, certainly no paradox: Parliament cannot legislate 'Parliament cannot legislate everything' for the simple and sufficient reason that the rule of recognition says it can't. Such an enactment would be an invalid statute (a norm which is not recognized). And if on the other hand the rule of recognition is that Parliament can legislate everything including 'Parliament cannot legislate everything' there is also no paradox. Parliament can legislate 'Parliament cannot legislate everything', and this, being in accordance with the rule of recognition, will be a valid statute, and like any other operative until repealed. But can this statute be repealed? This is a question which has caused much trouble (there are literally hundreds of articles on it).

However, if one is careful to distinguish statute from rule of recognition the puzzle that attaches to the question dissipates. If the new enactment (call it enactment *A*) is a statute it derives its validity from the (old) rule of recognition, and it would follow that the validity of a repealing enactment would be similarly dependent. Thus the question of the repeal of enactment *A* as a statute is answered by the rule of recognition (either in its terms, or if its terms are not clear in its terms filled out by interpretation). If, on the other hand, enactment *A* is not a statute it must either be a nullity (invalid) or a rule of recognition. If it is a nullity no question of its repeal arises. If it is a rule of recognition (which would entail its having been established by revolution rather than by valid enactment) it is by definition ultimate and here, too, as with any rule of recognition, no question of its repeal arises, only a question of its revolutionary overthrow.

These distinctions cannot be made if one talks of an ultimate constitutional rule justifying *its own* amendment or repeal. This terminology will always in this context create confusion by running together the two things, rule of recognition and statute. A rule of recognition cannot ever justify its own amendment because any amendment which it justifies (validates) must by definition be a statute, something conceptually separate, not something part of itself (of course government printing conventions are quite irrelevant).

Alf Ross proposed (1958) that a constitutional rule could not justify its own repeal or amendment because: (a) self-reference was logically objectionable, and (b) when analysed the conclusion of such a process of reasoning was inadmissably inconsistent with a premise. Thus it would follow, Parliament could not bind itself. Hart (1964, 307) exposed some inadequacies in Ross's argument. Ross then re-affirmed his earlier position on the logic of the matter, but developed a compromise solution (1969). This compromise, however, indeed the whole debate, is flawed by confusions induced mainly by (a) a failure to distinguish rule of recognition from statute, and (b) a failure clearly to state the terms of recognition (the terms of the rule of recognition, or if the rule of recognition does not cover the case in hand, the terms of the consequently required hard decision on recognition).

Ross's original position was stated by reference to article V of the United States Constitution:
According to art. V any amendment of the Constitution requires the ratification by three-fourths of the states. If by this majority it is decided that in the future a ratification by four-fifths of the states shall be required the new rule of amendment cannot be regarded as derived from the old one. If that were the case it would be possible to amend the new basic norm in the same procedure in which it had been created, that is, by a majority of three-fourths, and the present amendment rule would continue to be the highest norm of the system. (1958, 83)

As soon as Ross referred to the new article V as 'the new basic norm' (meaning: new rule of recognition) his argument became confused. The new article V would be a statute not a rule of recognition, for it derives its validity from the old article V, the rule of recognition. It would only be a (new) rule of recognition if it replaced the old one by revolutionary act. What procedure is required to amend this statute obviously depends upon recognition, and close attention to the terms of what is still the rule of recognition solves all problems (or if its terms do not cover the case in hand, attention to the terms of the consequently required hard decision). The rule of recognition or the hard decision of recognition might be either:

(a) the new article V can only be amended in the old way, or
(b) the new article V can only be amended in the new way (the way it institutes itself).

The second of these would be the case if the terms of the old article V, interpreted or decided by hard decision, were: amend this article only by the three-quarters procedure or if under the three-quarters procedure a new procedure is established only by the new procedure. If the terms were: amend this article only by the three-quarters procedure, then that would be the only way to amend it, and the new article 5 contradicting this would be invalid; being unauthorized by the rule of recognition it could not be recognized as a statute. In either case there is no logical problem (there are many other possibilities for the interpretation of the old article V. These I ignore. None creates any logical problem).

Ross saw most of this in his second attempt at the problem (1969); but unfortunately the solution which he presented was again confused because of a failure to attend to the terms of recognition (the rule or, if incomplete, the hard decision of recognition).

Article 88 of the Danish constitution is now his example. For simplicity we can say that article 88 prescribes that the constitution may be amended by procedure *C*. Ross thinks that the procedure of Article 88 could not be used to amend article 88 itself because, adhering to his original conception of the logic of the matter, this would involve objectionable self-reference and also contradiction between premise and conclusion:

> Now, if we suppose art. 88 to be amended according to its own rules with the result that it is replaced by art. 88′ (with a content contrary to that of art. 88) the validity of art. 88′ is based on an inference of the following pattern:
>
> art. 88: The constitution may be amended by a process in accordance with [condition *C*] and only by this process;
>
> art. 88′ stating that the constitution may be amended by a process [*C*′] has been created in accordance with condition [*C*].
>
> ∴ art. 88′ is valid, that is, the constitution may be amended by a process in accordance with [condition *C*′] and only by this process.
>
> As the meaning of art. 88 is to indicate the *only way* in which the constitution may be amended, this is an inference in which the conclusion contradicts one of the premises, which is a logical absurdity. (Ross, 1969, 5)

It is I think quite obvious that Ross has failed to formulate the article 88 of his inference clearly enough. Earlier, when looking at a similarly vaguely formulated norm, 'Parliament can legislate everything', we wanted to know exactly what 'everything' meant. Did it include 'Parliament cannot legislate everything'? And so on. Now, looking at Ross's formulation of article 88, we would want to know what exactly 'only by this process' means. It could mean 'only by this process until a new process is substituted and then only by that process until . . .' or it could mean 'for all time only by this process'. Those who have read the account which Ross has given of Danish constitutional law in his article know the answer.

Danish constitutional law allows a new process to be substituted. Ross said:

> people (in Denmark, as elsewhere) think and act as if the basic norm (article 88) may be amended in accordance with its own rules. There is no doubt that any attempt to change art. 88 in any other way would be considered illegal by the people, the leading politicians and the courts. So it must be accepted as Danish constitutional law that art. 88 may be amended by the legal process described in the article itself. (ibid., 6)

Ross means here that the accepted legal interpretation of article 88 is that 'only by this process' means 'only by this process until a new process is substituted and then only by that process until . . .'. Article 88, therefore, when filled out in the ordinary way by hard decisions stands as something like the following:

> The constitution may be amended by process *C* and only by this process until by this process the process of amendment is changed to process *C'* and then only by that process until by that process the process of amendment is changed to process *C"* . . .

It is obvious that if we put this formulation of article 88 and a corresponding one of article 88' into Ross's inference there is no contradiction. The contradiction was produced only by Ross's failure to attend carefully enough to the formulation of article 88.

Article 88 is the rule of recognition; article 88', since it derives its validity from the rule of recognition, is a statute. This difference in logical status removes the problem of self-reference. Ross, himself, saw this logical fact, but he then proceeded to establish the necessary levels of logical status by inventing a basic norm above article 88. This was his solution to the problem. But it was a fiction bound to create a terrible mess (see Raz, 1972b). And it was quite unnecessary; the already existing differing logical statuses of articles 88 and 88' were sufficient for Ross's purposes. Ross's mistake was to look the wrong way; when confronting his rule of recognition, to look up (into the air) rather than down to statute.

XI

THE WORLD

XI.1

The world is all the particulars, including the particular attachment
of all the (universal) properties and relations. Putting aside I for
the moment (see XI.9), there is nothing but the world (though the
world is mysterious). Thus the basis of moral (including legal)
thought in hard cases is the particular facts of the world; and the
paradigm of a hard case is ABC weighed against XYZ, where each
letter stands for a particular fact. These particular facts are
unconditional reasons for or against action (I.10).

There is nothing else that could activate hard cases (there is
nothing but the world). There are no *a priori* moral truths
(IV.3–IV.4). There are certainly my desires (my basic physiological needs), but my desires are part of the world, giving
unconditional self-regarding reasons for action (I.1). My wants,
which we call projects, give conditional reasons for action and are
not fundamental (I.1); the fundamental question about a project is
the hard case of the adoption of the project based upon the
unconditional reasons for and against it. And there are certainly
(man-made) norms; but these, too, if they are applied externally
rather than internally (IV.2), are particular facts in the world.

The paradigm, ABC weighed against XYZ, might nevertheless
be thought too simple on a number of grounds.

Suppose A is a fact about a human being and X a fact about a
tree. Must not the relationship between these two facts as reasons
for action be an ordinal one and not the cardinal relationship

implied by the weighing paradigm? Is not the priority of man over thing (ordinary definition) absolute? How, then, could A be weighed against X?

A second problem is the one given by Ivan Karamazov to his brother (in the literature of moral philosophy there are now hundreds of variations):

'. . . imagine that it is you yourself who is erecting the edifice of human destiny with the aim of making men happy in the end, of giving them peace and contentment at last, but that to do that it is absolutely necessary, and indeed quite inevitable, to torture to death only one tiny creature, the little girl who beat her breast with her little fist, and to found the edifice on her unavenged tears – would you consent to be the architect on those conditions? Tell me and do not lie!'

'No, I wouldn't,' Alyosha said softly.

(Or will you punish an innocent man if to do so is an effective deterrent?) Let ABC be all the facts of the future happiness of mankind and X the torture of the little girl. Is there not also here an (ordinal) priority of X over ABC?

Thirdly, the truth of a deontological theory of morality would be difficult to accommodate. Of course, there are man-made norms, but if, beyond these, moral truth itself were in the form of norms it would not fit ABC against XYZ. The theory that there are *a priori* moral truths is certainly an example of this, and a certain form of rule-utilitarianism may be another.

And a fourth problem relates to intention. It is commonly thought that my intention is an important element in the rightness of any moral judgment I might make. Now, obviously, an intention can be a fact and therefore fit the ABC against XYZ paradigm. For instance, I might be a judge and the case the question of what punishment to impose for a crime; in such a case there is no difficulty in regarding the criminal's intention as one fact and one reason for action. But the problem arises with my own intention. Is that not a component of the rightness of my judgment in my case, ABC against XYZ, but not itself a fact of the case? The difficulty is brought out by Germain Grisez, who has proposed an analysis of the problem of double effect which requires reference to my intention. We shall have either to deal with this or modify the paradigm.

The next four sections are concerned with these questions. We then return to the general problem.

XI.2

The argument that facts about human beings are not commensurate with facts about, say, trees depends upon a conception of rational autonomy. By introspection I know that I am rationally autonomous; that is, that I am not the slave of my ends, but ultimately free to choose them. *I* am not a means to an end. And if I am not to be a solipsist I shall accord an equivalent status to others – they also are not means to ends under this basic Kantian idea, which we can call respect. Now, clearly, this form of respect is required only in the case of other rationally autonomous creatures, not for instance for trees. How then if *A* is a fact about a human being can it be weighed against *X*, a fact about a tree?

However, Kant's is not the only argument available to establish respect as the basic moral concept.

That I respect you is a prerequisite of my freedom. If you are my slave or my tool then I see you not as an individual person but as a means for the satisfaction of one of my projects, not sharply distinguished from my other tools. I do not see you as particular: any tool or slave of a certain class will do. I am myself in the moral sense the prisoner of my project, for it prevents me from seeing you as an individual; as a particular with beauty. My attention, which might otherwise be to your beauty (and to the rest of the world), is held inward as I contemplate my project. Moral freedom, my moral freedom, is my struggle to attend to you as a particular person independent of me; when I do this, I am free (you, of course, though I was using you, may have been free in the real sense all along). This sort of respect is love. It is the attention that Iris Murdoch examines (V.9). For the present it is sufficient to say that there is no reason to hold that the only objects of such respect are human beings. If I see the non-human world, merely or dominantly, as a means to an end (a forest as newsprint, a valley as the walls of a dam, a whale as money in the bank) I fail to see it as independent of me and my projects. Again I am a prisoner, cut off from the beauty of the world.

Thus all of *A*, *B*, *C*, *X*, *Y* and *Z* are to be respected; no one of them is absolute by virtue of requiring respect, such as would break the cardinal weighing paradigm into some more complex set of orders. Thus if I can be justified in, say, killing one man in defence of another there is no set of orders which excludes my being justified in killing the human attacker in defence of a whale (or a valley, or the Parthenon). Perhaps you might think that in these cases the value of the human life would outweigh the other values; but all I wish to claim is that this is a cardinal not an ordinal judgment.

XI.3

There is a short answer available to Ivan Karamazov's problem (XI.1). To purchase the future happiness of mankind by the murder of the little girl is to use her as a means to an end; it is therefore to fail to accord her due respect. Thus the short answer is that *ABC* against *XYZ* (all respected) is not properly set up. Unfortunately it can be properly set up. Another example is clearer (this is taken from Williams, 1973, 98).

Jim is in the presence of twenty Indians in South America. He is told that either he kills one of them or Pedro will kill all of them (we shall assume that there is good reason to believe this). If he kills one of them the others will be released. The problem, I think, is much harder if the one to be killed is designated in advance, for then we may presume that he does not consent to the enterprise; so we shall take it in that way. Can this moral case be represented as simply as *ABC* against *XYZ*?

It is clearly possible to give an answer to the case not having set the problem up properly. As with Ivan Karamazov's little girl, Jim may decide in a simple way to purchase nineteen lives with the twentieth, using the latter, therefore, in the Kantian terms, as a means to an end (there would be a conditional reason to kill the twentieth – it would be conditional upon the project of saving the others and it would be weighed against, and in the circumstances easily defeat, other similarly conditioned reasons, e.g. trying to kill Pedro). The twentieth would not have been respected, thus *ABC* against *XYZ* would not have been properly set up. But unfortunately this does not solve the problem, for it is not necessary that Jim decide in this way. He might respect all Indians

The World

equally, give full weight to the dignity and needs of each of them as individual human beings (we can amend the facts to give him the time to do this, should it be thought necessary), or putting the point in another way, look them all in the eye, including the twentieth (Nagel, 1979, 53–74); or, yet another way, decide reactively rather than objectively (Strawson, 1974, 1–25). Now I think we have a problem of *ABC* against *XYZ*, all respected and thus properly set up, and in the absence of a rule such as that which Catholic theology or some other deontology makes available it must be decided as that hard case, *ABC* against *XYZ*.

There is no escape from this. I cannot avoid the problem by saying that I am responsible only for my own acts, for I am responsible for my own omissions too. Respect for the nineteen (nineteen individuals) requires that I not omit to attend to their needs, just as in a different situation I might be required to pull them (strangers whom I have just happened upon) from a lake. Sometimes the point is put in terms of integrity or keeping my own conscience clear, but my integrity is compromised and my conscience burdened by my omissions as well as by my acts. This is clearly shown by the lake case. And that matter of integrity and conscience, that requirement not to omit to help, does not disappear because it is forced into competition with another (*ABC*, the reasons to save the nineteen, does not disappear as a set of reasons for action just because of the appearance of *XYZ*). So I cannot avoid *ABC* against XYZ.

However, the various attempts to avoid it are not without truth. There is always a strong reason not to act; the mystery of the world always seems to suggest, in the case of any of its particulars, that there is reason to leave the world as it is.

We called this reason *X* in IX.3, note 7; but it is not a reason like others. It is part of the passionate response to mystery, and thus an element of the weight of all reasons (for all particular facts contain the mystery of the world). It is not always a reason not to act (more accurately, not always something diminishing the weight of reasons to act), for in the case of self-regarding reasons for action it seems to operate the other way: I leave the world as it is only if I continue to perform various natural functions such as feeding myself. This is a consideration of some importance – otherwise a kind of saintly indifference to action might have seemed attractive

236

as a moral aspiration.

So far as our case is concerned we can say that ABC, the probable twenty deaths at Pedro's hand, is diminished in weight by this reason to leave the world as it is (I leave the world as it is if Pedro kills the twenty; I do not if I kill the one). I have no clear opinion which way to decide this case (though the more difficult it is and the more profound the questions it raises the greater seems to be the weight of X, for we begin to see that we don't own the world). But whatever the decision, I cannot see how its structure is other than I have stated.

XI.4

There is one form of rule-utilitarianism which need not delay us; for it can be accepted that there are reasons for rules, not just rules of thumb, but rules of the sort analysed in this book, and it may often be for the best that we take and keep rules. These are strategic cases of reasons for and against the various actions involved in the taking and keeping of a rule, and they clearly fit the paradigm of ABC against XYZ (there are various problems with subsequent single cases where the rule gives the wrong decision – see VI.7, IX.13, and X.7 – but these, we have argued, do not affect the fact that ABC reasons for taking a rule can outweigh XYZ reasons against it). For reasons that will be clear, we usually call this case of reasons for and against rules DEF against UVW.

The really puzzling form of rule-utilitarianism is one that would have it that moral truth itself takes a normative form. I have in mind a rule-utilitarianism which maintains something like: what is right in any case is to be decided by reference to the most optimific set of rules (this is, of course, much simplified, but it is the basic type of the rule-utilitarianism proposed by, for example, Brandt, 1963). If this sort of theory can be maintained then at least some of A, B, C, X, Y and Z are rules; and our analysis would be much complicated.

Now, the objection to such a theory is that either it is vacuous, or it is inconsistent, or it collapses. It is vacuous if it proposes a too-simple rule or set of rules; for instance, if it proposed the simple rule 'act optimifically' it would be an example of rule-utilitarianism in name only. If, on the other hand, there is substance in the rule or set of rules, it seems necessary that it contain inconsistencies and that the theory either allow these to stand or allow itself to collapse into a theory of reasons for action (*ABC* against *XYZ*).

We are talking of what in our terminology are not rules, but norms, and we are considering the possibility that there are natural norms. If there were natural norms it would seem necessary that they be inconsistent in some cases; for it is easy, given typical candidates, let us say for example 'promises ought to be kept' and 'those in need ought to be helped', to dream up situations where they are inconsistent (I promise to do something for you but I cannot because I have to take someone to hospital).

Now, this situation as it stands is unsatisfactory. A set of natural inconsistent norms is a quite implausible account of the world – as though the world itself were a tragedy! – and measures are commonly taken to avoid it. For example, the deontologist, W. D. Ross (1930) suggested that such norms were of *prima facie* force. Thus in cases of conflict between two *prima facie* norms a decision (which we call weighing) must be made between them.

As far as it goes this is acceptable. But we have argued that a *prima facie* norm (or a *ceteris paribus* norm, or a norm to be weighed – we do not distinguish these things) is not really a norm at all but a principle. Principles are universalized reasons for action (IV.2), and the latter has primacy, hence *ABC* and *XYZ*, where each letter stands for a relevant fact, i.e., a reason for action. We shall not repeat the reasons for this primacy (IV.1–IV.2) but one reason is especially pertinent in the present context. The two principles mentioned, 'promises ought to be kept' and 'persons in need ought to be helped' vary indefinitely in weight. The weight of the former depends, among other things, on the seriousness of the promise, and the latter on the seriousness of the need. The variation in the weight of these principles is indefinite because each of these things, seriousness of the promise and seriousness of the need, is open to indefinite gradation (IV.3). The weight will depend simply upon the facts of each case, hence the primacy of facts and reasons, hence the form *ABC* against *XYZ*.

Like the theory that there are *a priori* moral norms (IV.3–IV.4), rule utilitarianism attempts to establish that moral truth itself takes a normative form. In fact a very great deal of moral philosophy has proceeded on the basis that what were fundamentally controversial in human moral discourse, what put moral truth in issue, were the norms, principles, values or maxims by which hard cases were decided; and correspondingly in legal discourse, the 'rules of law' by which hard decisions were made (IX.5). But this is a mistake. What are fundamentally controversial in the sense that they produce differing decisions about moral and legal questions, are the differing passionate responses to the particular facts of the world, that is to say the weight of reasons for action (a condition of our properly using the word 'controversial' here is the account already given in chapter V of the objectivity and freedom of reasons: if passionate responses were simply subjective or allowed no room for freedom there could be no controversy between moral agents).

All that is needed for this account of moral truth is I and the world; hence the form of hard case *ABC* against *XYZ*, where *ABCXY* and *Z* are all particular facts in the world, to which I respond passionately.

XI.5

My intention when I deliberate about a proposed action is not part of the world (not one of *A*, *B*, *C*, *X*, *Y* or *Z*); thus it is no part of my moral judgment what to do. It is something which follows that judgment, something which accompanies my decision to act (it may be part of the world for my next case).

Thus in Ivan Karamazov's dilemma (kill one little girl to save mankind) my intention forms no part of the problem. If confronted with the problem I should hope to say: I shall intend, and do now intend, to do what is right, all things considered. Of course, when I act and you try to describe my action, reference must be made to my intention. And in the next case which, let us say, is concerned with my guilt or otherwise for what I did in the first case, the intention I had is a fact forming part of the case.

Germain Grisez, interpreting a long-standing natural law tradition, has argued for an ethical position that would have it that if I kill the little girl I intend her death, and that that is impermissible. This is to be contrasted with a case of self-defence (let us say I shoot at my assailant's heart thinking it the only practicable way of stopping him shooting me), where I do not, Grisez argues, intend the death (1970, 64–96).

This natural law position requires a standard or conception of good that is in some sense independent of my case. Then, it makes sense to require that I decide my case by, and intend the implementation or furtherance of, that standard or good (just as for Kant it made sense to require that I act out of respect for duty rather than for some meaner motive). But there are no *a priori* standards or goods (IV.3–IV.4); and man-made standards or goods (in our terms rules and projects) are not able in themselves to provide moral justification.

In the absence of *a priori* standards and goods there can be nothing in the natural law tradition but a confusion of cases. My deliberation and decision is one case. Then, after I act or omit to act, there is another case of my responsibility and possible guilt. In this second case what intention I had when I acted or omitted to act is a fact clearly relevant. But in the first case it is not a fact and, as I hold, not relevant. (Anscombe, perhaps, makes a similar confusion of cases (1967, 16–17):

> Similarly if there are a lot of people stranded on a rock, and one person on another, and someone goes with a boat to rescue the single one, what cause, so far, have any of the others for complaint? They are not injured unless help that was owing to them was withheld. There was the boat that could have helped them: but it was not left idle; no, it went to save that other one. What is the accusation that each of them can make? What wrong can he claim has been done him? None whatever: unless the preference signalizes some ignoble contempt.

But their claim to have been wronged, not to have been given what is owed, (to sue), raises a separate case. When deciding what to do in the primary case I should hope to pay scant regard to this other case, so difficult is the primary one.

Much that Grisez says is very disturbing:

> If he [who chooses to kill as a means to an end] is to be a killer through his own self-determination he must regard himself in any situation as the lord of life and of death. The good of life must be rated as a measurable value, not as an immeasurable dignity. (1970, 76)

But I am the lord of life and of death if I kill in self-defence. I could there, too, leave the world to work itself out, and die a good man. But I don't. I intervene. I claim the right to do so. A saving-grace of these awful dilemmas is that they begin to teach one how awful is that claim; and to give weight to X, the reason to leave the world as it is.

XI.6

The particular facts of the world constitute reasons for or against one action or another; and in a hard case the action is decided by weighing these reasons. The metaphor of weighing is simple and easy; so much so that many philosophers (quite rightly) distrust it.

Germain Grisez has said of another theory that requires measurement in the nature of weighing:

> If 'greater good' is to be meaningful in the formulation of a criterion of morality, three conditions must be fulfilled: 1) 'good' must have a single meaning; 2) what is good in this unique sense must be measurable; and 3) the result of measurement must settle moral issues either directly or indirectly. (1978, 31)

I take the first of these requirements to be simply that the units in any balance must be commensurate (this is a logical require-ment). We have argued that there is one world; the particular facts of this world give reasons for action; why should the reasons thus given not be commensurate? Further, I am one man, and I am the one who must decide in any case. What more could there be to commensurability than this? The thrust of this argument is that the reasons in a case are commensurate because I am the balance. Now, this looks a very crude argument indeed; rather like saying of an ordinary scales that everything that you can place on it is commensurate because it *will* weigh. And putting it like this exposes a fundamental issue.

Germain Grisez has made an argument which suggests that any moral theory involving a single and total commensurability is unacceptable because it denies moral freedom (1978, 21). If the argument presented in this book were incompatible with moral freedom I accept that it would have to be rejected; but I don't believe it is.

Grisez's argument is against a form of consequentialism which has it that all goods are commensurate (thus that there is a single and total commensurability), and that moral decision is a matter of weighing the consequences of any action in terms of these goods and deciding. Grisez's view is that fundamental goods (life, friendship, play . . .) are incommensurate, and the nub of his argument is that this is necessary for the existence of moral freedom. If these goods were commensurate, that is to say if they were all part of one good, then it would not be possible knowingly to do wrong:

> An analogy will help to make clear the force of this argument. If one were literally interested in nothing whatsoever except acquiring money, whenever one considered possible courses of action one would look for only a *single* thing: how much money one might acquire if one chose each course. When one saw that a certain possibility was not the best bet, one could not choose it. Likewise, since one who chooses can be interested in various possibilities only insofar as they promise good, whenever one deliberates one considers what good one can hope for by choosing each possibility. If one could see that a certain possibility promised measurably less good, one could not choose it. (1978, 44)

Now, our analysis does not use the concept good, either distinct goods or one commensurate good – reasons for action are the units of hard decisions. But the same difficulty obtains: are these reasons commensurate, and if they are commensurate, if there is only one standard by which to decide, how is there moral freedom? The problem of akrasia or weakness of the will, which is the problem of showing how I can do other than what I ought to do, has always fascinated moral philosophers, and Grisez by clarifying its connection to moral freedom has shown why.

In hard cases weakness of the will is not possible (V.13). To weigh a reason for action is to make a real passionate response to a particular fact in the world (chapter IV); thus it is not possible for me to decide against the balance of reasons as I experience it. Am I not, then, the slave of my passions? Where is my freedom? (So Grisez would argue.)

Freedom, however, is not the uncontrolled leaping of the will between goods (and though Grisez talks of moral deliberation, and pictures his moral hero thinking calmly about his choices (1978, 42–3), he gives no content to deliberation on the choice: there is much deliberation on what is to count as a good, and the hero can deliberate on this good and that, but not on the choice between them. At the actual moment of choice there must be for Grisez, as for the existentialists, a leap of the will). Freedom is not this. It is the more disciplined, more gradual, less heroic process of attempting to attend clearly to the particulars of the world (V.9). At the simplest level my moral freedom is my ability to move from violent to calm passions and judge (weigh) accordingly; the freedom that Achilles had, sitting in his tent cherishing his wrath (*Iliad*, bk 2, 769), to project his attention outward towards the great events on the plains of Troy. And when such an act of freedom is accomplished it is obvious that the weights of the various reasons for action change (Achilles will leave his tent and go out to fight). And at the deepest level my moral freedom is my ability to contemplate and respond to the mystery of the world.

Consider whether Abraham ought to have decided to kill Isaac. Abraham had a hard case. On the one hand, God's command was a reason to kill Isaac; on the other, Isaac's innocence, and individuality . . . were reasons not to. Now, Grisez's position here is that morally speaking either is permissible: killing Isaac is a pursuit of the good of devotion to God and not killing him is a pursuit of the good of respect for life; these are incommensurate goods, thus morally speaking there is a free choice between them; there is no moral truth immediately at stake in that choice (1970, 90).

But in this example one choice or the other must be disastrously wrong, and immediately so. If God did not command Isaac's death then Abraham, out of commitment to fantasy, has decided against his son's individuality and innocence, and if He did command it, to choose against that command would seem to be the ultimate disaster. Now, I am claiming only that it matters which answer is given to Abraham's hard case, that is, that there is truth at stake. I am not claiming that the case is easy. In fact the answering of it is a lifetime's work, and more. But that is what freedom is like: the gradual orientation towards, and the infinitely difficult understanding of the particularity of the world and the mystery it contains. One does not often make much progress with this freedom; and those who do are saints not heroes (Grisez talks, as he must do, of Socrates, Jesus, St Thomas More and Joan of Arc as moral heroes: this is very revealing).

Nothing turns on the use of the word 'moral'. There is no doubt mixed in this argument what is ordinarily called moral, the theological and what Grisez calls the pre-moral. I am quite happy to abandon the word 'moral': Abraham's hard case is a practical problem, and the only question of interest is the structure of his problem of deciding what to do.

Grisez's second requirement is that the units in any balance must be measurable. There is a simple answer to this: passionate responses are measured by their intensity (not their violence: the calmest passion has a greater intensity than the most violent). The objectivity of this measure is guaranteed by the objectivity of the particular facts of the world to which the passions respond (V.11).

Grisez's third condition is that the result of measurement must settle moral issues. The word 'moral' doesn't matter very much. Can there be more to the substance of this condition than that the measurement must result in a conclusive judgment, one for which there is responsibility, and one which has admitted unconditional other-regarding reasons for action?

Of course, weighing is just a metaphor. And a very poor one; an everyday metaphor, not a profound one like Plato's of the cave and the sun (*Republic* 514A–516B). But then law is an everyday matter, so its analysis needs everyday metaphor (imagine trying to construct an analysis of precedent on the model of the cave and the sun). We shall stick with weighing but note its main defects:

1 It gives no sense of reflection. A real scales cannot think about itself, but I, the scales in my hard cases, can; and adjust accordingly. I weigh with all my passions; but I can order and control them.

2 It gives no sense of moral freedom (the same point as 1, really); and, related to that, it makes moral judgment look easier than it really is. Moral freedom is something going on behind the metaphor. A better metaphor would present this duality. Perhaps one could think of a batsman in cricket: playing each ball on its merits; but behind this, building his innings, getting the pace of the pitch, the strength of the wind, gradually coming to grips with the tricks of the bowler

and the lurking threat of the cover-point; waiting, perhaps, for them to tire; and the whole performance quickened by the knowledge that the game finishes at six o'clock.

All sorts of metaphors might have their point. Mary Midgely, referring to conflicts between love and honour, art and friendship, order and freedom, says: 'Different sides of our nature demand them; the disasters springing from their withdrawal are of different kinds. Where there is conflict, we have to resolve it by deciding which disaster strikes nearer the core of our being' (1978, 193). But this metaphor of the core of one's being has its disadvantages, too. The main one is that it suggests an ordinal and not a cardinal judgment. But whereas on one set of facts love will be closer to the core of one's being than honour, on another the positions will be reversed. The possibility of indefinite variation here (according to the indefinite variety of facts) makes moral judgment cardinal not ordinal (IV.3). Perhaps the chief merit of the balance metaphor, apart from its everydayness, is to display this truth.

XI.7

There is one world; this one world is the source of moral values (unconditional reasons for action); yet discontinuity and seeming incommensuration have commonly been experienced. Why is this?

Thomas Nagel lists five types of values which often appear incommensurate with one another (1979, 129):

1 Specific obligations to family, community and the like. These values seem incommensurate with duties to others further removed.
2 Rights. I think he has in mind here something like Dworkin's idea of trumping. A claim of right, for instance in a court, overrides (not just outweighs, but overrides in the sense of trumps) a seemingly greater, usually consequential, value (see e.g. Dworkin, 1977, 366).
3 Utility. Remote consequences.
4 The intrinsic value of certain things such as artistic creation, scientific discovery, space exploration . . .
5 The value of one's own projects.

It is important to attempt to explain these feelings of discontinuity. Nagel himself suggests that this may not be possible: 'it is naive to suppose that there is a solution to every moral problem with which the world can face us. We have always known that the world is a bad place. It appears that it may be an evil place as well' (1979, 74). As though the world itself, rather than our attempts to cope with it, were discontinuous! As though tragedy were part of the structure of the world!

The incommensurateness of my projects can easily be explained. If I have a project *p* I have numerous reasons conditional on *p*; and these are certainly incommensurate with unconditional or differently conditioned reasons (III.12). It is no doubt difficult for me to abandon my project (often as difficult as it is to abandon rules); but there may be unconditional reasons to do so. The difficulty here is that to attend to these unconditional reasons I have first to abandon my commitment to the project (abandon the internal acceptance of the norm that my decision to adopt the project constitutes: III.12). When I do that the case is an ordinary one of unconditional reasons *ABC* for the actions involved in the project against *XYZ* reasons against (nothing is assumed). There is no discontinuity in the moral nature of things evident here; merely a psychological difficulty in abandoning a comfortable assumption. This psychological difficulty may look like incommensurateness.

The intrinsic value of artistic creation, scientific discovery, space exploration and the like (Nagel's fourth type of value) is the beauty of the world. It is the other side of the sort of incommensurateness just discussed. Ultimately, however, when my rules, projects and special loves are abandoned there is one world and no discontinuity.

Special loves are cases of eros. Nagel's first type of value, obligations to family and community, are cases of eros. Eros is not Eris, but it is discordant and incommensurate. If I love you in this way, erotically, I exclude others, and the point extends to community: I can love my community and, on the wings of eros so to speak, say my country right or wrong (VI.4).

This is the most difficult question in moral philosophy. Eros is the energy of love. To attend to you lovingly and clearly, as something free and independent, I need eros. It carries my attention. Then, attending, in love (so to speak), where is the rest of the world? (Excluded and incommensurate, our analysis

246

answers). But when I see your beauty do I not see also the beauty of others?

It seems necessary to speak as Plato did in the *Symposium* of progressive stages of love (. . . so that, having his eyes fixed upon beauty in the widest sense, he may no longer be the slave of a base and mean-spirited devotion to an individual example of beauty . . .: 210C). In conventional terms the progression is from eros to agape; and it is precisely a movement away from the incommensurate and discontinuous. Eros, by itself, is not a true witness to the nature of the world.

Remote consequences are obviously in a sense incommensurate. For want of a nail a shoe was lost, for want of a shoe a horse was lost, for want of a horse a charge was lost, for want of a charge a battle was lost, for want of a battle the war was lost; but how could the blacksmith tell? The fate of the war is obviously a relevant (future) fact in the practical case that the blacksmith has of shoeing the horse (will I go looking for the extra nail, or will I not?); but not something easily commensurate with the inconvenience, the matter of personal integrity and the other immediate reasons for and against action that obtain.

We have said that future facts have weight as reasons for action according to their probability (I.6). And this is true, but not a sufficient answer to our present problem, for the degree of probability may be as difficult for the blacksmith to calculate as the actual outcome of the war.

It seems clear that in all practical cases rules are applied at one point or another terminating the search for further relevant facts. This is obviously so in courts of law where there are strict rules of relevance, so-called. And it must be so for all practical cases, for the simplest action has consequences which radiate indefinitely. This demonstrates no incommensurateness in the nature of the world: I could spend the rest of my life on the next practical problem I encounter (how exactly will the next word I write affect the world's ink resources, what are the possibilities of someone being put out of work, with what consequences?). Now, you might say that such future facts are not likely to be significant; and you are probably right, but this is a reason for a terminating rule of the sort described. The incommensurateness produced in the assessment of remote consequences is, therefore, the simple incommensurateness of a rule. (The complexity of practical cases necessarily containing such rules, even on the simplest point, has been noticed in chapter VIII.)

The remaining category in Nagel's list is rights.

Americans (Nagel and Dworkin, for example) tend to say that there are legal rights which trump other values. I don't think there are rights in any fundamental sense. Respect for you gives reasons for action in regard to you; and this translates better into my duty than into your right (I owe respect: I have a duty of respect). Of course, right and duty are often correlative, but it is important which is fundamental; and, anyway, rights as correlatives of *commensurate* (non-trumping) duties would themselves be commensurate – they would have the (necessarily commensurate) weight of their correlatives, that is to say, the weight of whatever reasons for action constituted the duties, and no more. Dworkin thinks that the idea of a trumping right is part of that theory of adjudication which best explains (best fits) the American legal systems. But this theory of adjudication as an explanatory device fails (as has been argued in chapter IV).

Still, the intuition that there are rights as trumps is common amongst Americans. Why is this?

There is one simple explanation. There is a set of rules in the United States legal system called the Bill of Rights, and these trump other values (by excluding them) in the way that rules do. An American lawyer accepts a norm of the Bill of Rights and any question under it is simply a question of naming things for the purposes of the norm (X.13). Other values are relevant only to this, not at large, not relevant in their own right – and in this sense we can say they are trumped. But this is not a complete explanation of the American view. At bottom I think there is Ivan Karamazov's dilemma. Will you torture one little girl to secure perpetual happiness for mankind? No, answers Aloysha softly, thereby trumping the latter consideration.

This is a great dilemma. But we have already argued that much of its power derives from the vagueness of its formulation. When it is set up properly so as to exclude conditional reasons (people as means to ends) it is a great dilemma still; but, since unconditional other-regarding reasons for action are commensurate, there are no trumps available to foreclose it.

There is one world and therefore no moral discontinuities stemming from the nature of the world. The discontinuities commonly experienced in moral thought are the result of human acts which create rules, decisions, projects and erotic loves (VI.10). These are absolutes which when they clash must break. It is they that (thereby) create tragedy, rather than tragedy being part of the structure of the world.

XI.8

There is one world, however, there is also I, both part of the world and not. Here, at the edge of the world, so to speak, there is the most difficult problem of commensuration. Harold and I are in an open boat and I am in control of just enough food to save one of us. What is the status of Harold's hunger as a reason for my action as compared with my own hunger? It is necessary to say there is an equivalence and therefore a commensurateness between Harold's hunger and mine, for what sort of reason for action could Harold's hunger be if it were not equivalent to the only hunger of which I have any primary knowledge, viz., my own?

There is no reason why my hunger should not be regarded by me as a particular fact in the world. What is out of the world is I, the free, willing subject.

XI.9

The unity of moral thought is the product of ontological parsimony. I am one man surrounded by one world. That world as facts provides reasons for action. At this fundamental level of moral thought I can know no discontinuities: no fact carries a mark of some category or another, such as might enable me to say 'this is a legal reason for action, that, another sort'. A reason for action can obtain only by its weight (if a fact has no weight it is not a reason for action), and, since I am the only balance and I am one man, it has only one weight. It follows that there are no uniquely *legal* reasons or principles (chapter IV); and if I am to say there are legal hard cases I can mean only that there are hard cases in legal situations (for example, in courts). It is obvious that such a qualification or definition is unimportant.

Now, 'I', 'we', 'a judge', 'a court' . . . are used for the most part interchangeably in this book. This is not simply a methodological convenience; it is a consequence of the ontological parsimony just stated. There is only I and the world. Thus a judge must either be equivalent to I or part of the world. As willing subject, the decider of cases (that which is practical philosophy's main focus of interest), a judge is equivalent to I. As fact a judge is part of the world (as, for instance, one who in fact has decided a precedent case).

What a judge will decide, said Holmes, is what I mean by the law. This definition of law as prediction is partly demolished by Hart's objection that it will not do for the judge himself: the judge cannot decide by predicting his own decision (1961, 10). The equivalence just stated between I and a judge completes the demolition. No idea of prediction can obtain, for prediction of one's own decision is logical nonsense (unless one is schizophrenic – but then 'one's own' doesn't apply). Of course, the prediction of someone else's decision may state a future fact, relevant to a practical decision. A definition of law as such a future fact would be harmless enough, but without interest to practical philosophy, whose concern is with the willing subject, the decider of (practical) cases, I.

XI.10

Commonly, great judges talk of their lives as lives of service to the law; of clear-headed, reverential respect, rather than heroic idiosyncrasy.

Now, if we are to have rules we shall clearly have such judges. Rules cut off (idiosyncratic) questions; truth is assumed not engaged; and the moral life (the legal life, since we are talking about judges) is at least partly a life of submission. And if we are to have rules it makes little sense for each to have his own rules (VI.2). Thus submission is to the law (that set of public norms identified by the rule of recognition), and the judicial life is its service.

Are we to have rules? In the second chapter we offered a rather vague formulation of the moral doubts that attach to this question. Rules appropriate the mystery of the world, which is the foundation of moral thought. A rule subsumes the mysterious particulars of the world into a normative class suitable to be applied absolutely by those in its service. But this matter of application is not to be overlooked. The relationship of rule and single case is fundamental to the moral status of rules.

In a well-known article (1967) John Rawls distinguished two concepts of rules. There are rules of thumb where the single case clearly has logical priority: the rule has no independent status – it is merely a guide to logically prior single-case decisions – and if in any single case it gives the wrong decision there is no question of following the rule. The second concept of a rule is close to that examined in this book. Here, says Rawls, the rule itself has logical priority over the single case. Now, there is a sense in which we can accept this. If I make a rule decision I do not make a hard decision, and the fact that the right hard decision might be contrary to what the rule requires is irrelevant to (because excluded by) my rule decision. However, Rawls makes a very important mistake here. He overlooks that it nevertheless is possible in this situation (indeed sometimes morally required) to make the hard decision.

> Where a form of action is specified by a practice there is no justification possible of the particular action of a particular person save by reference to the practice. In such cases then action is what it is in virtue of the practice and to explain it is to refer to the practice. There is no inference whatsoever to be drawn with respect to whether or not one should accept the practices of one's society. One can be as radical as one likes but in the case of actions specified by practices the objects of one's radicalism must be the social practices and people's acceptance of them. (1967, 169)

This is made clear by the example of a promise to a dying father where the disutility of secret breach after death can be supposed to be slight:

> How do these remarks apply to the case of the promise known only to father and son? Well, at first sight the son certainly holds the office of promisor, and so he isn't allowed by the practice to weigh the particular case on general utilitarian grounds. Suppose instead that he wishes to consider himself in the office of one empowered to criticize and change the practice, leaving aside the question as to his right to move from his previously

assumed office to another. Then he may consider utilitarian arguments as applied to the practice; but once he does this he will see that there are such arguments for not allowing a general utilitarian defence in the practice for this sort of case. For to do so would make it impossible to ask for and to give a kind of promise which one often wants to be able to ask for and to give. Therefore he will not want to change the practice, and so as a promisor he has no option but to keep his promise. (1967, 166)

Two categories of decision are admitted by Rawls:

1 single-case decision applying a rule, and
2 strategic decision about a rule ('criticize and change the practice').

What he leaves out is:

3 single-case non-rule (hard) decision.

The son in Rawls's example judges that there is a balance of reasons in favour of an absolute (or fairly absolute) rule to keep promises (Rawls talks of utility, but the point transfers to reasons for action); and Rawls thinks it follows from this that 'he has no option but to keep his promise'. But it does not. There may be a balance of reasons in favour of a certain rule, and one not making any exceptions, but a balance of reasons against its application in a certain single case; for I can say simply: there should be this rule, but it should not be applied in this case. There can be a balance of reasons in favour of the promising rule without any exception for the dying father case, but a balance of reasons against deciding in accordance with it in the (single) dying father case. As we put it earlier (the case of the judge deliberating about the application of a rule of recognition to an iniquitous statute (X.7) and the case of the low court judge deliberating whether to follow a high court decision wrong in the strong sense (IX.13)), it may be the case both that DEF (strategic) reasons for a rule to p outweigh UVW reasons against, and at the same time in a single case that ABC reasons to p are outweighed by XYZ reasons against. When we add to this the fact that a decision of the single case cannot be avoided we have the primacy of the single case.

Thus the son in Rawls's example can say consistently; there ought to be an absolute rule about promising, and I ought not to keep my promise in this case. He may even say (if he thinks he needs a personal rule): I ought to have an absolute rule about promising, and I ought not to keep my promise in this case. In the case of public rules it is obvious that there can be reasons for the unqualified (absolute) rule rather than the qualified rule: because of human proneness to error a qualified rule may produce more wrong decisions in the interpretation of the qualification than the unqualified rule produces in the single cases of the sort we are considering. But this applies for private rules, too, and for my personal adoption of public rules: I, too, am prone to error, and qualifications of simple rules may exacerbate this.

Rawls's argument takes some plausibility from the fact that often rules are in command of the appropriate language. Thus one can only decide to steal a base in the baseball game if one makes a rule decision. A non-rule single-case decision could not be to 'steal a base', but only to move from one place on a field to another. I don't think there is anything in this point at all. The moral question (*the* practical question) is the same whatever the language we use to express it. Anyway, in most important cases (and notably in Rawls's two important cases of promising and punishment) the rule is not in command of the language. I can quite sensibly wonder whether to keep a promise to you whether or not there is a rule: at heart I shall be wondering whether your reliance on what I have said I would do is a sufficient reason to do it. And in the case of punishment I can deliberate on the question whether to punish you whether or not there is a rule. I might decide not to, but the question, the language, makes sense without the rule. Perhaps the word is borrowed from the rule; but perhaps not: the question is of no consequence.

It must be admitted that the primacy of the single case causes a certain difficulty in the case of some attempts at promising, and this difficulty may be at the heart of Rawls's point. But it has nothing to do with rules. In the dying father case if the son says to his father 'I promise . . .' knowing that in the (single) case that must ensue there will be a balance of reasons against his doing what he said he would do he has not made a promise (for he cannot have intended to keep it). But this is so whether or not there is a rule about promising. All the moral issues here are quite in order.

It is important to see that our argument is not an argument for a limited rule. As we saw with the rule of the authority of high courts (IX.13) and with the rule of recognition (X.7) a rule with an exception of those cases where it gives the wrong single-case decision would cause more trouble than it was worth; and the same is probably true of a promising rule. If there is a balance of reasons for these rules it is for absolute rules. But nevertheless in certain single cases the balance of reasons is against their application.

There is certainly an appearance of paradox here; not unlike the paradox of the Prisoners' Dilemma (see IV.5), which exposes a number of logical facts, including the logical primacy of the single case. Each prisoner is rationally required (in the game-theorists' sense of rationality: not, as we have seen (I.12) in the full sense of rationality) to decide his single case in favour of defection (i.e. confession). The rational *joint* action, however, is for neither to defect. But, even having undertaken joint action, it remains rational in any single case treacherously to defect.

The paradox, however, in both cases is more apparent than real. In the Prisoners' Dilemma the paradox depends upon overlooking other-regarding reasons for action (I.12). In the rule case we must say: that *DEF* (the reasons for the rule) outweighs *UVW* (the reasons against) does not entail that in a particular single case *ABC* (the reasons for the action that conforms to the rule) outweighs *XYZ* (the reasons against) (specific values are given to *DEF*, *UVW*, *ABC* and *XYZ* in IX.13 and X.7). And this is true notwithstanding the fact that there is a considerable correspondence of *DEF* to *ABC* and *UVW* to *XYZ*. *ABC* are the reasons in a single case to act in accordance with the rule, and there is a considerable correspondence between *ABC* and *DEF*, for *ABC* substantially represents the damage that would be done to the values of *DEF* by the single-case breach of the rule (if we fail to apply a statute perhaps disobedience will spread, and so on). *XYZ* are the reasons against applying the rule in the single case (for instance, in the case of the statute requiring the execution of blue-eyed babies, the iniquity of the statute and the social divisiveness of its implementation) and there is some correspondence here, too, because the possibility of damage to the values of *XYZ* is envisaged in *UVW*, which are reasons concerned with an absolute rule (one including the single case in question). But it is clear that there is insufficient correspondence between the two sets of reasons for one in any sense to entail the other. *ABC* is only the partial loss of the values of *DEF*; and *UVW* includes only the possibility of the iniquity in question, *XYZ*, on the other hand, its certainty. There is no plausibility at all in the idea that because I think there is a balance of reasons in favour of a rule (*DEF* outweighs *UVW*) I am committed to its application in any single case (*ABC* outweighs *XYZ*). I can quite rationally decide both to take a rule and in any single case decide not to apply it. These decisions do not conflict. They would conflict only if I decided not to apply the rule in all or a substantial number of single cases; and such a decision, of course, is not required of me in any single case.

There is no way that a judge can avoid the single case. Let us say that he decides the strategic case *DEF* against *UVW*, deciding to adopt the rule (if he does this in the single case it is, of course, more likely to be simply a re-affirmation of the rule). The parties before him are entitled to say: please decide our case, you have not yet done so; the adoption of a rule (or its re-affirmation) even though it covers our case is not the decision of the case. You, responsible for your actions, must decide it. So he must go on to the single case and decide it, either by his just-adopted rule or by the hard case *ABC* against *XYZ*. If he decides it by the rule he decides wrongly, for *ABC* does not outweigh *XYZ*. But it is necessary that he decide it one way or the other with moral responsibility. Moral responsibility attaches to his disposal of the case because it is entailed (as was argued in chapter II). There is no way that a judge can avoid this. He might (illogically) think that in disposing of the single case all he was deciding was to accept a rule (*DEF* against *UVW*); but he would still be responsible in reason for the single case (*ABC* against *XYZ*). We may call this necessity the primacy of the single case. It is a necessity which attaches to every single action of an individual. It is the necessity that he be responsible in reason for whatever action he takes.

It is recorded that German machine-gunners in the First World War were happy to be chained to their guns (Ullman-Margalit, 1977, 30–41). Their situation was a version of The Prisoners' Dilemma: that is, it was rational to undertake the joint action of defending a position, but the joint action was unstable because of the possibility of individual (single-case) defection, and it was therefore rational to try to counter this instability. The solution chosen by the Germans was the solution of brute force. Their (rational) strategy could not be subverted by single-case decisions because single cases were, by the brute force of the chains, prevented from coming about.

Alternatively, and more conventionally, there might have been sanctions against desertion. These, of course, would have tended to stabilize the action and preserve the strategy; but they would not have pre-empted the single case, and any machine-gunner might still have decided that *ABC* (including the sanction) was outweighed by *XYZ*, and therefore have deserted.

Now a leviathan might be instituted in a community to operate by real brute force; to use chains rather than rationally motivating sanctions; like the German machine-gunners, actually to determine events. The chains might be psychological controls or some devilish contraption; or fear, used not as a rational motivation but brutally, and with psychological sophistication, as a real determinant of events (Hobbes said: covenants without the sword are but words (*Leviathan*, ch. xvii); but did not distinguish a sword which determined events by fear from a sword which stood as a reason for action). And it might be rational to agree in advance to this (*DEF* outweighs *UVW*), and as it were, hold out one's hands to receive the chains.

It is not difficult to think of ways of constructing a real leviathan (one that really locks the chains). Erect over the world a network of cameras and highly accurate gas ejectors, connected to a computer (the mortal god), the whole fuelled for a thousand years. When wrong action is perceived, including turning off or tampering with the system and going out of sight of the cameras, immobilizing gas is applied.

Hobbes would not have accepted a leviathan which had no moral authority. But this contraption would have the authority that Hobbes requires: we who switched it on would be the moral authors of its power, and we could therefore not complain.

There would be no judges under a real leviathan, for there would be no single cases; just a programme in a computer.

Hobbes never had to face this issue clearly. A technologically sophisticated leviathan was in his time inconceivable: the parts in a leviathan such as Hobbes could conceive were necessarily free moral agents, and anyone of them at any time was in this sense free to decide a single case against the leviathan (decide that *ABC* did not outweigh *XYZ*). A real leviathan actually determines events; no single cases can arise.

The positivistic conception of law rejected in chapter II tends to see judges as computers; as, at least in clear cases, simply certifying what in fact the law is on certain facts, without necessary moral commitment. Now, such a state of affairs could be instituted: real computers could be substituted for judges, and their 'decisions' would obviously entail no moral justification. But this would be insufficient to establish the positivistic conception. The single-case responsibility would fall totally to those charged to execute the law; they would necessarily become the judges, and the arguments of chapter II would apply to them. One taking the positivistic conception of law seriously would have to determine in a real way execution as well as adjudication. In the example taken in chapter II, if the adjudication only was determined, the hangman would necessarily become judge as to whether the norm certified by the computer ought to be implemented – there would be no way he could avoid that single case (II.3); and the philosophy of law would then focus its attention on his decision. Thus the positivist toying with the idea of a computer as a judge is, if he wishes to carry his conception through, required to make it executioner too: consider a rather more devilish contraption into which those charged might be fed to be tried and either in its bowels executed or ejected, innocent.

Now, this leviathan is not to be taken lightly, for *DEF* does outweigh *UVW*, that is, there are reasons for a determination in the rule way of a class of cases including certain single cases where it is wrong on single-case reasons (*ABC* against *XYZ*) so to decide. Thus if there are reasons for such a rule there may be reasons for the establishment of the equivalently programmed leviathan. Perhaps no wrong would have been done, for *DEF* outweighs *UVW*, and *ABC* against *XYZ* simply does not arise because no moral agent has to decide it.

These reflections suggest it is possible to avoid the single case *ABC* against *XYZ*, and anyone's moral responsibility for it, by the real establishment of a technologically sophisticated leviathan; and all of Hobbes's arguments stand to support that course (*DEF* outweighs *UVW*). But it would not be a case of law: we would not call the contraption a legal system. The reason for this would be that it lacked judges. There is only I (equivalent to a judge) and the world. By the implementation of such a leviathan we would have modified the world and cancelled the I.

A rule of recognition in a legal system tends towards such real determination by virtue of the subjective determination of the will involved. It is as though I am programmed. If the assumption constituting the rule were merely the sort of provisional assumption that one makes concerning part of a complex problem when that part may turn out not to be critical, it would not determine the will. But the assumption of bindingness in rules is an assumption of ultimate (moral) bindingness – it is not provisional but determines action without (further) hard judgment. A rule of recognition with the statutes valid under it is in this way a large-scale programme, which might be treated by those in its service as though it were equivalent to the programme of such a leviathan as we have imagined. The crucial issue here is whether the possibility of single-case decisions against the rule is admitted. Legal positivists deny that there can be single-case *legal* decisions against the rule. Faced by an iniquitous statute a judge as judge (as servant of the law) must either apply it or resign: according to legal positivism, he cannot ever say in the single case 'this statute because of its iniquity is not the law'.

This is equivalent to denying that it is possible to be a judge. Legal positivism reduces to this: either one applies the programme of the rule of recognition as the arm, so to speak, of a computer, or one resigns. Hart advocated in the case of an iniquitous statute the latter course, resignation (or, which is equivalent, sitting tight and saying of the statute 'this is the law but I shall not apply it'). But the appearance of a morally satisfactory solution which this presents should not disguise the view which is taken of law. There are no judges in the positivist view; for either the programme is applied without judgment or, one unwilling to do that (unwilling to see himself as the arm of a computer) has no course but to resign.

No amount of theorizing about judgment and discretion in peripheral cases where rules are not clear can disguise this central fact. Under the perfect leviathan single cases are not judged; they are determined by the gas ejectors. According to legal positivism, in cases where a clear rule of recognition identifies a clear statute judges are equivalent to the gas ejectors; with the one saving grace that they are allowed just enough intelligence to incapacitate themselves (cease to be gas ejectors). This intelligence, of course, is by the positivists' definitions not a legal intelligence (judges resign for what are explicitly said to be moral not legal reasons). Thus whilst it is a saving grace it does not save the positivists' concept of *law*. So far as the law is concerned judges (in clear cases) are nothing but gas ejectors. Or, more accurately, since there is no judgment in this, there are no judges in law.

When great judges speak of their lives as service they must be taken to mean service to the community as judges in law. Service to community can include service of (submission to) its rules (a disposition not to play gaily with new ideas); indeed it must, for its rules are part of a community's works, and, moreover, *DEF* outweighs *UVW*. But it cannot be limited to service to rules if the service is to be service as a judge in law.

XI.11

Plato thought that life was to be lived as play (*Laws*, VII, 803). The meaning of this is that there is something behind life of such importance and power that the passing events of life are as nothing – mere playthings. And illusions. In the metaphor of the cave and the sun we are from birth shackled in a cave, our vision constrained towards the back wall. On that wall there are the shadows of a puppet show conducted behind us, projected by the light of a fire burning yet further behind us. Beyond the fire there is the mouth of the cave, and outside is the sun. Shadow is mistaken for reality (*Republic*, 514A–516B).

What is of ultimate seriousness (what is of such power that all else is as nothing) is the mystery of the world. This mystery obtains for every particular in the world, for any one of them might be the world (there might be only one particular in the world), and it would constitute the same mystery. In the case of the world the mystery is that the world exists; thus in the case of any particular the mystery is that this particular exists. The power of the mystery of existence lies partly in the awe that it evokes; but more significantly in the fact that it provides the only purely objective determination of the will (universals make a programme: only a response to particulars is purely objective: I.10).

Being infinite, existence is a power beyond anyone's measure (if you believe there is an intervention somewhere in this infinity of existence, a beginning or an end to existence, then let that intervention be, as it was for Plato and for most people in the history of this human race, the power beyond measure: the point is, it seems, there must be either infinite existence or God). From the perspective of the infinity of existence how could the events ('plaything') of life matter? This perspective is the perspective of agape (God's love – God's attention – God's view of the world: when Lear through tragedy became God's spy, taking upon himself the mystery of things, the passing events of life ('who loses and who wins; who's in, who's out') were as nothing).

Now you might think that these reflections are a bit large to be of interest to the philosophy of law – the philosophy of practical cases. You would be wrong. The infinity of existence is the most purely practical thing. For it is particulars which are intrinsically practical (I.10), and every particular is, beneath its attached (universal) properties and relations, pure existence (and for every particular the particular attachment of each of these (universal) properties and relations is at *its* core, stripped of *its* (universal) properties and relations, pure existence, too). And there seems no way to separate the ideas infinity of existence and pure existence. The word 'mystery' encompasses both without discrimination.

The significance of the *practicality* of this conception is not to be underestimated. For without it, we are all practical solipsists lacking significant freedom. Without particulars as practical, what could be the point of moral freedom? To choose between one (universalized) programme and another? But what is freedom if it is merely freedom to choose a programme? (Or, alternatively, what is a programme if I am free to ignore it in the next case?) Particulars (the infinity of existence) give at the same time both moral freedom and objectivity.

Now, it is particulars which stand behind rules. They are subsumed into the classes which the rules constitute; so that when a rule decision is made the only question is of membership of the class which the norm of the rule constitutes (inference (D) in IV.2: all whales ought to be killed. This is a whale. Therefore, this ought to be killed. One ought to exercise care towards anyone in front of one's car. Harold is in front of my car. Therefore, I ought to exercise care towards Harold). There is no question here of a

passionate response to the particulars of the case, as there would
be if I were to make a hard decision: the practical content of the
rule decision is given by the subjective determination of the will to
apply the norm of the rule, the major premise in inference (D).
Particulars in this sense transcend rules. The rule appropriates the
whole universe of discourse on cases to which it applies. It creates
an absolute. But beyond that absolute, transcending it, ever
present and available for hard decision, are particulars. And so
long as there is law not leviathan, as there is so long as I am free to
unprogramme myself, single cases are available to reassert these
particulars. And it is they which are of ultimate seriousness, they
which contain the mystery of the world.

Think of the statute requiring the execution of blue-eyed babies
(who might be Jews at Auschwitz). Where there is a real leviathan
the blue-eyed babies die, should that be the programme, their
particularity unnoticed. But where there is law there is the single
case. If I decide it by rule (the rule of recognition as stated by the
conventional doctrine of the omnipotence of Parliament) and send
the babies to their deaths by virtue of their membership of the
class constructed by the rule, their particularity unnoticed, I shall
have made the awful mistake of confusing law with leviathan; for I
did not *have* to decide the case by rule; I did not have to allow my
will to be determined subjectively, for I was free to respond
(objectively) to the particulars. A rule tends towards leviathan
because of the psychological hold of its programme. But it is not
leviathan. I am free to abandon the programme (and therefore the
assumption of bindingness) and respond to the particulars of the
case.

And much the same is true of projects. If I have a project, for
instance that which is the fundamental legal project, preserve the
community, I have a multitude of reasons conditional upon that
project, by which I can decide cases (III.12). As with rules this
creates an absolute area of discourse, within which these conditional reasons operate. And any particular caught up, so to speak,
in the project is used, its particularity unnoticed, as a means to the
end of the accomplishment of the project. Its particularity is
unnoticed because any means of the relevant type will do. Such
decisions are not made by passionate response: a balance of
conditional reasons is theoretical rather than practical – simply a
measurement of efficiency in accomplishment of the project. The

The World

practical content of the decision is given by my adoption of the project (III.12). This, as in rules, creates a subjective determination of the will. And here, too, particulars transcend the (absolute) project: they are ever-present, available for a passionate (practical) response and hard decision, such as would put the project itself in issue. I am free to decide not to use the particulars caught up in the project as (universal) means, and to respond passionately to them as particulars.

The third normative absolute is erotic love, where my fixation on one particular as well as excluding others is by that exclusion a degraded attention to the one ('the slave of a base and mean-spirited devotion to an individual example of beauty', *Symposium*, 210C). Here, in the matter of law, I say my country right or wrong, and exclude other particulars. But they are available, ever-present. And more importantly the one particular is available for truer attention. Eros is a profound moral concept. Analysis of the sort offered in the case of rules and projects is never attempted: the philosophy of love speaks in metaphor. Eros is a grace, the correlative of the grace of beauty; and on the wings of Eros, it is said, I can ascend to a higher love (agape).

In all three cases there is appropriation of an area of moral thought thereby creating an absolute; and transcending this absolute there are particulars containing the mystery of the world. And there is my freedom to break the absolute and attend or attend more truly to the particulars.

The difficulty of making this response is not to be underestimated. Any mind at ordinary moral levels is full of these absolutes. For one thing they are comfortable. There is the illusion of truth in them, which is a consolation to us; and many other side-benefits of certainty. The mystery of the world, by contrast, is distinctly uncomfortable; a power beyond measure, a power against which I am nothing. Plato's metaphor of the cave and the sun is in order here: 'And if he were compelled to look at the light itself would that not pain his eyes, and would he not turn away. . .?' (*Republic*, 515E). If there is grace in this ('compelled to look'), it is at least partly the grace of the beauty of the particulars of the world.

Now, we cannot decide all cases by hard judgment on the particulars. We adopt rules (VI.3–VI.4) (projects and erotic loves, too). And, anyway, even if we could eschew rules there are reasons for them (*DEF* outweighs *UVW*), which reasons are themselves particulars (*DEFUV* and *W* are no less particulars than *ABCXY* and *Z*). But the shadow ought not to be mistaken for the reality; *DEFUV* and *W* may be reality but the programme of the rule, the subjective determination of the will, is shadow. That which is not of ultimate seriousness ought not to be mistaken for that which is. The rules, the projects and the erotic love of a legal system, which by some further grace have the logical structure of ordinary games (VII.9–VII.11), are to be lived as play. Not that this is not serious in its way – the way that games are serious.

If I lose this sense of game I take the absolutes of a legal system too seriously. The more seriously I take them the harder it is to release them (and the nearer I come to Auschwitz). Of course, I am free to release them, always. But a sense of playfulness is more conducive to the exercise of this freedom (Christopher Robin, as an exemplar, rather than Athene: II.13).

The release of the absolutes of a legal system is a condition of agape/reality/freedom, but not a sufficient condition. All the other absolutes, consoling fantasies and violent passions that constrict my practical attention remain. My struggle for perfect freedom has hardly begun. The philosophy of love here takes over from the philosophy of law.

What has my freedom (my love) to do with law? I and a judge are equivalent (XI.9). Adjudication, the activity of judging, is what distinguishes law from leviathan. Adjudication is the decision of single cases. Thus a judge's freedom to respond to the particulars of those cases is at the basis of law. Thus my freedom is at the basis of law.

Me, I'm in the law game: my professional accomplishments and acceptance in the law are such as to allow me to think that my thought in and about the law, the structure and nature of which this book is an analysis, is not too idiosyncratic to prevent me claiming that the book's concern is the concept of law (the arguments in pursuit of that concern may of course be mistaken). Perhaps this reflection is nonsense: there is after all just I and the world. A better way of making the claim may be as follows:

The 'law' in this analysis is general or conceptual (the *concept* of law) in the following sense: If someone raises an analytical fact about law which is true but does not fit satisfactorily into or out of this analysis, then either the analysis must be modified or there is an unresolved problem of the translation of whatever the world is for 'law' (it might be 'law') in the language from which the fact comes. I do not want to underestimate the difficulty of saying which. All I want to claim here is that the fact that there is no third possibility (for instance, that the analytical fact which does not fit into or out of this analysis is a fact about a case of law (the word properly translated) but a different kind of case from my own) makes 'law' in this analysis as general or conceptual as it is possible for a word to be.

BIBLIOGRAPHY

Anscombe, G. E. M (1957), *Intention*, Oxford.
— (1958a), 'Brute Facts', *Analysis*, 69.
— (1958b), 'Modern Moral Philosophy', *Philosophy*, XXXIII, 1.
— (1967), 'Who is Wronged?', *Oxford Review*, 16.
Armstrong, D. M. (1978), *Nominalism and Realism*, Cambridge.
Becker, Lawrence (1973), 'The Finality of Moral Judgments', *Phil. Rev.*, 82, 364.
Benson, J. (1968), 'Oughts and Wants', *Aristotelian Society Supp.* vol. XLII, 155.
Brandt, R. B. (1963), 'Towards a Credible Form of Utilitarianism', in *Morality and the Language of Conduct* (eds Castaneda and Nakhnikian), Detroit, 1963.
Chayes, A. (1976), 'The Role of the Judge in Public Law Litigation', *H.L.R.*, 89, 1281.
Cross, R. (1977), *Precedent in English Law*, 3rd edn, Oxford.
Dicey, A. V. (1885), *The Law of the Constitution*, London (9th edn, 1939).
Diplock, Lord (1965), 'The Courts as Legislators', Presidential Address, Holdsworth Club.
Dworkin, Ronald (1977), *Taking Rights Seriously*, London.
Edgley, Roy (1969), *Reason in Theory and Practice*, London.
Foot, Philippa (1972), 'Morality as a System of Hypothetical Imperatives', *Phil. Rev.*, 81, 305.
Goodhart, A. L. (1931), 'The Ratio Decidendi of a Case', in *Essays in Jurisprudence and the Common Law*, Cambridge.
Grisez, Germain (1970), 'Towards a Consistent Natural-Law Ethics of Killing', *Am. J. of Jurisprudence*, 15, 64.
— (1978), 'Against Consequentialism', *Am. J. of Jurisprudence*, 23, 21.
Hampshire, Stuart (1978), *Public and Private Morality*, Cambridge.
Hare, R. M. (1952), *The Language of Morals*, Oxford.
— (1957), 'Are Discoveries About the Use of Words Empirical?', *J.P.*, LIV, 741.

Bibliography

— (1963), *Freedom and Reason*, Oxford.

— (1964), 'The Promising Game', *Revue Internationale de Philosophie*, 398; reprinted in Foot (ed.), *Theories of Ethics*, Oxford, 1967, 115, to which page references are given.

Hart, H. L. A. (1961), *The Concept of Law*, Oxford.

— (1963), 'Kelsen Visited', 10 U.C.L.A. *Law Rev.*, 709.

— (1964), *Self-Referring Laws, Festkrift till Karl Olivecrona*, Stockholm.

— (1976), 'Law in the Perspective of Philosophy', *N.Y.U.L.R.*, 51, 538.

Hudson, W. D. (1945), 'The Is–Ought Controversy', *Analysis*, 25, 191.

Kelsen, Hans (1965), *General Theory of Law and State*, New York.

— (1967), *The Pure Theory of Law*, Berkeley.

Kydd, Rachel M. (1946), *Reason and Conduct in Hume's Treatise*, Oxford

MacCormick, Neil (1978), *Legal Reasoning and Legal Theory*, Oxford.

Mackie, J. L. (1977), 'The Third Theory of Law', *Phil. and Pub. Aff.*, 7, 3.

— (1978), *Ethics*, Harmondsworth.

Midgely, Mary (1974), 'The Game Game', *Philosophy*, 49, 231.

— (1978), *Beast and Man*, Hassocks.

Murdoch, Iris (1959), 'The Sublime and the Good', *Chicago Review*, 42.

— (1959–60), 'The Sublime and the Beautiful Revisited', *Yale Review*, 49, 247.

— (1970), *The Sovereignty of Good*, London.

Nagel, Thomas (1970), *The Possibility of Altruism*, Oxford.

— (1979), *Mortal Questions*, Cambridge.

Nowell-Smith, P. H. (1958), 'Choosing, Deciding and Doing', *Analysis*, 18, 65.

Pound, Roscoe (1908), 'Common Law and Legislation', *H.L.R.*, 21, 383.

Rawls, John (1967), 'Two Concepts of Rules', in Foot (ed.), *Theories of Ethics*, Oxford.

Raz, Joseph (1972a), 'Legal Principles and the Limits of Law', *Y.L.J.*, 81, 823.

— (1972b), 'Professor A. Ross and Some Legal Puzzles', *Mind*, LXXXI, 415.

— (1975), *Practical Reason and Norms*, London.

— (1979), *The Authority of Law*, Oxford.

Reid, Lord (1972), 'The Judge as Law Maker', *J.S.P.T.L.*, XII, 22.

Ross, Alf (1958), *On Law and Justice*, London.

— (1969), 'On Self-Reference and a Puzzle in Constitutional Law', *Mind*, LXXVIII, 1.

Ross, W. D. (1930), *The Right and the Good*, Oxford.

Searle, J. R. (1969), *Speech Acts*, Cambridge.

— (1978), 'Prima Facie Obligations', in Raz (ed.), *Practical Reasoning*, Oxford.

Smart, J. J. C. (1955), 'The Existence of God', in *New Essays in Philosophical Theology* (eds Flew and MacIntyre), London.

Solomon, William David (1975), *Moral Reasons*, *A.P.Q.*, 12, 331.

Strawson, P. F. (1974), *Freedom and Resentment*, London.

Stephen, Leslie (1882), *The Science of Ethics*, London.

Bibliography

Ullman-Margalit, Edna (1977), *The Emergence of Norms*, Oxford.
Warnock, G. J. (1971), *The Object of Morality*, London.
Williams, B. A. O. (1973), 'A Critique of Utilitarianism', in Smart and Williams (eds), *Utilitarianism For and Against*, Cambridge.
— (1978), 'Ethical Consistency', in Raz (ed.), *Practical Reasoning*, Oxford.
Wolff, R. P. (1970), *In Defence of Anarchism*, New York.

INDEX

Action, 1, 162, 169, 180–2; in rule cases, 182; *see also* Practical and theoretical; Reasons for action
Aeschylus, 40–2
Analogy, 183, 210–13
Anscombe, G.E.M., 62, 70–1, 75, 240
Aquinas, 145
Aristotle, 130–1
Armstrong, D.M., 14
Authority, 141–2, 171; contrasted with education, 198; high court and low court, 204–8; incompatible with reasons, 196–8; *see also* Precedent; Ratio decidendi

Barwick v. English Joint Stock Bank, 187
Beauty, 7–8, 119–21
Benson, J., 1
Bill of Rights (United States), 217, 224–5, 248–9
Bourhill v. Young, 192
Brutus v. Cozens, 169–71

Cases, xvii, 11, 162–73, 239–41; *see also* Single case, primacy of
Cassell v. Broome, 205–7
Charter v. Race Relations Board, 102–4
Christopher Robin, 42–3, 263
Commensurateness of moral thought, 232–50
Constitution, contrasted with statute, 226–31; *see also* Rule of recognition

Courts, equivalent to I, 249–50; *see also* Authority; Judge; Precedent; Ratio decidendi
Cross, R., 191–2, 203–4

Decisions, 64–72; internal attitude to, 66–72
Desire, *see* Want
Dicey, A.V., 216, 224, 225
Diplock, Lord, 204
Discontinuity, feelings of, *see* Commensurateness of moral thought
Discretion, judicial, 108–15, 120, 148–50, 208
Dixon, Owen, 46–7
Donoghue v. Stevenson, 151, 172–3
Dworkin, Ronald, 60, 73–105, 125–7, 142, 149, 151, 167–9, 225, 245

Edgley, Roy, 2, 182
Education, 88–90, 178–9
Edwards v. Bairstow, 163
Example: incompatible with norm, 174–9; precedent as example, 174–9

Facts, 184–6, 187–8; brute, 11–12, 62; evidential, 12; fact and law distinguished, 163–4, 169–71; *see also* Reasons for action, facts as
Forms of action, 104
Freedom, moral, 73, 99, 105, 116–22, 145–6, 241–5, 260, 263

269

Index

Reid, Lord, 154, 204
Respect, 3–8, 234–7
Revolution, 50, 222–3
Riggs v. Palmer, 83, 190, 193–4
Rondel v. Worsley, 188
Ross, Alf, 228–31
Rule of recognition, 58, 59–60,
  198–201, 215, 258; iniquitous statute,
  215–26, 258–9, 261; recognition of
  judicial decisions, 198–201, 214
Rules, xvii, 21–2, 33–4, 67–72, 75,
  100–2, 103, 143–6, 147, 184, 206–8,
  237–9, 247–9, 250–9, 260–3;
  assumptions, constituted by, 48–64,
  186–7; external attitude, 48–9, 52,
  60, 124; internal attitude, 33, 45–64,
  67–72, 124; interpretation, 164–70;
  norms contrasted, 74, 125–6, 238;
  particulars subsumed by rules,
  260–3; reasons and, 100, 123–46,
  206–7, 217–19; reasons for, 123–46,
  206–7, 217–19

Searle, J.R., 12–13, 63–4, 143
Single case, primacy of, 252–3, 257–8,
  262–3

Smart, J.J.C., 5
Solomon, W.D., 2
Stephen, L., 216–17, 224
Strawson, P.F., 236

Theoretical, see Practical
Tragedy, 143–6, 246, 249

Ullman-Margalit, E., 255
Universalization, 77–8; see also Particulars

Want, distinguished from desire, 1–2
Warnock, G.J., 3, 44, 129–30
Weight of reasons for action, xvii, 12,
  13, 70, 73–107, 115, 117, 121,
  168–9, 178; the balance metaphor,
  241–5
Will: determination of, subjective and
  objective, 16, 72, 116–22, 258, 259,
  262; weakness of, 30–1, 115–16,
  121–2, 242
Williams, B.A.O., 35, 143, 235
Wittgenstein, L., 4, 17, 144
Wolff, R.P., 196–7

271